The Digital Divide

The Digital Divide
Facing a Crisis or Creating a Myth?

edited by
Benjamin M. Compaine

MIT Press Sourcebooks

The MIT Press
Cambridge, Massachusetts
London, England

This book was set in QuarkXpress in Sabon by Asco Typesetters, Hong Kong, and was printed and bound in the United States of America.

Library of Congress Cataloging-in-Publication Data

The digital divide: facing a crisis or creating a myth? / edited by Benjamin M. Compaine.
    p.   cm. — (The MIT Press Sourcebooks)
Includes bibliographical references and index.
ISBN 0-262-53193-3 (pbk.: alk. paper)
    1. Digital divide—United States. 2. Information technology—Social aspects —United States. I. Compaine, Benjamin M.
HN90.I56 D54   2001
303.48′33—dc21   00-048964

Source notes can be found on p. 341.

Contents

Foreword

Taken together, the chapters of *The Digital Divide* show that perceived gaps are closing among various ethnic, racial, and geographical groups in access to the Internet. At least two factors account for the rapid diffusion of Internet technology: steadily decreasing costs of use, and steadily increasing ease of use. In the coming months I believe that these trends will continue and that controversies about the "digital divide" will fade away.

As Internet technology becomes pervasive and cheap, it will offer an enormous opportunity to diminish a different, but real, divide. This is the critical divide between those who can read well and take full advantage of the treasures of information that will be so widely available, and those who are not fully literate and cannot take advantage of easily accessible information resources.

As Internet technology is diffused and bandwidth increases, there will be more use of the Internet for video and audio. However, because of the disparities in usable bandwidth between the Internet and television, the Internet is unlikely to displace television sets as the preferred means of viewing video. For the foreseeable future the Internet will continue to be most hospitable to print and graphics. To use it well one must be able to read.

Among the skills of information reception, reading has a special place. The proficient reader has access to knowledge that is denied the less-skilled reader. The written word remains the storehouse of the world's wisdom and knowledge. Reading also opens the door to symbolic thought, and without that skill the citizen is severely handicapped. The corollary skill of writing also has special cultural value: as a means of ordering and communicating thought, the discipline of writing is a powerful antidote to sloppy thinking.

Too many children and adults are unable to read well. The reasons include poor teaching, home environments that do not support reading, popular culture that glorifies other values, language barriers, and shame at not having such a skill. Internet technology offers the opportunity to develop individualized programs to teach reading at all levels of skill. There should be a wide variety of roads to reading varying in format, entertainment value, content, and approach. Unlike classroom instruction, anyone who might be interested could study anytime and at his or her own pace. The investment necessary to develop many different courses to teach reading on the Internet would be a small fraction of the federal investment in wiring the schools. The long-term return would likely be far greater.

No technology, in itself, will ever eliminate the differences that arise among people who effectively utilize a technology and those who do not. The Internet, however, is a technology that can give people the opportunity to learn the very skills that maximize the value of the technology. Internet content can be created that allows everyone the opportunity to learn to read, and as readers, take full advantage of the cornucopia of information resources that exist and are being created. The divide between those who can read well and those who cannot is a real divide. Rather than being a "digital divide," the Internet can be a road to information freedom.

Lloyd Morrisett

Preface

The digital divide, as anyone who has picked up this book should know, refers to the perceived gap between those who have access to the latest information technologies and those who do not. If we are indeed in an Information Age, where information is power, where content is king, where ... well, whatever ... then not having access to this information is considered in some quarters to be a handicap. And, according to some versions of the scenario, those who have access will further their distance from those who do not.

I should lay my cards on the table (the page?) immediately. I'm skeptical of the entire digital divide concept. But the objective of this volume is to present some documents that make the case for such a public policy issue, as well as material that questions the existence or at least the severity of the issue. The readings have been selected to describe the issues and then see it within a multi-layered context.[1] That is:

1. What are the underpinnings of the digital divide: the data that substantiated the concept?
2. What is its historical context?
3. What do some advocates say about the consequences or the remedies for the divide?
4. What research or analysis provides other perspectives on this issue?

I started as an agnostic in the early 1980s, when the catch phrase was information "haves and have-nots." Back then the Internet was not the driving force. Rather it was the Apple II and the original IBM PC. There was writing about the wealthy schools that would have computers and the poor ones that would not. I was a research director at the Program on Information Resources Policy at Harvard, so I did what such a program should do: I initiated research on the topic. I had no preconceived agenda. In the midst of the research my colleagues and I determined that this was, in fact, a non-issue (not that some advocates did not persist in making it one). I wrote up my findings, a version of which is re-published in this volume as chapter 4.

I need not repeat here what is available in that chapter. But the short version is that there have been and will continue to be many gaps—between those who knew how to farm and those who did not in the Agriculture Age; those who could fix an engine and those who could not in the Industrial Age; and those who could use a computing appliance and those who could not in the Information Age.

But the larger finding was, that when it came to gaps related to technology, they tended to be relatively transient. Television sets went from zero to universality in about a decade. VCRs likewise, as their prices went from thousands of dollars to a few hundred. Automobiles cost less today in terms of hours worked than in the days of the Model T and seem to sit in front of homes in even the poorest neighborhoods. Telephone service was much longer in coming. Why? Cost perhaps. Yet for the first 60 or 70 years of telephone service there was little incentive for households to have one unless they knew some other people with one. In the "old" days when most people lived and died within a small geographic community, there was not the usefulness that we take for granted today.

What Are the Stakes in the Digital Divide?

Whether one buys into the notion of a digital divide with substantial societal consequences is not of simply intellectual curiosity. It has very substantial economic and political implications: from the taxes on telephone service that are targeted to fund remedies in rural areas and poor neighborhoods to the broader skills that will be available in the work force. When President Clinton asked Congress for $50 million to provide computers and Internet access for poor families in his State of the Union address in 2000 (chapter 16), that had political ramifications. The same for his proposal for $2 billion in tax incentives for digital divide—

inspired programs (chapter 12). When the chairman of the Federal Communications Commission (FCC) makes proposals to Congress and his fellow commissioners for legislation and rules (chapter 8), that is a political process. So clearly the political players have raised the stakes.

This filters down to the costs. The specific costs are those taxes on telephone bills that are earmarked for digital divide subsidies. This includes the Universal Service Fund Fee. This is a tax on telephone companies that they typically pass on to their customers. As of April 2000, MCI, for example, was adding a 10% surcharge to the bills of their interexchange phone customers. In 2000, the FCC was requiring telecommunications carriers to contribute nearly 6% of their interstate and international calling revenues to subsidize schools and rural areas, an amount well in excess of $4 billion.[2] The economic stakes are considerable.

There are the human stakes. Access to the information available from networked devices may be critical in the education process—for both teachers and students. It will be useful in finding and improving jobs. It will be part of the routine everyday life. But will the stakes be as high as some prognosticators proclaim? FCC chairman Kennard writes, "The high-skilled, well-paid jobs of tomorrow demand the ability to use computers and telecommunications." Car mechanics and engineers were good occupations for some. Yet today does one need to know anything about the workings of the internal combustion engine and transmission differentials to use an automobile? Will knowledge of computers be essential to use them as they continue to get smarter, smaller, and less visible?

The Boundaries of the Digital Divide

The digital divide may have varying connotations. Already mentioned was how the chairman of the FCC incorporated a broader agenda of ownership of media into the concept. In the original iteration of the National Telecommunications and Information Agency (NTIA) surveys (chapter 1), it meant primarily personal computer ownership. More recently it has come to incorporate Internet access. The latest noises is that it further delineates those with high speed (broadband) access from slower dial-up modem access. In effect, it may be a moving target.

The term "digital divide" achieved mass media attention when it became part of the title of the second NTIA survey in 1998. Donna Hoffman, Thomas Novak, and Ann E. Schlosser, in their paper in chapter 3, credit Lloyd Morrisett with coining the term. However, while admitting that it may have been him, he told me, "I am not at all certain that is true. My best guess is that someone else did it." Wherever it came from, it was a catchy label and was applied with great effect by NTIA to its study, which received widespread attention.

Before there was a digital divide, even before there was a movement identifying information haves and have-nots, there was the universal service issue. This is explained in the introduction and readings in Part II. Although the political and financial mechanisms of universal service did not spring full bloom following the Communications Act of 1934 that made it a matter of national policy, it ultimately did lead to the phenomenon of nationwide averaging of telephone rates. That is, residential phone users paid roughly the same for a given level of telephone service regardless of the cost of providing that service. Thus, residential users in communities that were relatively inexpensive to serve, such as high-density urban areas where there may be hundreds or even thousands of subscribers in a square mile, were generally charged more by the phone companies—with the urging and blessing of the state regulators—than the cost of providing the service. This excessive "profit" helped subsidize subscribers in low-density areas—such as suburban and rural areas. Here there might be dozens or fewer subscribers in a square mile.

Although the goal of universal service was to make access to a dial tone affordable to all, it was never extended to incorporate subsidies for the actual *use* of the telephone. That is, long-distance calls were, until after the breakup of AT&T in 1984, priced well above cost to further help subsidize local basic service. Information that could be accessed by phone—from time and weather to pay-per-call services such as 900 exchange calls—were not part of the universal service contract. But the digital divide debate has included some component of the cost of information that could be available online.

Finally, then, there is the question of whether the cost of information should be part of the policy debate of the digital divide. If in fact there a disadvantaged population on the short end of the divide, is providing hardware and access enough—or should there be a provision to, in effect, subsidize the digital equivalent of newspapers, magazines, and books? And although it does not get discussed in much detail in these readings, where would one draw the line between information and entertainment? Much of what is available on cable and DBS, on newsstands and online is reasonably characterized as content for entertainment. If policy makers even wanted to somehow make content available to some disadvantaged groups, should they or could they differentiate between public affairs that might be useful to the body politic and the digital equivalent of "Beverly Hillbillies" reruns?

Stakes for Democracy

Are there stakes for democracy? Yes and no. In the long term—perhaps over 25 years—new ways of communication will become mainstream and prevalent. What is today the Internet, that is, a packet-switched multi-node network utilizing both wired and wireless components, will likely become *a*—if not *the*—primary carrier. So access to that network will be critical. On the other hand, what is the likelihood that this network *will* indeed become universal and central to communications if virtually everyone did not first have access to it?

Will people need high-tech skills to participate in this democracy in the future? Probably not. In fact, probably less than is needed today. This was a common trend even in the Industrial Age. In the early days of the automobile, the machines were so unreliable that a basic familiarity with their mechanics was helpful. Today, few users have ever looked under the hood. The first radios required a hobbyist approach, not only in building the sets but adjusting them to receive imprecise signals. Today, we pop in a battery and turn it on. The early days of computers similarly were reserved for those who enjoyed the challenge of making them work —or could employ a staff of engineers. Today, with some luck (we're not *quite* there), a novice can take a unit out of the box, plug in the power cord and a telephone line and have a reasonably good chance of getting online in a few minutes.

And the skill level to use intelligent devices keeps getting lower. Even programming is easier today with higher level languages than the totally foreign machine languages that were needed in the earliest years of computing.

It may be argued that even pre-Internet the mass audience has failed to take advantage of the tools it has for political participation: newspaper circulation per household has been declining for decades. Viewership of the evening national news programs fell through the 1990s. Audiences of the quality public affairs television shows are miniscule compared to viewership of even low-rated entertainment programming.

Perhaps a tougher question to address is how these technologies will enhance—or undermine—democracies. Providing a rich diversity of viewpoints may be a blessing—or the curse of a fragmenting society. Allowing individuals to inexpensively communicate with a nation or the world may be a democrat's utopia. Or it may open up new avenues for demagogues. The bottomless vat of text as well as unregulated audio and video that may become a reality must be weighed with the current and growing concerns about the privacy and security issues that seem to accompany the benefits of the digitally networked world.

The readings in this volume will not settle any of these issues. It is my own view, after picking through the digital divide literature, that this is not the issue to expend substantial amount of funds nor political capital. I summarize my reasoning in the final chapter. On your way there, there should be plenty of ammunition for whatever side of the debate you wish to argue. Thanks for coming along for the trip.

Ben Compaine

Notes

1. Or, as I first heard from Lee Fritschler, the former president of Dickinson College, "I've never seen a pancake so thin it didn't have two sides."

2. Proposed First Quarter 2000 Universal Service Contribution Factor, CC Docket No. 96–45, Public Notice, DA 99–2780 〈http://www.fcc.gov/Bureaus/ Common_Carrier/Public_Notices/1999/da992780.doc〉 and Separate Statement of Commissioner Furchtgott-Roth 〈http://www.fcc.gov/Bureaus/Common_ Carrier/Public_Notices/1999/d992780a.doc〉.

Acknowledgments

This book owes its existence to Bob Prior, executive editor, computer science, at The MIT Press. He pitched the idea to me—a turnaround from the usual order of events in book publishing. He then followed up with the support I needed to get this out in a timely fashion. From that point I owe considerable thanks to Katherine Innis, whose title, assistant acquisitions editor, computer science, belies her active role in shepherding the book to completion. Along with production editor Deborah Cantor-Adams, who turns the manuscript as best she can into a literate and well-designed volume (meaning any errors are mine), they are typical of the skilled and pleasant professionals I have worked with at The MIT Press. There are others at the publisher as well who work behind the scenes and perform their roles wonderfully—indexers, designers, and production coordinators. Thanks to you all.

Finally, I extend my appreciation to the researchers and writers who permitted their work to be published in this volume. Each in his or her own way has contributed to our awareness, understanding, and discussion of the policy issues around information and communications access.

I

The Set-Up: Documenters of the Digital Divide

Before there was a "digital divide" there were the "information haves and the have-nots." Commentators started making references to access to personal computers almost as soon as the first school anywhere installed an Apple II in 1980. By 1983 a survey found that two-thirds of the schools in the wealthiest school districts had personal computers, but "only" 41% in the poorest districts.

The first high-profile survey by the federal government to address the have and have-not issue was initiated in 1994 by the National Telecommunications and Information Administration (NTIA) within the Department of Commerce. That was the year that the World Wide Web got its first national attention and that Netscape commercialized an early graphical interface, the Mosaic browser. Although the Internet traces its origins to 1968 and the World Wide Web to 1991, they remained a relatively obscure preserve for academics and defense contractors until the graphical browsers made the Web user-friendly. Thus, it should come as no surprise that the first NTIA survey, "Falling Through the Net," all but ignored Internet access. "Internet" was mentioned twice, once in an endnote to the first reference. The Web was only mentioned in that same endnote. Its focus was on access to telephone service, personal computers, and modems. PCs with modems were for the most part still used to connect to proprietary online services, such as CompuServe, Prodigy, and America Online.

So the first chapter, "Falling through the Net: A Survey of the 'Have-Nots' in Rural and Urban America" is a rather short document. To no one's surprise, it reported that the poorest households had the lowest telephone, computer, and modem penetration. But it further subdivided the poor by where they lived: rural, central city, and urban, as well as by racial and ethnic group, age, and education. Although I have provided the full report (except for the section on methodology), I only included 8 of the 30 tables. The text of the report itself actually does a rather succinct job of summarizing the key tables. There are a few noteworthy twists for those willing to mine the data. One is that telephone penetration is higher among the rural poor than among the central-city poor. The paradox is that telephone-rate cross subsidies have long been aimed at "overcharging" urban subscribers subsidizing rural subscribers (regardless of income).

By 1998, NTIA's follow-up survey had taken on the digital divide as its subtitle and included several tables covering online access. I have not included this report because a report issued a year later, included here as chapter 2, is not only more timely but was a substantially more extensive report than its predecessors. By 1999 the subtitle was "Defining the Digital Divide." This report continues the series in measuring telephone and computer penetration, but for the first time specifically addresses Internet penetration. Because of its expanded size, I have substantially abridged it for publication here. I removed sections on telephone penetration, reasoning that not only doesn't this change much year to year at its current high level of penetration, but it is subsumed by the more relevant measurement of computer and Internet access. I have also skipped the section on how people use the Internet, not because it is is irrelevant but again because it is slightly off the point of access. As with all the chapters in this section, I have included the URL links to the complete reports for those who want the unabridged version.

The final report in this section was the latest research (at the time of this compilation) from Donna Hoffman and her colleagues at Vanderbilt University. Professor Hoffman was one of the pioneers in tracking and interpreting Internet usage. "The Evolution of the Digital Divide" is an extensive study, though based on data gathered by third-party sources. Stimulated by some research that suggested that even when adjusting for income and education African Americans and Hispanics were less likely to own computers than whites, they set out to look for differences based on race over time, albeit a rather short time—late 1996 to mid 1998. Chapter 3 presents a substantial portion of the study, including tabular data.

The Hoffman, Novak, and Schlosser research probes deeper than the gross numbers and percentages of the NTIA studies, leading to more nuanced findings. For example, focusing on the most recent Web users they find few if any differences between Whites and African Americans. They also noted that rates of cable and satellite dish penetration among African Americans is increasing dramatically, making that group better prospects than whites for high-speed Internet access.

Still, all three of these studies suffer from a major failing: they have been light on use of statistical measures for determining the significance of the differences in their findings among groups. They have not generally employed analysis of variance or similar measures that can help factor out the spurious from the valid factors (e.g., ethnicity, income, education, age, gender, etc.) that can help us know which factors really matter. Contrast with chapter 14, which does employ such methods to identify the measures that do matter in determining digital access.

1

Falling through the Net: A Survey of the "Have-Nots" in Rural and Urban America

National Telecommunications and Information Administration

I Background

At the core of U.S. telecommunications policy is the goal of universal service—the idea that all Americans should have access to affordable telephone service. The most commonly used measure of the nation's success in achieving universal service is telephone penetration—the percentage of all U.S. households that have a telephone on the premises.[1] There currently exist two principal sources for nationwide data on telephone penetration: First, the Current Population Survey (CPS), conducted by the U.S. Bureau of the Census, U.S. Department of Commerce, three times each year, includes questions on telephone subscription. Second, the Federal Communications Commission's (FCC) Industry Analysis Division, within the Common Carrier Bureau, uses the CPS data to produce regular reports that provide a detailed demographic profile of telephone subscribership in the United States.

Although these statistics have provided an invaluable empirical foundation for the universal service debate, they are incomplete in at least two respects. The publicly available CPS data does not include a geographic identifier for the households surveyed, primarily to preserve the confidentiality of household-specific information. As a result, the FCC's periodic reports cannot indicate how telephone subscribership varies geographically—how, for example, telephone penetration in rural areas compares to penetration in suburbia or central cities.

Additionally, the subscribership data typically collected are limited to telephone service. There are legitimate questions about linking universal service solely to telephone service in a society where individuals' economic and social well-being increasingly depends on their ability to access, accumulate, and assimilate information. While a standard telephone line can be an individual's pathway to the riches of the Information Age, a personal computer and modem are rapidly becoming the keys to the vault. The robust growth recently experienced in Internet usage illustrates this promise as new and individual subscribers gravitate to online services.[2] This suggests a need to go beyond the traditional focus on telephone penetration as the barometer of this nation's progress toward universal service.

As the President's principal adviser on telecommunications policy, the Commerce Department's National Telecommunications and Information Administration (NTIA) has taken two steps to fill these lacunae in the nation's universal service database. In July 1994, NTIA contracted with the Census Bureau to include questions on computer/modem ownership and usage in the CPS conducted in November 1994.[3] Further, after the CPS was concluded, NTIA asked the Census to cross-tabulate the information gathered according to several specific variables (i.e., income, race, age, educational attainment, and region) and three geographic categories—rural, urban, and central city.[4]

By supplementing the existing database in these two critical respects, NTIA has developed a more expansive profile of universal service in America—a portrait that includes computers and modems as well as telephones. The data in the attached tables provide fresh insights into the make-up of those who are not connected to the National Information Infrastructure (NII). More particularly, this research has explored the characteristics of the have-nots in rural versus urban settings. In addition, the agency has gained new insights about the information disadvantaged in America's central cities, enabling policy makers for the first time to array these characteristics against rural and urban profiles. NTIA's examination reveals the usage habits of PC/modem users in accessing online services, an important input for policy development in the nascent Information Age.

A Closer Look

In essence, information have-nots are disproportionately found in this country's rural areas *and* its central cities. While most recognize that

Table 1.1
Percent of U.S. Households with a Computer, 1994: By Income, by Rural, Urban, and Central-City Areas

	Rural	Urban	Central City
Less than $10,000	4.5	8.1	7.6
$10,000–$14,999	7.0	9.1	9.3
$15,000–$19,999	11.0	12.6	13.0
$20,000–$24,999	15.7	15.9	16.3
$25,000–$34,999	18.1	22.0	21.1
$35,000–$49,999	32.7	34.9	34.7
$50,000–$74,999	46.0	48.4	47.4
$75,000 or more	59.6	64.4	63.1

Table 1.2
Percent of U.S. Computer Households with a Modem, 1994: By Income, by Rural, Urban, and Central-City Areas

	Rural	Urban	Central City
Less than $10,000	23.6	44.1	43.9
$10,000–$14,999	28.9	40.6	44.8
$15,000–$19,999	32.4	30.7	28.3
$20,000–$24,999	28.5	38.2	36.8
$25,000–$34,999	32.6	41.1	43.3
$35,000–$49,999	34.4	45.6	48.0
$50,000–$74,999	46.7	49.8	49.2
$75,000 or more	52.2	58.1	56.4

poor people as a group have difficulties in connecting to the NII, less well-known is the fact that the lowest telephone penetration exists in central cities. Concerning personal-computer penetration and the incidence of modems when computers are present in a household, however, no situation compares with the plight of the rural poor (tables 1.1 and 1.2).

An examination by *race* reveals that Native Americans (including American Indians, Aleuts, and Eskimos) in rural areas proportionately possess the fewest telephones, followed by rural Hispanics and rural Blacks. Black households in central cities and particularly rural areas have the lowest percentages of PCs, with central-city Hispanics also

Table 1.3
Percent of U.S. Households with a Computer, 1994: By Race/Origin, by Rural, Urban, and Central-City Areas

	Rural	Urban	Central City
White—non-Hispanic	24.6	30.3	29.4
Black—non-Hispanic	6.4	11.8	10.4
Hispanic	12.0	13.2	10.5
American Indian, Aleut, Eskimo—non-Hispanic	15.3	23.7	25.5
Asian or Pacific Islander—non-Hispanic	33.7	39.5	35.9
Other—non-Hispanic	11.8	33.7	27.2

Table 1.4
Percent of U.S. Computer Households with a Modem, 1994: By Race/Origin, by Rural, Urban, and Central-City Areas

	Rural	Urban	Central City
White—non-Hispanic	40.2	48.6	49.7
Black—non-Hispanic	41.7	41.2	37.6
Hispanic	45.0	42.3	36.0
American Indian, Aleut, Eskimo—non-Hispanic	28.3	44.9	35.4
Asian or Pacific Islander—non-Hispanic	26.7	45.9	44.1
Other—non-Hispanic	33.4	43.8	28.2

ranked low (table 1.3). For those households with computers, Native Americans and Asians/Pacific Islanders registered the lowest position among those possessing modems (table 1.4).

On the basis of *age*, the single most seriously disadvantaged group consists of the youngest householders (under 25 years), particularly in rural areas. Overall, they rank lowest in telephone penetration and near the bottom relating to computers on-premises. While senior citizens (55 years and older)—regardless of the type of area—surpass all other groups with respect to telephones, rural seniors rate lowest in computer penetration (see table 1.5). Among households with PCs, the youngest in rural areas also fare worst in modem penetration, followed by rural middle-aged and senior citizens (table 1.6).

Table 1.5
Percent of U.S. Households with a Computer, 1994: By Age, by Rural, Urban, and Central-City Areas

	Rural	Urban	Central City
Under 25 years	12.3	20.7	21.0
25–34 years	22.3	27.8	25.0
35–44 years	34.7	36.6	31.4
45–54 years	32.5	36.8	31.8
55 years and older	11.9	13.8	12.0

Table 1.6
Percent of U.S. Computer Households with a Modem, 1994: By Age, by Rural, Urban, and Central-City Areas

	Rural	Urban	Central City
Under 25 years	27.4	44.4	46.6
25–34 years	44.0	52.3	51.0
35–44 years	41.5	47.6	48.2
45–54 years	38.0	48.4	47.9
55 years and older	38.4	41.7	39.2

Generally, the less that one is educated, the lower the level of telephone, computer, and computer-household modem penetration. For a given level of *education*, however, central-city households generally have the lowest penetration for both telephones and computers (table 1.7), while rural households with computers consistently trail urban areas and central cities in terms of modem penetration (table 1.8). Northeast central cities rank as the *region* with proportionately the most telephone and computer have-nots, followed by southern central cities and rural areas. Modem penetration among computer households is lowest in rural areas, specifically in the West, then the Midwest and the South.

Empowering the Information Disadvantaged

NTIA's research reveals that many of the groups that are most disadvantaged in terms of absolute computer and modem penetration are the most enthusiastic users of online services that facilitate economic uplift and empowerment. Low-income, minority, young, and less-educated computer households in rural areas and central cities appear to be likely

Table 1.7
Percent of U.S. Households with a Computer, 1994: By Educational Attainment, by Rural, Urban, and Central-City Areas

	Rural	Urban	Central City
Elementary: 0–8 years	2.6	2.8	2.6
High School: 1–3 years	6.5	6.1	4.7
High School: 4 years	16.5	15.3	12.2
College: 1–3 years	32.7	29.9	27.5
College: 4 years or more	51.2	50.7	47.0

Table 1.8
Percent of U.S. Computer Households with a Modem, 1994: By Educational Attainment, by Rural, Urban, and Central-City Areas

	Rural	Urban	Central City
Elementary: 0–8 years	23.7	32.9	35.4
High School: 1–3 years	22.4	36.7	44.7
High School: 4 years	31.2	37.8	36.0
College: 1–3 years	40.4	45.0	42.3
College: 4 years or more	48.9	53.5	53.9

to engage actively in searching classified ads for employment, taking educational classes, and accessing government reports, online via modem.

The Facts
More specifically, our findings point to the following information have-nots:

• Poor in Central Cities and Rural Areas—Overall, the poorest households (incomes less than $10,000) in central cities have the lowest *telephone* penetration (79.8%), followed by rural (81.6%) and urban (81.7%) areas. However, the rural poor are lowest in terms of *computer* penetration (4.5%) and—among those households with computers—*modem* (23.6%) penetration compared to central cities (7.6% and 43.9%) and urban areas (8.1% and 44.1%). Interestingly, among the most likely users of *online* classes are low-income users ($10,000–$14,999) in all areas (rural, central-city, and urban).

• Rural and Central-City Minorities—Native American households (American Indians, Aleuts, and Eskimos) in rural areas have the lowest *telephone* penetration (75.5%). Rural Blacks have the lowest *computer* rates (6.4%), followed by central-city Blacks (10.4%), central-city Hispanics (10.5%), and urban Blacks (11.8%). Computer households composed of Asian/Pacific Islanders (26.7%) and Native Americans in rural areas have the least *modem* penetration. Albeit Whites in urban areas have the highest telephone penetration (96.2%), an urban minority group (Asians or Pacific Islanders) leads all others in terms of computer penetration (39.5%). Regarding usage of online services, minority groups surpassed Whites in percentage of: *classified ad searches*—urban and central-city Native Americans (48.6%, 27.0%) and rural Hispanics (22.1%); *taking courses*—rural Native Americans (51.7%) and rural Blacks (33.4%); and *accessing government reports*—rural, urban, and central-city Native Americans (45.4%, 46.4%, 41.8%) and rural Hispanics (52.8%).

• Young and Old—Regarding *telephone* penetration, the youngest households (under 25 years) in rural areas trail all others. In terms of *computers*, rural senior citizens (55 years and older) possess the lowest penetration (11.9%), followed by seniors in central cities (12.0%) and the youngest in rural areas (12.3%). These two groups are also very low-ranking in terms of *modem* penetration as a percentage of computer households, all in rural areas: the youngest (27.4%), 45–54 years old (38.0%), and seniors (38.4%). Yet the youngest households with computers in rural areas rank number one in taking courses (21.7%) and second in classified ad searches (10.7%). The youngest householders in central-city areas are also among the most likely to search classified ads (9.2%) and access government reports (21.0%) among *online services*.

• Less-Educated in Central Cities—With some exceptions (most notably, telephone penetration for the two lowest education categories), the fewer the number of years of education, the lower the telephone, computer, and computer-household modem penetration. For a given level of education, however, central-city households generally have the lowest *telephone* and *computer* penetration rates, while rural households with computers consistently trail other areas with respect to *modems*. For those taking *online* courses, the highest degree of participation is among those with the lowest level of education (zero to eight years) located in urban (31.8%) and rural (24.3%) areas, and the lowest in the central cities (13.7%).

• Northeastern Central Cities and the South—The lowest *telephone* and *computer* penetration is in northeastern central cities (89.5%, 16.4%), plus central-city (91.2%, 22.0%) and rural (91.3%, 18.6%) areas in the South. *Modem* penetration among households with computers is lowest in rural areas in the West (35.3%), Midwest (37.2%), and South (40.7%). Yet households in the rural South (7.3%) and north-eastern central cities (9.4%) are among the most active in searching classified ads, and the latter region in accessing government documents (20.9%). In taking classes, the rural South (22.3%) and central cities (20.3%) topped all other areas, followed by northeastern central cities (18.8%).

Where We Go from Here—and Why ...

More work needs to be done to better assess the characteristics of these have-nots. For example, it is not clear whether the same low-income dis-advantaged are also those who are minorities or the less educated or the young or old. Additional evidence is required for determining whether, e.g., mobility of households is an important determining factor of in-formation exclusion within central cities or rural areas. Once superior profiles of telephone, computer, and online users are developed, then carefully targeted support programs can be implemented that will assure with high probability that those who need assistance in connecting to the NII will be able to do so. NTIA anticipates working in a collaborative effort with federal, state, and local policy makers, as appropriate, to meaningfully achieve these goals.

The broad policy implications for these findings should not be over-looked. By identifying those who are truly in need, policy makers can prudently and efficiently target support to these information disadvan-taged. Only when this point is reached can *all* those who desire to access the NII be possibly accommodated. However, connectivity to all such households will not occur instantaneously; rather, there is a pivotal role to be assumed in the new electronic age by the traditional providers of information access for the general public—the public schools and libraries. These and other community access centers can provide, at least during an interim period, a means for electronic access to all those who might not otherwise have such access. Policy prescriptions that include public safety nets would complement the long-term strategy of hooking up all those households who want to be connected to the NII.

[*Part II, Methodology and Definitions, is omitted.*]

Notes

This report was published by NTIA in July 1995.

1. As of November 1994, telephone penetration in the United States was 93.8 percent. See Alexander Belinfante, Federal Communications Commission, Telephone Subscribership in the United States, Table 2 at 14 (April 1995).

2. Recent evidence accumulated by the University of Michigan Business School suggests that more than half of Net users subscribe through a private Internet access provider—using their PCs and modems. Steve Lohr, Technology: On the Net; Out, Damned Geek! The Typical Web User is no Longer Packing a Pocket Protecter, *New York Times*, July 3, 1995, 1, at 39. Moreover, a 1994–95 survey of 12,000 users conducted by the Interactive Services Association found that for the first time, consumers that have been online for a year or less will make up a majority of all online users by the end of 1995. *Communications Daily*, May 22, 1995.

3. The November, 1994 Current Population Survey reports data collected from a sample of 54,000 U.S. households.

4. See discussion in part II, "Methodology and Definitions."

2

Falling through the Net: Defining the Digital Divide

National Telecommunications and Information Administration

I Household Access

A Introduction

Over the last five years, NTIA has measured household connectivity as a means of determining which Americans are connected to the nation's telecommunications and information infrastructure. Part I updates the earlier household penetration surveys released in NTIA's *Falling through the Net: A Survey of the "Have-Nots" in Rural and Urban America* (July 1995) and *Falling through the Net II: New Data on the Digital Divide* (July 1998).[1]

As in our earlier surveys, we have measured household telephone, computer, and Internet penetration rates across America to determine which Americans own telephones and personal computers (PCs) and access the Internet at home.[2]

The 1998 data reveal that, overall, U.S. households are significantly more connected by telephone, computer, and the Internet since NTIA issued the first *Falling through the Net* report, which was based on 1994 Current Population Survey (CPS) results.[3] Penetration rates have risen across all demographic groups and geographic areas. Nevertheless, penetration levels currently differ—often substantially—according to income, education level, race, household type, and geography, among other demographic characteristics. The differences in connectivity are most pronounced with respect to computers and Internet access.

The following examples highlight the breadth of the digital divide today:

• Those with a college degree are more than *eight times* as likely to have a computer at home and nearly *sixteen times* as likely to have home Internet access as those with an elementary-school education.

• A high-income household in an urban area is more than *twenty times* as likely as a rural, low-income household to have Internet access.

• A child in a low-income White family is *three times* as likely to have Internet access as a child in a comparable Black family, and *four times* as likely to have access as children in a comparable Hispanic household.

• A wealthy household of Asian/Pacific Islander descent is nearly *thirteen times* as likely to own a computer as a poor Black household, and nearly *thirty-four* times as likely to have Internet access.

• Finally, a child in a dual-parent White household is nearly *twice* as likely to have Internet access as a child in a White single-parent household, while a child in a dual-parent Black family is almost *four times* as likely to have access as a child in a single-parent Black household.

The data reveal that the digital divide—the disparities in access to telephones, personal computers (PCs), and the Internet across certain demographic groups—still exists and, in many cases, has *widened significantly*. The gap for computers and Internet access has generally grown larger by categories of education, income, and race.

These are just a few of the many disparities that persist across the United States today. As discussed below, however, the divide among households with telephones is narrowing. Some gaps for computer ownership (between certain income and education levels) are also closing. As the following discussion explains, Internet access remains the chief concern, as those already with access to electronic resources make rapid gains while leaving other households behind.

[*Section B, Telephone Penetration, is omitted.*]

C **Access to Electronic Services**

While telephone penetration has remained stable across the nation, significant changes have occurred for personal computer ownership and Internet access. For the latter two categories, household rates have soared since 1994 for all demographic groups in all locations. These increases indicate that Americans across the board are increasingly embracing electronic services by employing them in their homes.

Despite increasing connectivity for all groups, in some areas the digital divide still exists and, in a number of cases, is *growing*. Some groups (such as certain minority or low-income households in rural America) still have PC and Internet penetration rates in the single digits. By contrast, other groups (such as higher-income, highly educated, or dual-parent households) have rising connectivity rates. One promising sign of change is that the gap between races for PC ownership has narrowed significantly at the highest income level (above $75,000).

1   Expanding Access to Electronic Services   Americans of every demographic group and geographic area have experienced a significant increase in computer ownership and Internet access. Nationwide, PC ownership is now at 42.1%, up from 24.1% in 1994 and 36.6% in 1997 (an increase of 74.7% and 15.0%, respectively). Households across rural, central-city, and urban areas now own home computers in greater numbers; each area experienced at least a sixteen percentage point increase since 1994, and at least a five percentage point increase since 1997. Similarly, households of all ethnic groups, income levels, education levels, and ages have experienced a significant increase. Black and Hispanic households, for example, are now twice as likely to own PCs as they were in 1994.

Internet access has also grown significantly in the last year: 26.2% of U.S. households now have Internet access, up from 18.6% in 1997 (an increase of 40.9%).[4]

As with computer ownership, Internet access has increased for all demographic groups in all locations. In the last year alone, for example, Internet access increased 40.5% for White households, 45.4% for Black households, and 44.8% for Hispanic households.

2   Disparities in Access to Electronic Services   Despite these gains across American households, distinct disparities in access remain. Americans living in rural areas are less likely to be connected by PCs or the Internet—even when holding income constant. Indeed, at most income brackets below $35,000, those living in urban areas are at least 25% more likely to have Internet access than those in rural areas. Additionally, groups that already have low penetration rates (such as low-income, young, or certain minority households) are the least connected in rural areas and central cities.

The following demographic and geographic breakdowns are significant determinants of a household's likelihood of owning a computer or accessing the Internet from home:

Income   PC and Internet penetration rates both increase with higher income levels.[5] Households at higher income levels are far more likely to own computers and access the Internet than those at the lowest income levels. Those with an income over $75,000 are more than *five times* as likely to have a computer at home and are more than *seven times* as likely to have home Internet access as those with an income under $10,000.

Low-income households in rural areas are the least connected, experiencing connectivity rates in the single digits for both PCs and Internet access. The contrast between low-income households (earning between $5,000 and $9,999) in rural America and high-income households (earning more than $75,000) in urban areas is particularly acute: 8.1% versus 76.5% for computer ownership, and 2.9% versus 62.0% for Internet access.

The impact of income on Internet access is evident even among families with the same race and family structure. Among similarly situated families (two parents, same race), a family earning more than $35,000 is two to almost six times as likely to have Internet access as a family earning less than $35,000. The most significant disparity is among Hispanic families: two-parent households earning more than $35,000 are nearly *six times* as likely to have Internet access as those earning less than $35,000.

Race/Origin   As with telephone penetration, race also influences connectivity. Unlike telephone penetration, however, households of Asian/Pacific Islander descent have the clear lead in computer penetration (55.0%) and Internet access rates (36.0%), followed by White households (46.6% and 29.8%, respectively). Black and Hispanic households have far lower PC penetration levels (at 23.2% and 25.5%), and Internet access levels (11.2% and 12.6%).

Again, geography and income influence these trends. Urban Asians/Pacific Islanders have the highest computer penetration rates (55.6%) and Internet access rates (36.5%). By contrast, rural Black households

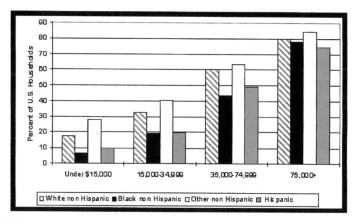

	Under $15,000	15,000-34,999	35,000-74,999	75,000+
White non Hispanic	17.5	32.5	60.4	80.0
Black non Hispanic	6.6	19.4	43.7	78.0
Other non Hispanic	27.8	40.1	63.4	84.4
Hispanic	9.4	19.8	49.0	74.8

Figure 2.1
Percent of U.S. households with a computer, by income and by race, 1998.

are the least connected group in terms of PC ownership (17.9%) or Internet access (7.1%). Black households earning less than $15,000 are also at the opposite end of the spectrum from high-income Asians/Pacific Islanders for PC ownership (6.6% versus 85.0%). (See figure 2.1.)

The role of race or ethnic origin is highlighted when looking at similarly situated families. A White, two-parent household earning less than $35,000 is nearly *three times* as likely to have Internet access as a comparable Black household and nearly *four times* as likely to have Internet access as Hispanic households in the same income category.[6]

Education Access to information resources is closely tied to one's level of education. Households at higher education levels are far more likely to own computers and access the Internet than those at the lowest education levels. Those with a college degree or higher are more than *eight times* as likely to have a computer at home (68.7% versus 7.9%) and are nearly *sixteen times* as likely to have home Internet access (48.9% versus 3.1%) as those with an elementary-school education. (See figure 2.2.)

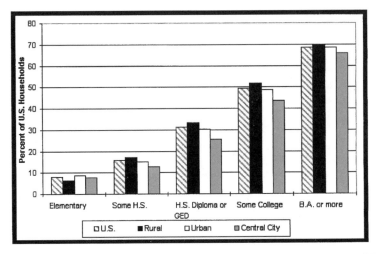

	U.S.	Rural	Urban	Central City
Elementary	7.9	6.3	8.7	7.7
Some H.S.	15.7	17.2	15.0	12.7
H.S. Diploma or GED	31.2	33.2	30.3	25.6
Some College	49.3	51.7	48.6	43.7
B.A. or more	68.7	69.7	68.5	65.8

Figure 2.2
Percent of U.S. households with a computer, by education and by U.S., rural, urban, and central-city areas, 1998.

In rural areas, the disparity is even greater. Those with a college degree or higher are more than *eleven times* as likely to have a computer at home (6.3% versus 69.7%) and are more than *twenty-six* times as likely to have home Internet access (1.8% versus 47.0%) as those with an elementary-school education.

Household Type   As with telephones, the makeup of the household influences the likelihood of the household's access to electronic services. Computer ownership lags among single-parent households, especially female-headed households (31.7%), compared to married couples with children (61.8%). The same is true for Internet access (15.0% for female-headed households, 39.3% for dual-parent households).

When holding race constant, it is clear that family composition can still have a significant impact on Internet access. Overall, dual-parent

White families are nearly *twice* as likely to have Internet access as single-parent White households (44.9% versus 23.4%). Black families with two parents are nearly *four times* as likely to have Internet access as single-parent Black households (20.4% versus 5.6%). And, children of two-parent Hispanic homes are nearly *two and a half times* as likely to have Internet access as their single-parent counterparts (14.0% versus 6.0%).[7]

These differences are modified somewhat when income is taken into account. Nevertheless, even when comparing households of similar incomes, disparities in Internet access persist. At all income levels, Black, Asian, and Native American households with two parents are twice as likely to have Internet access as those with one parent. For Hispanics and White households with two parents, on the other hand, clear-cut differences emerge only for incomes above $35,000. For these households, Whites are *one and a half times* more likely and Hispanics are *twice* as likely to have Internet access.[8]

Age   Age also plays a role in access to information resources. While seniors have the highest penetration rates for telephones, they trail all other age groups with respect to computer ownership (25.8%) and Internet access (14.6%). Young households (under age 25) exhibit the second lowest penetration rates (32.3% for PCs, 20.5% for Internet access). Households in the middle-age brackets (35–55 years) lead all others in PC penetration (nearly 55.0%) and Internet access (over 34.0%). The contrasts among age groups are particularly striking between rural seniors (23.3% for PCs, 12.4% for Internet) and young, rural households (27.7% for PCs, 13.3% for Internet) on the one hand, and urban 45–54 year-olds on the other (55.3% for PCs, 36.5% for Internet).

Region   The region where a household is located also impacts its access to electronic services. The West is the clear-cut leader for both computer penetration (48.9%) and Internet access (31.3%). At the other end of the spectrum is the South at 38.0% for PC penetration and 23.5% for Internet access. (See figure 2.3.) Looking at the degree of urbanization, the lowest rates are in northeastern central cities (30.4% for PCs, 18.7% for Internet access); the highest are in the urban West (49.2% for PCs, 32.0% for Internet access).

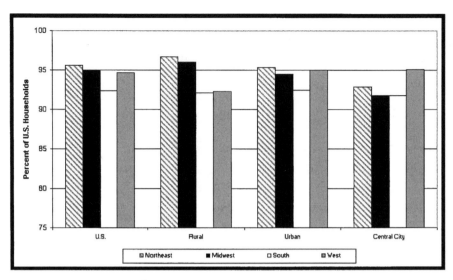

	U.S.	Rural	Urban	Central City
Northeast	95.6	96.7	95.3	92.9
Midwest	94.9	96.0	94.5	91.8
South	92.4	92.1	92.5	91.8
West	94.7	92.3	95.0	95.1

Figure 2.3
Percent of U.S. households with a telephone, by region, by rural, urban, and central-city areas, 1998.

State   As with telephones, computer penetration among states is grouped according to tiers due to the ranges of certainty created by the use of 90% confidence intervals).[9] The top tier ranges from Alaska's 62.4% to Wyoming's 46.1%. The middle grouping is bounded by Arizona (44.3%) and Pennsylvania (39.3%). The low tier includes principally southern states, ranging from Oklahoma (37.8%) to Mississippi (25.7%). Regarding Internet access, the ordering of the states—ranging from Alaska (44.1%) to Mississippi (13.6%)—tracks relatively closely the PC rankings, but often with wider confidence intervals at the 90% level.

In sum, disparities with respect to electronic access clearly exist across various demographic and geographic categories. Similar to telephone penetration, electronic access comes hardest for Americans who are low-income, Black or Hispanic or Native American,[10] less educated, from single-parent families (but especially single-female householders), young heads of households, and who live in the South, rural areas or central cities. Dissimilar to the phone profile, however, senior have-nots are less connected in terms of electronic access. And Asians/Pacific Islanders have reached a leading status with respect to computers and Internet access that they have not enjoyed in telephone comparisons.

3   The Expanding Digital Divide   The chief concern with respect to household computer and Internet access is the growing digital divide. Groups that were already connected (e.g., higher-income, more-educated White and Asian/Pacific Islander households) are now far more connected, while those with lower rates have increased less quickly. As a result, the gap between the information haves and have-nots is growing over time. The increasing divides are particularly troublesome with regard to Internet access.

Divide Based on Race/Origin   The digital divide has turned into a "racial ravine" when one looks at access among households of different races and ethnic origins. With regard to computers, the gap between White and Black households *grew 39.2%* (from a 16.8 percentage point difference to a 23.4 percentage point difference) between 1994 and 1998. For White versus Hispanic households, the gap similarly *rose by 42.6%* (from a 14.8 point gap to 21.1 point gap).

Minorities are losing ground even faster with regard to Internet access. Between 1997 and 1998, the gap between White and Black households *increased by 37.7%* (from a 13.5 percentage point difference to a 18.6 percentage point difference), and *by 37.6%* (from a 12.5 percentage point difference to a 17.2 percentage point difference) between White and Hispanic households.

Even when holding income constant, there is still a yawning divide among different races and origins. At the lowest income levels, the gap has widened considerably for computer ownership.[11] For households earning less than $15,000, the gaps rose substantially: by 73.0% or an additional 4.6 points between White and Black households, and by 44.6% or an additional 2.5 points between White and Hispanic households. For the households earning between $15,000 and $34,999, the disparities between White and Black households have increased by 61.7% (or 5.0 percentage points), and 46.0% or (4.0 percentage points) between White and Hispanic households.

For the same period, the increases for the $35,000–$74,999 bracket are much smaller for both the White/Black gap (a growth of 6.4%, or 1.0 percentage points) and the White/Hispanic divide (a growth of 15.2%, or 1.5 percentage points). The most striking finding, however, concerns the highest income level of $75,000 or more. For that income range, the gap between White and Black households has *declined* substantially (by 76.2%, or 6.4 percentage points), while the gap between White and Hispanic households has grown by 4.9 percentage points.

Divide Based on Education Level   Households at higher education levels are now also much more likely to own computers and access the Internet than those at the lowest education levels. In the last year alone, the gap in computer use has grown 7.8% (from a 56.4 to a 60.8 percentage point difference). The divide with respect to Internet access has widened 25.0% (from a 36.6 to a 45.8 percentage point difference). Not all groups, however, are lagging further behind the front-runners. Those with some college education and those with a high school diploma are now closing in on those with a college education.

Divide Based on Income   The digital divide has widened substantially when comparing households of different incomes. In the last year, the divide between the highest and lowest income groups grew 29.0% (from a 42.0 to a 52.2 percentage point difference) for Internet access. The same trends are recurring with respect to all income levels lower than $50,000. Interestingly, however, the gap appears to be narrowing for the mid-range and upper income groups. Households earning between $50,000–$74,999 are now actually closer (by 0.4 percentage points) to those at the highest income level than they were in 1997.

Middle-income households are faring far better with regard to computers. A significant drop of 11.1% (from a 15.3 to a 13.6 percentage point difference) occurred between the highest ($75,000+) and second highest ($50,000–$74,999) income brackets. And the gaps are also narrowing—though less significantly—for those earning more than $25,000.

D   Conclusion

The Census data reveal a number of trends. On the positive side, it is apparent that *all* Americans are becoming increasingly connected—whether by telephone, computer, or the Internet—over time. On the other hand, it is also apparent that certain groups are growing far more rapidly, particularly with respect to Internet connectivity. This pattern means that the haves have only become more information-rich in 1998, while the have-nots are lagging even further behind.

As the Internet becomes a more mature and pervasive technology, the digital divide among households of different races, incomes, and education levels may narrow. This pattern is already occurring with regard to home computers. Race matters less at the highest income level, and the gap is narrowing among households of higher income and education levels.

Even so, it is reasonable to expect that many people are going to lag behind in absolute numbers for a long time. Education and income appear to be among the leading elements driving the digital divide today. Because these factors vary along racial and ethnic lines, minorities will continue to face a greater digital divide as we move into the next century. This reality merits a thoughtful response by policy makers consistent with the needs of Americans in the Information Age.

II   Internet Access and Usage

A   Introduction

This section provides an in-depth examination of Internet (or Net) access and usage. In contrast to part I, which looks at household access, part II focuses primarily on trends among *individuals*. This is a new analysis in the *Falling Through the Net* series, which we have included for at least two related reasons. First, given the Internet's robust growth, the Internet has assumed an importance in Americans' everyday lives that compels us to probe more deeply into this new medium. Second, a sufficient number of people are now online, enabling meaningful surveying and statistically significant analyses.

Many of the findings in this new section will be useful to the stakeholders in the new Information Age. They may be particularly useful for policy makers concerned with ensuring affordable access to the Internet. Key findings include:

• Despite the Internet's only recent emergence as a new media, approximately one-third of all Americans already have Internet access from some location, either at home or outside of the home. Almost one-fourth of Americans have access at home.

• Whites are more likely to have Internet access *at home* than Blacks or Hispanics are from *any* location.

• Approximately two-thirds of households with PCs or WebTVs®[12] have Internet access. Those households that do not have Internet access cite "cost" or the fact that they "don't want it" as leading reasons for never having used the Internet. Cost is also the leading reason for discontinuing Internet use.

• Americans' use of the Internet varies tremendously among demographic groups. Email, however, overwhelmingly represents the most popular type of use for all groups, whether access occurs at home (three-fourths) or at an outside location (almost two-thirds).

• Groups that are less likely to have Internet access at home or work (such as certain minorities, those with lower incomes, those with lower education levels, and the unemployed) tend to access the Internet at public facilities, such as schools and libraries. These same groups also tend to engage in online activities that can result in their economic advancement, such as taking educational courses, engaging in school research, or conducting job searches.

The Internet is a nascent, rapidly diffusing technology that promises to become the economic underpinning for all successful countries in the new global economy. Understanding who is connected to the Net, and how it is being used, is critical to the development of sound policies in this area. In the sections that follow, we examine both Internet access and its usage through a variety of measurements.

B   Where People Access the Internet

1   General Access to the Internet   Many people have the option of accessing the Internet from more than one place. A person can connect from home; select another site, such as at work, a school, library, or community center; or use a combination of the two. Among all Americans, 22.2% currently use the Internet at home, and 17.0% use it at some site outside the home. Almost one-third (32.7%) use the Internet somewhere, while approximately two-thirds (67.3%) do not use it at all.

Demographic and Geographic Variables   Levels of Internet access differ dramatically among different groups and geographic areas. A cross-sectional analysis based on the seven variables set forth below illustrates this theme. Where a given variable is cross-tabulated with the degree of urbanization (such as rural or central city), significant differentials also typically occur.

• *Income.*   As a basic proposition, usage of the Internet is directly related to one's income level. (See figure 2.4.) For those at the lower end of the income scale ($5,000–9,999), 12.1% use the Internet, either at home or at an outside location. This contrasts with 58.9% of those in the highest bracket ($75,000+) accessing the Internet at any location. Where one accesses the Internet also correlates with income levels. Thus, persons with incomes of less than $35,000 use the Internet more often outside the home, while the reverse is true for those earning $35,000 or more annually.

• *Race/Origin.*   How often and where the Internet is used differ by race or ethnic origin. Whites (37.7%) and Asians/Pacific Islanders (35.9%) use the Internet much more than Blacks (19.0) and Hispanics (16.6%). (See figure 2.5.) Only Asians/Pacific Islanders and Whites have relatively greater access at home, while American Indians/Eskimos/Aleuts, Blacks, and Hispanics more often turn to access outside the home. In fact, Blacks and Hispanics are less connected everywhere (such as at home, school, library, or community center) than Whites are at home. Internet usage is affected by geography, as well as by race. Households of all races lag significantly in Internet access—whether at home, outside home, or for any location—in rural areas. Regarding home access, the highest usage is by urban Whites (29.4%), while the least usage is found among rural Blacks (6.3%). Outside the home and at any location, respectively, the pattern is similar, with the two extremes being represented by Whites in central cities (21.8%, 41.3%) and rural Blacks (8.2%, 12.8%).

• *Education.*   The level of education and Internet usage are highly correlated. Considering any access site, least usage occurs among those persons with an elementary-school education or less (6.6%). Those with four-year college degrees have a usage rate more than nine times higher (61.6%).

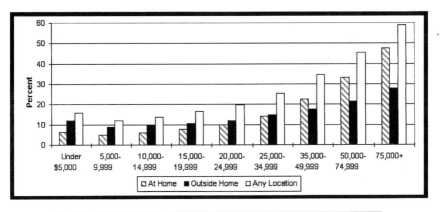

	At Home	Outside Home	Any Location
Under $5,000	6.5	12.1	16.0
5,000-9,999	5.1	8.7	12.1
10,000-14,999	6.0	9.5	13.9
15,000-19,999	7.7	10.5	16.6
20,000-24,999	9.9	12.1	19.9
25,000-34,999	14.1	14.9	25.3
35,000-49,999	22.5	17.7	34.7
50,000-74,999	33.1	21.7	45.5
75,000+	47.7	28.0	58.9

Figure 2.4
Percent of U.S. persons using the Internet, by income, by location, 1998.

• *Household Type.* In terms of total (home and external) Internet access, married couples with children less than eighteen years of age exhibit the highest usage among all household groups (37.6%), while female householders with children have the least (22.3%). Married couples and family households without children use the Internet at home more than elsewhere. This contrasts with families led by single males and females, which typically make greater use of the Internet outside the home. This pattern holds true no matter where the single-parent families live, except that single fathers in urban areas use the Internet more at home than outside the home. Factoring in location also produces new highs and lows. At the highest end are urban married couples with children (38.4%) and at the lowest are female-headed households in central cities (18.8%) for access at any location.

• *Age.* Internet usage rises with age until people reach their senior (55+) years. Seniors not only change the pattern, but actually rank low-

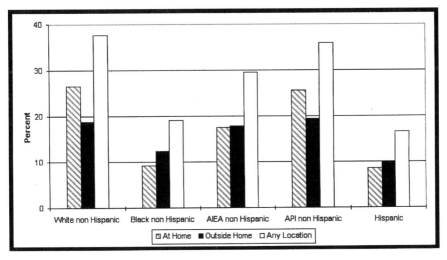

	At Home	Outside Home	Any Location
White non Hispanic	26.7	18.8	37.7
Black non Hispanic	9.2	12.4	19.0
AIEA non Hispanic	17.5	17.8	29.5
API non Hispanic	25.6	19.4	35.9
Hispanic	8.7	10.0	16.6

Figure 2.5
Percent of U.S. persons using the Internet, by race/origin, by location, 1998.

est among all age groups, whether at home (11.0%), away from home (5.5%), or at any location (14.4%). The highest usage at home is among 35–44-year-olds (29.2%), but 25–34-year-olds lead all others in terms of external access or usage anyplace.

• *Region.* The West leads in at-home (25.1%) and total (35.5%) usage. The Midwest ranks above others in non-home access. The South trails in all three categories of home (20.0%), outside the home (15.6%), and total usage (29.8%).

• *Gender.* Both sexes use the Internet more at home than elsewhere. Males generally access the Internet by about three percentage points more, regardless of location, and equal 34.3% in total access.

This discussion has attempted to present a broad assessment of which Americans access the Internet. In the section that follows, we narrow the focus to patterns of access for those who go online at sites other than home.

2   Points of Access outside the Home   Of those people who go online outside the home, there are significant differences as to where people access the Internet. Certain demographic groups are particularly likely to have access at work. Those same groups are far less likely to access the Internet at schools, public libraries, or through someone else's computer. The converse is also true. Those groups with lower access rates at work or at home are far more likely to use the Internet at a public place, such as a school, library, or a community center. These findings suggest that Americans without ready access to the Internet (at home or at work) are making use of public resources.

Access at Work   By far the most popular place to access the Internet outside the home is at work. Of those who access the Internet outside of home, more than half (56.3%) of Americans access it at work, particularly in urban (58.8%) and central city (58.7%) areas. Certain groups have particularly high rates of access at work. Those with college or advanced degrees are the most likely to have access at work—about *ten times* more likely than those with only some high-school education (87.2% versus 8.7%). Similarly, those earning at least $75,000 are nearly six times more likely to have work access than those earning less than $5,000 (72.9% versus 12.3%). Families without children and non-family households who access the Internet externally also rank high in accessing the Internet from work—69.4% and 68.4%, respectively (compared to 32.8% for male-headed households, 29.0% for female-headed households, and 50.4% for dual-parent households).

There are also notable disparities based on race. Whites and Asians/Pacific Islanders who use the Net outside the home are more likely to be connected at work (58.8% and 56.6%, respectively), compared to American Indians/Eskimos/Aleuts, Hispanics, and Blacks (34.8%, 39.1%, and 49.3%, respectively). Men are also more likely than women to access the Internet at work (58.7% compared to 53.8%).

Not surprisingly, those demographic groups with higher access from work tend to be the same groups that have higher rates of access at home. (See discussion above.) They are also the same groups that exhibit lower usage rates from public access points, such as schools, libraries, or community centers.

Access at K–12 Schools   The second most frequently used access point is the kindergarten through 12th grade (K–12) school, particularly in rural areas (30.0%). These figures may be higher than other public access points because they include school-aged children, many of whom use the Internet at school. The inclusion of children who access the Internet at school could account, in part, for the particularly high levels of usage among those with lower education levels, lower incomes, and those "not in the labor force."

Nevertheless, certain groups who access the Internet outside the home are particularly likely to go online at K–12 schools. American Indians/ Eskimos/Aleuts and Hispanics are particularly high users (36.5% and 35.1%, respectively), compared to Asians/Pacific Islanders (19.4%), Whites (20.0%), and Blacks (26.6%). Hispanics and American Indians/ Eskimos/Aleuts are especially likely to use schools for access if they live in rural areas (e.g., 46.6% for Hispanics). Single-parent households are also far more likely to use K–12 schools (43.6% for female-headed households, 38.5% for male-headed households) than are dual parent households (33.7%), families without children (5.8%), or non-family households (4.3%).

Access at Public Libraries and Community Centers   Many Americans who obtain Internet access outside the home rely on such places as public libraries (8.2%) and community centers (0.6%).[13] Public libraries, in particular, are used by certain groups with some regularity. Unemployed persons who access the Internet outside their homes are nearly *three* times more likely to use public libraries as the national average (21.9% versus 8.2%). Those Americans who are "not in the labor force," such as retirees or homemakers, are twice as likely to use the public libraries for access (16.1%). Both groups are even more likely to use public libraries in urban, as opposed to central-city or rural, areas (22.8% and 17.9%, respectively).

Other groups that also use public libraries more frequently include those earning less than $25,000, those with less than a high-school education, those in female-headed households, and American Indians/ Eskimos/Aleuts, Blacks, and Hispanics. Of these groups, American Indians/Eskimos/Aleuts are especially likely to use libraries in urban areas (17.3%), while Blacks are more likely to use libraries in rural areas (16.3%). Those in female-headed households are also more likely to gain Internet access in libraries in central cities (16.4%).

Using a logistic regression analysis, we also compared the likelihood of a group's using public libraries or community centers for online access. Our analysis pertained only to those people who reported usage of the Internet from outside the home.[14] This regression analysis revealed the additional interesting comparisons:

• Those earning less than $20,000 who use the Internet outside the home are two times more likely (2.12 times) to get their access through a public library or community center than those earning more than $20,000.

• Blacks using the Internet outside the home are nearly two times more likely (1.91 times) to use a public library or a community center as Whites. "Other non-Hispanic" minorities (including Asians/Pacific Islanders, American Indians, Eskimos, and Aleuts) are 1.24 times more likely to use these resources as Whites.

• People without home computers are almost 1.5 times more likely than people with home computers to get outside access to the Internet through public libraries or community centers.

• People without college degrees are also significantly (1.4 times) more likely to use public libraries or community centers for their outside Internet access than those who have earned a college degree.

These findings support our general conclusion that those who are less likely to have Internet access at home or work (e.g., those earning less than $20,000, certain minorities, and those without a college degree) are relying on the resources of public facilities.

C How Households Access the Internet

1 Type of Internet Access Device   The 1998 Census survey also asked how people access the Internet from home. Personal computers with modem capability have been historically, and are currently, the mode of choice for Internet access. Among those households that have a computer or a WebTV®, 61.0% connect to the Internet via PCs, 1% obtain access via WebTV®, and 38.0% do not use the Internet at all.[15] Already there are signs that alternative modes—for example, Internet phones—will soon become available for browsing the web or e-mailing.

Whether or not a household with a PC is also an Internet user depends on various demographic characteristics. For instance, usage varies by race/origin, ranging from high levels of use by Asians/Pacific Islanders (65.0%) and Whites (63.5%) to lower usage levels by American Indians/ Eskimos/Aleuts (53.2%), Hispanics (48.7%), and Blacks (47.4%). Breakdowns by type of household also reveal differing usage rates, ranging from married couples with children (63.4%) to single-parent households with children; either male-headed (55.2%) or female-headed (46.4%) families.

2 Type of Internet Service Provider   An important part of the linkage in being able to go online is to connect to an Internet Service Provider (ISP). Currently there is a tremendous variation in market share among the types of ISPs to whom households choose to subscribe. National service providers have captured the bulk (69.0%) of the market. Local phone companies rank second (14.0%), followed by long-distance companies (4.0%), cable TV systems (2.0%), and wireless firms (1.0%). An "other" category, comprised of types of ISPs that are too small to be broken out, accounts for the rest of the total (10.0%).

3 Why Households with Computers Have Never Had Internet Access
Multiple reasons exist as to why households with computers at home have never used the Internet there.[16] In the 1998 CPS supplement survey, the most common response given was that the household's occupants "don't want" such access (25.7%). The second major reason among respondents concerns "cost" (16.8%), which is further disaggregated into the monthly service charge (9.7%), the need to make a toll call in order to reach one's ISP (4.8%), and other costs (2.3%). Following cost are such categories as "can use elsewhere" (9.6%), "no time" (8.7%), "computer not capable" (8.3%), "future access planned" (but none at home currently) (7.5%), "concern with children" (6.0%), and "not useful" (5.6%). Some people gave "not user friendly" (2.7%) and "problem with service provider" (1.3%) as reasons for not having Internet access at home. Myriad other responses whose percentages are quite small appear under the headings "other cost" and "other."

These profiles were gleaned from an analysis of Internet "non-users" by demographic variables.

• *Income.* Not surprisingly, the lower a household's income, the more likely a household cites "cost" as the reason for not having Internet access. Thus, 7.2% of those with incomes of $75,000 or more cited cost as a reason for no usage, contrasted with 33.2% for the $5,000 to $9,000 bracket. The "don't want it" response generally increases with income, with a few exceptions.

• *Race/Origin.* The cost factor is most important to Hispanics (23.4%), surpassing the "don't want it" response (19.6%). However, "don't want it" ranks higher than cost in the case of Whites (26.7% versus 15.6%), Blacks (24.0% versus 22.0%), and "other" (21.8% versus 17.4%). The reason "can use elsewhere" is much less important to all except for "other non-Hispanic" households (15.1%).

• *Education.* Generally, cost becomes more important the lower the level of education. The response "don't want it" generally increases as the level of education decreases. Viewed head-to-head, "don't want it" dominates across all education levels relative to cost and "can use elsewhere." For example, this holds for the least educated (33.3% versus 25.3% versus 1.3%) and for the most educated (24.2% versus 13.2% versus 16.7%). Solely in the case of those with a college education, "can use elsewhere" ranks higher than cost.

• *Household Type.* Cost is the most important factor for single-parent families, both compared to other types of households and relative to other reasons for non-use of the Internet. For male householders with children, cost (23.2% of respondents) exceeds "don't want it" (18.7%). A similar scenario exists for female householders with children (29.4%, 19.4%). For all other household types, the reverse is true, i.e., "don't want it" is a more important reason than cost.

• *Age.* Cost prevails as the biggest reason for not having Internet access (20.4%) for those householders under 25 years old, although "can use elsewhere" is a close second (19.1%). For other age groups, "don't want it" prevails, by a modest amount through 44 years old and much more significantly for 45–54 years and particularly 55 and older (35.7% versus 12.1%).

• *Employment.* One's labor force status affects reasons for non-use as well. Far and away the most important reason for abstention by the unemployed work force is the cost factor (38.2%), dwarfing "don't want it" at number two (13.3%). This contrasts with employed workers, where "don't want it" prevails over "cost" (25.5% versus 16.5%).

In sum, the most important reasons why certain households have never used the Internet is that they "don't want it" or it is too expensive. Although the former is the more important reason overall, the cost factor dominates among low-income groups, Hispanics, single-parent families, the youngest householders, and the unemployed. Policymakers should therefore consider the role of cost as a deterrent to expanding online access.

4 Why Households with Computers Have Discontinued Internet Use
Internet churn—the incidence of households discontinuing Internet use —represents another area that policy makers have begun to examine. In the 1998 CPS supplement survey, respondents identified "cost, too expensive" (15.0%) as the most important reason for dropping off the Internet. The second most compelling reason is "no longer owns computer" (14.0%), followed by "not enough time to use it" (10.0%), followed by "can use elsewhere" (9.0%), "don't want it" (7.0%), and "moved" (7.0%). "Other" accounts for the rest (17%).

[*Section D, How People Use the Internet, is omitted.*]

E Conclusion
For the first time in our *Falling through the Net* series, the Commerce Department has collected and analyzed wide-ranging data with respect to Internet usage by Americans. These statistics will advance our knowledge base with respect to whether, where, and how people in this country are making use of the Internet.

These data provide concrete evidence that the Internet is being used by an increasing number of Americans. More than one-third of Americans go online from any point, either at home or outside the home. Approximately one-quarter access the Internet at home. For those households with a computer, approximately two-thirds have Internet access. Households that do not have Internet access most frequently explain that they either do not want it or that it is too expensive; for those households that have dropped off the Net, cost is the most important reason.

While Americans are becoming increasingly connected, there are still significant discrepancies in access: Blacks and Hispanics, for example, are less connected anywhere than Whites are at home. Those groups with lower access rates at work or home are much more likely to use the Internet at a public place such as a school, library, or community center. They are also more likely to use the Internet to take courses or to conduct job searches than other groups. These and other findings—present and future—will provide an important factual foundation for the sound policy making needed to ensure socioeconomic success in the Information Age.

III   Challenges Ahead

Traditionally, our notion of being connected to the nation's communications networks has meant having a telephone. Today, Americans' increased use of computers and the Internet has changed that notion. To be connected today increasingly means to have access to telephones, computers, and the Internet. While these items may not be necessary for survival, arguably in today's emerging digital economy they are necessary for success. As the Department of Commerce has found in its *Emerging Digital Economy* reports,[17] the dramatic growth of electronic commerce and the development of information technology (IT) industries are changing the way Americans work, communicate, purchase goods, and obtain information. Jobs in the new economy now increasingly require technical skills and familiarity with new technologies. Additionally, obtaining services and information increasingly requires access to the Internet.

Policy makers have achieved high levels of telephone connectivity through the implementation of two key initiatives. Pro-competition policies at the state and national levels have resulted in lower prices for consumers of telephone services. Universal service policies have helped assure that most Americans can enjoy affordable access today. Assistance for low-income households (e.g., the Federal Communications Commission's (FCC) Lifeline Assistance and Link-Up America and state programs) and support for high-cost regions of the country (e.g., the FCC's Universal Service Fund; other state and federal rate-averaging) are prime examples of such programs. And the U.S. Department of Agriculture's Rural Utilities Service (RUS) provides targeted lending and technical advice to help ensure that advanced telecommunications infrastructure is in place for rural communities.

With the data in this report, we are in a better position to identify where and how to reach everyone. Policy makers should explore ways to continue to boost telephone penetration, particularly among the underserved, and to expand computer and Internet connectivity. For some individuals, it is an economic solution. Lower prices, leasing arrangements, and even free computer deals will bridge the digital gap for them. For high-cost communities and low-income individuals, universal service policies will remain of critical importance. For other individuals, there are language and cultural barriers that need to be addressed. Products will need to be adapted to meet special needs, such as those of the disabled community. Finally, we need to redouble our outreach efforts, especially directed at the information disadvantaged.

A   Promoting Competition and Universal Service

To some extent, the surging use of computers and the Internet among American households reflects the success of our nation's pro-competition policies. A significantly higher percentage of households owned PCs in 1998 (42.1%) than in 1997 (36.6%) and experienced greater Internet access during the same period (26.2% versus 18.6%). The increased competition among PC providers and lower costs of manufacturing have resulted in PCs selling for well below $1000. The increasing use of other Internet-accessing devices, such as televisions, palm computers, and Internet phones, should further invigorate competition among manufacturers and reduce prices for consumers.

While competition has made computers and the Internet increasingly affordable, these technologies still remain beyond the budget of many American households. When asked why they lacked Internet access, a significant portion of households (16.8%) responded that it was too expensive. Respondents particularly cited the cost of monthly bills, followed by toll calling for ISP access. A significantly higher percentage of minority and low-income households reported that Internet access was cost prohibitive. In addition, cost ranked highest among reasons given by those who discontinued Internet use. And, the proportion of non-use would surely be higher still for those who do not yet own PCs or other

Internet access devices. Policy makers, such as the Federal-State Universal Service Joint Board, State Public Service Commissions, and the FCC should carefully consider these facts in their attempts to evaluate the new universal service and access needs.

These findings suggest that further competition and price reductions will be vital to making information tools affordable for most Americans. Going forward, it will be important to promote policies that directly enhance competition among companies manufacturing computers and other Internet devices, as well as among Internet service providers. Expanding competition in rural areas and central cities is particularly significant, as these areas lag behind the national averages for PC ownership and household Internet access.

At the same time, the data demonstrate the need for continued universal service support for telephony, particularly in rural and other high-cost areas. And we need to encourage the buildout of broadband networks to rural and other underserved areas of our nation, so that all Americans can take full advantage of new information technologies and services.

B   Expanding Community Access Centers

Competition is a significant answer to providing affordable access to computers and the Internet, but it is not the total solution. It is highly unlikely that, in the foreseeable future, prices will fall to the point where most homes will have computers and Internet access. As a result, a digital divide may continue to exist at home between the information rich and the information poor. Given the great advantages accruing to those who have access, it is not economically or socially prudent to idly await the day when most, if not all, homes can claim connectivity. Part of the short-term answer lies in providing Internet access at community access centers (CACs), such as schools, libraries, and other public access facilities.

The 1998 data demonstrate why providing public access to the Internet at these external sources is critical. To begin with, these sources tend to be used by groups that lack Internet access at home or at work; chiefly, minorities, people earning lower incomes, those with lower education levels, and the unemployed. Households with incomes of less than

$20,000 and Black households, for example, are twice as likely to get Internet access through a public library or community center than are households earning more than $20,000 or White households. Similarly, low-income households and households with lower education levels are obtaining access at schools at far higher rates.

Moreover, the same households that are using community access centers at higher rates are also using the Internet more often than other groups to find jobs or for educational purposes. CACs are, therefore, providing the very tools these groups need to advance economically and professionally.

The data support the continued funding of CACs by both industry and government. Industry has already come forward with significant assistance. Companies are supporting the creation of community technology centers, helping connect schools through "NetDays," and donating computers and software to schools and neighborhood centers. NTIA's Telecommunications and Information Infrastructure Assistance Program (TIIAP) has funded a number of pioneering CAC efforts.[18] The U.S. Department of Education's new Community Technology Centers (CTC) program will enable the funding of CACs in economically distressed communities on a broader scale.

The 1998 data also underscore the importance of the Administration's efforts to ensure that all schools and libraries have affordable access to the Internet. Under the E-rate program, telecommunications carriers are providing eligible schools and libraries with a discounted rate for telecommunications services, internal connections among classrooms, and Internet access. As a result, the E-rate program is helping to connect more than 80,000 schools and libraries and is enabling children and adults to both learn new technologies and have new points of access. The data demonstrate that these community access centers are, indeed, used by people who lack access at home and merit further funding.

In addition, we should look to other community-based organizations that can help us achieve these goals—traditional community centers, churches, credit unions, housing projects, senior centers, museums, fire and police stations, and more. Each community knows best how to reach and connect its residents.

C   Building Awareness

While many Americans are embracing computers and the Internet, there are many others who do not realize that this technology is relevant to their lives. We need to reach out to these communities and let them know why they should care—how new technologies can open new opportunities for them and their children.

We also need to find out *why* people are or are not connected. While such outreach works best at the local level, this type of information should be shared with policy makers at all levels of government—local, state, tribal, and federal. Only when we have a good understanding about why different communities do or do not have access to digital tools can we fashion appropriate policies.

D   Addressing Content Concerns

The data show that Americans are concerned about invasions of their privacy caused by accessing the Internet. Almost two-thirds of Americans are either "very concerned" or "somewhat concerned" about confidentiality on the Internet. There are legitimate concerns regarding the collection and transmission of personal information via the Internet, especially information gathered from children. The Administration has set forth an Electronic Bill of Rights, proposing that every consumer have: the right to choose whether her personal information is disclosed; the right to know how, when, and how much of that information is being used; the right to see that information; and the right to know if information is accurate and to be able to correct it if it is not.

The Administration believes that the private sector should take the lead in implementing meaningful, consumer-friendly privacy regimes. We would like for companies to take steps to notify customers of their privacy policies, process consumer privacy preferences, protect customer data, and handle inquiries and complaints. Several promising private-sector initiatives are underway, such as BBBOnline and TRUSTe, which require merchants to adhere to fair trade practices. These programs provide a seal to businesses that post privacy policies that meet certain criteria.

Parents are also concerned about their children's safety while using the Internet. The data show that one of the reasons that households with a computer have never used the Internet is "concerns with children." The

Administration is committed to empowering parents, teachers, and other guardians with tools to keep children safe while online. The Administration has encouraged private-sector initiatives, such as "One Click Away," which are designed to give parents technology and educational resources to protect their children from material that they deem to be inappropriate and to know who to contact when their children encounter dangerous situations online. The Administration has also promoted the concept of "greenspaces"—educational, age-appropriate, non-commercial content that is easily identifiable for families online.

E Continued Monitoring

Good public policy requires a good factual foundation. Continued studies—public and private—are vital to permitting policy makers to make prudent decisions. Policy makers should explore ways to improve the availability of reliable penetration data for historically small but vitally important groups, such as Native Americans and Asians/Pacific Islanders. Potential solutions include "over-sampling" as part of a broader-based survey or conducting special studies that target these groups. A new analytical tool to gauge the status of Internet connectivity could be a Household Access Index (HAI), designed to highlight progress or deficiencies in this regard. A composite index could be developed that represents the country's combined penetration for telephones, computers, other Internet access devices, and the Internet. In 1998, the HAI for U.S. households would have equaled 162.4%, increasing from 149.0% in 1997.

In the final analysis, no one should be left behind as our nation advances into the 21st century, in which having access to computers and the Internet may be key to becoming a successful member of society.

Notes

This report was published by NTIA in 1999.

1. Households were asked the same survey questions to permit easy comparison of penetration rates across the last five years. The Trendline Study in the appendix to this report [not included here] provides a historic overview, comparing penetration rates for certain categories since 1984. We have provided nearly identical tabulations and charts for these surveys.

2. Part II of this report expands on the earlier reports by examining Internet access at sources outside of the home, as well as other Internet-related issues. A number of other studies have been developed on the subject of U.S. households' electronic access to information. See, e.g., Susan Goslee (1998), *Losing Ground Bit by Bit: Low-Income Communities in the Information Age*, Benton Foundation; Donna L. Hoffman and Thomas P. Novak, "The Evolution of the Digital Divide: Examining the Relationship of Race to Internet Access and Usage Over Time," a paper presented at the conference, "Understanding the Digital Economy: Data, Tools and Research," May 25–26, 1999 (forthcoming); Robert Kraut et al. (1996), "HomeNet: A Field Trial of Residential Internet Services,"*ACM Research*; Shelley Morrisette et al. (1999), "Consumers' Digital Decade," Forrester Research, Inc. ⟨www.forrester.com⟩; U.S. Internet Council (1999), *State of the Internet: USIC's Report on Use & Threats in 1999* ⟨www.usic.org⟩; and Anthony Wilhelm (1998), *Closing the Digital Divide: Enhancing Hispanic Participation in the Information Age*, The Tomas Rivera Policy Institute.

3. As discussed in the "Methodology" section [not included here], the Census Bureau collected CPS supplemental data on telephones, computers, and Internet use by conducting interviews of 48,000 sample households (57,000 in 1994). Significant advantages of the Census approach relative to others include its scientifically selected large sample and the employment of home visits by interviewers rather than strict reliance on telephone surveys, thereby reaching important households (e.g., those without telephones) that otherwise would likely be missed.

4. Because we have data on Internet access only for 1997 and 1998, a comparison before 1997 is not possible. As explained in the Trendline Study, household Internet access was not measured until 1997. Prior to 1997, the Census Bureau measured which households had "modems" in place. While modems provide a means to access the Internet, they do not necessarily mean that a household actually has Internet access. This measurement therefore does not provide an exact proxy for Internet access.

5. PC-penetration and Internet access are closely correlated to income for all but the lowest income level (households earning under $5,000). This income level shows slightly higher rates than the next income level ($5,000–$9,999), which may be explained by the high number of students included in the lowest income category.

6. These calculations are derived from NTIA's own cross-tabulation of the Census data.

7. Ibid.

8. Ibid.

9. Precise rankings cannot be assigned because in some cases, confidence intervals (i.e., positive or negative values that identify the range within which it is 90% certain that the true penetration number falls) do not permit a stable ranking system.

10. This report uses "Native Americans" as a shorthand reference to American Indians, Eskimos, and Aleuts.

11. Data for Internet access by race and income was unavailable. This discussion pertains to computer ownership only.

12. For the first time in these studies, NTIA sought information regarding means of accessing the Internet other than personal computers. The Census CPS survey asked respondents whether they owned a WebTV®, which is the most widely used system for accessing the Internet through television sets. A WebTV® unit connects to a television set, much like a VCR, and to a telephone line to send and receive data. This data is then displayed on the television, rather than a computer monitor. WebTV® Networks, Inc. is a subsidiary of the Microsoft Corporation. We note that WebTV® is not the only vendor of non–PC-based access to the Internet.

13. Community centers are generally a new and growing point of access to the Internet. We are unable to conduct an independent, meaningful analysis of those Americans using community centers, however, because the numbers involved generally fall below statistical levels of significance. Nevertheless, the Census Bureau data suggest that—as with public libraries—community centers are used more often by low-income persons, Blacks, American Indians/Eskimos/Aleuts, and the unemployed than by other groups.

14. The logistic regression analysis was conducted according to the model set forth in the methodology section of the report. Logistic regression analysis requires a base reference group for purposes of comparison. The base group in this analysis is higher income, White, non-Hispanic, suburban, computer owner, and college-educated.

The dependent variable indicates whether someone has used the Internet from a public library or community center. The number of respondents who used the Internet at a community center was relatively small by itself. By combining them with public libraries, community centers could be included in the analysis. The sample was broken into two groups by income: those making above $20,000 a year and those making below. The $20,000 threshold isolates households in poverty from those with higher incomes. The race variables were disaggregated to separate Hispanics from all racial groups. Hispanics were then added into the regression. In the model "minorities" are considered to be all non-Hispanics not included in Black or White racial groups. The sample was also broken down into two segments: by suburban and non-suburban, with non-suburban combining non-metropolitan (rural) and central cities. Education was broken down into two categories, one for those who graduated from college and another for those who did not. The "computer at home" variable indicates whether or not households have a computer at home.

The fit of the model is significant with the Hosmer and Lemeshow Goodness-of-Fit test statistic of 7.6733 with 7 degrees of freedom ($p = 0.3623$). The model also shows relatively low col-linearity due to the breakdown of the binary variables.

15. Because of the small percentage of households with WebTV®, the term "PCs" includes WebTVs® for purposes of this section.

16. The CPS supplement questionnaire asked respondents to provide the *main* reason for non-use.

17. *The Emerging Digital Economy* (April 1998) and *The Emerging Digital Economy II* (June 1999).

18. *Networks for People: TIIAP at Work*, available on NTIA's web site, includes discussions of a number of TIIAP-funded CAC projects.

3

The Evolution of the Digital Divide: Examining the Relationship of Race to Internet Access and Usage over Time

Donna L. Hoffman, Thomas P. Novak, and Ann E. Schlosser

1 Introduction

That portion of the Internet known as the World Wide Web has been riding an exponential growth curve since 1994 (Network Wizards 1999; Rutkowski 1998), coinciding with the introduction of NCSA's graphically based software interface Mosaic for "browsing" the World Wide Web (Hoffman, Novak, and Chatterjee 1995).

Currently, over 43 million hosts are connected to the Internet worldwide (Network Wizards 1999). In terms of individual users, somewhere between 40 to 80 million adults (eStats 1999) in the United States alone have access to around 320 million unique pages of content (Lawrence and Giles 1998), globally distributed on arguably one of the most important communication innovations in history.

Enthusiasm for the anticipated social dividends of this "revolution in democratic communication" (Hoffman 1996) that will "harness the powerful forces of science and technology" (Clinton 1997a) for all members of our society appears boundless. The Internet is expected to do no less than virtually transform society. Nowhere is this confidence expressed more clearly than in President Clinton's aggressive objective to wire every classroom and library in the country by the year 2000 (NetDay 1998), followed by every home by the year 2007, so that "every 12-year-old can log onto the Internet" (Clinton 1997b).

Yet even as the Internet races ambitiously toward critical mass, some social scientists are beginning to examine carefully the policy implications of *current* demographic patterns of Internet access and usage (Hoffman and Novak, 1998; Hoffman, Kalsbeek, and Novak 1996; Hoffman,

Novak, and Venkatesh 1997; Katz and Aspden 1997). For while Clinton's "Call to Action for American Education" (Clinton 1997a) may likely guarantee universal access for our nation's next generation, are the approximately 200 million Americans presently over the age of 16 equally likely to have access to the Internet? The findings thus far are both obvious and surprising, with important implications for social science research and public policy.

Key demographic variables like income and education drive the policy questions surrounding the Internet. These variables are important because they are the most likely to differentially impact the consequences of interactive electronic media for different segments in our society. Looming large is the concern that the Internet may not scale *economically* (Keller 1996), leading to what Lloyd Morrisett, the former president of the Markle Foundation, has called a "digital divide" between the information "haves" and "have-nots."

For example, although almost 70 percent of the schools in this country have at least one computer connected to the Internet, less than 15 percent of classrooms have Internet access (Harmon 1997). Not surprisingly, access is not distributed randomly, but correlated strongly with income and education (Coley, Cradler, and Engel 1997). A recent study of Internet use among college freshman (Sax, Astin, Korn, and Mahoney 1998) found that nearly 83 percent of all new college students report using the Internet for school work, and almost two-thirds use email to communicate. Yet, closer examination suggests a disturbing disparity in access. While 90.2 percent of private college freshman use the Internet for research, only 77.6 percent of students entering public Black colleges report doing so. Similarly, although 80.1 percent of private college freshman use email regularly, only 41.4 percent of students attending Black public colleges do.

Further, although numerous studies (CyberAtlas 1999; Maraganore and Morrisette 1998) suggest that the gender gap in Internet use appears to be closing over time and that Internet users are increasingly coming from the ranks of those with lower education and income (Pew Research Center 1998), the perception persists that the gap for race is not decreasing (Abrams 1997).

Hoffman and Novak (1998) examined racial differences in Internet access and use at a single time point and found in 1997 that, overall,

Whites were significantly more likely than African Americans to have a home computer in their household and also slightly more likely to have PC access at work. Whites were also significantly more likely to have ever used the Web at home, whereas African Americans were slightly more likely to have ever used the Web at school. As one might expect, increasing levels of income corresponded to an increased likelihood of owning a home computer, regardless of race. Although income explained race differences in computer ownership and Web use, education did not. That is, they found that Whites were still more likely to own a home computer than were African Americans and to have used the Web recently, despite controlling for differences in education.

Their most striking findings, however, were for students. Hoffman and Novak (1998) found no differences among White and African American students when students had a home computer. However, among students without a computer in the home, White students were much more likely than African American students to have used the Web, and also more likely to have used the Web at locations other than home, work, or school. They concluded that "access translates into usage," and that Whites are more likely than African Americans to use the Web because they are more likely to have access.

In 1998, the Commerce Department's National Telecommunications and Information Administration (McConnaughey and Lader 1998) analyzed data on computer penetration rates from the October 1997 Census Current Population Survey (CPS) as part of an ongoing examination of the digital divide. This analysis represented an update from their 1995 study of similar data from the November 1994 CPS. The authors concluded that the gap between the technology haves and have-nots had *increased* between 1994 and 1997, with African Americans and Hispanics actually further behind whites in terms of home computer ownership and Internet access and with an even wider gap between individuals at upper and lower income levels.

More recently, Babb (1998) investigated home computer ownership and Internet use among low-income individuals and minorities. She found that African Americans and Hispanics were less likely to own computers, even after adjusting for income and education, and termed this finding, consistent across seven different data sets under examination, "the single most important finding" of her study.

Interestingly, some have suggested that United States policy itself may be a contributing factor in the growing digital divide. Cooper and Kimmelman (1999) argue that the Telecommunications Act of 1996 has had the unintended and unfortunate consequence of increasing the division between the telecommunications haves and have-nots. As evidence, they point to (1) increased concentration and less competition in the telecommunications and cable industries, (2) significant increases or flat prices, instead of declines, in cable, long distance, and local phone rates, and (3) a growing disparity among those market segments employing heavy use of telecommunications networks like the Internet and those whose use is more modest.

The consequences to American society of this race gap in Internet use are expected to be severe (Beaupre and Brand-Williams 1997). Just as A. J. Liebling observed for the freedom of the press (Liebling 1960), the Internet may provide for equal economic opportunity and democratic communication, but only for those with access. The United States economy may also be at risk if a significant segment of our society, lacking equal access to the Internet, wants for the technological skills to keep American firms competitive.

Given these concerns, we set out to systematically investigate the differences between Whites and African Americans in the United States with respect to computer access, which is the current prerequisite for Internet access, and Web use. We wished to examine whether observed race differences in access and use can be accounted for by differences in income and education, how access impacts use, and when race matters in the calculus of equal access. The particular emphasis of this research is on how such differences may be changing over time. We believe our results may be used as a window through which policy makers might view the job of ensuring access to the Internet for the next generation.

Objectives

[*Portion of text omitted.*] This work is intended to stimulate discussion among scholars and policy makers interested in how differences in Internet access and use among different segments in our society affects their ability to participate and reap the rewards of that participation in the emerging digital economy. For that reason, we have attempted to present the results in a manner that allows the data to "speak," as it were, for itself.

This paper is organized according to specific analysis objectives. In section 2 we begin by comparing the demographic composition of our three samples with U.S. Census data for a comparable time period. Overall, we find that the three CommerceNet/Nielsen IDS cross-sections are representative of the U.S. population, although results for some minority groups (Asian Americans and Native Americans) are based upon sample sizes too small to permit projectability to the U.S. population. Next, in section 3, we consider differences over time in Internet access and use among African Americans, Whites, and Hispanics in the United States over age 16. This is followed, in section 4, by an analysis of these differences in the context of key demographic variables, including student status, home computer ownership, education, income, gender, and the presence of children in the home. In section 5 [*omitted here*] we examine differences in Web shopping behavior and business uses of the Web. Finally, in section 6 we summarize the major issues surrounding minority use of the Internet and present a series of discussion and policy points relevant to the development of an open research agenda concerning the socioeconomic impact of the Internet and electronic commerce in the United States and globally.

2   Sample Composition

The three surveys used in this research are the: (1) Spring 1997 CommerceNet/Nielsen Internet Demographic Study (IDS) conducted in December 1996 and January 1997; (2) Fall 1997 IDS, conducted in August and September 1997; and (3) Spring 1998 IDS, conducted in May and June 1998 (Nielsen Media Research 1997a; 1997b; 1998). Hereafter, these studies will be referred to as the IDS 2, IDS 3, and IDS 4, respectively [*remainder of section omitted*].

3   Demographic Differences in Web Access and Use among African Americans, Hispanics, and Whites

Demographic Differences across Race/Access Segments
Three usage segments are compared in this section—respondents who have (1) no Internet access, (2) Internet access only, but have never used the Web, and (3) ever used the Web. Table 3.1 shows results for Whites,

Table 3.1
Demographic Differences over Time in Web Access and Use for Whites

	IDS2		
	no access	access only	Web user
N	2,825	569	1,365
Age:			
<25	7.41	15.66	25.39
25–45	38.95	50.04	52.74
46–64	29.61	25.52	19.52
>64	24.02	8.78	2.35
Total	100%	100%	100%
Education:			
less than h.s.	21.93	13.38	11.64
high school grad	40.18	30.74	17.46
some college	23.68	30.79	31.58
college grad	14.20	25.09	39.31
Total	100%	100%	100%
Occupation:			
Professional	12.28	22.33	26.33
White collar	28.51	38.76	39.16
Blue collar	13.68	9.64	5.63
Homemaker	13.92	9.32	3.80
Student	2.13	9.59	18.28
Retired	29.10	9.63	4.85
Total	100%	99.26%	98.06%
Household Income:			
<$10K	11.49	3.79	2.59
$10K–$19,9	14.12	6.73	5.34
$20K–$29,9	17.67	12.47	9.69
$30K–$39,9	17.62	16.20	11.36
$40K–$59,9	20.93	28.41	27.44
$60K+	18.17	32.39	43.57
Total	100%	100%	100%
Gender:			
Male	43.65	48.22	60.68
Female	56.35	51.78	39.32
Total	100%	100%	100%
% or column who ...			
Owns a PC?	26.52	63.43	81.86
PC access at work?	23.39	58.43	68.16

Table 3.1 (continued)

IDS3			IDS4		
no access	access only	Web user	no access	access only	Web user
3,183	569	2,227	1,630	285	1,522
6.81	11.14	26.58	7.10	8.50	23.49
36.02	46.90	48.75	34.81	46.30	50.57
29.63	34.15	22.93	29.99	38.09	22.35
27.54	7.81	1.74	28.10	7.11	3.59
100%	100%	100%	100%	100%	100%
21.99	12.33	14.66	25.04	9.62	13.22
42.23	35.75	17.69	43.01	37.84	18.60
22.37	30.18	30.13	21.39	38.78	29.77
13.41	21.74	37.51	10.56	13.76	38.41
100%	100%	100%	100%	100%	100%
11.33	17.51	26.24	11.00	17.67	27.64
27.16	38.27	38.95	23.76	37.82	38.40
15.16	15.14	7.04	16.65	15.96	7.34
13.94	11.16	4.47	16.43	9.38	4.29
1.64	7.46	17.78	1.42	5.78	15.27
30.77	10.45	5.52	30.40	12.74	5.78
100%	100%	100%	99.67%	99.36%	98.72%
12.80	3.10	2.87	13.60	5.51	2.53
15.87	8.65	5.01	15.91	9.11	4.47
18.97	14.28	9.63	17.39	15.60	10.16
17.35	14.37	13.48	18.31	12.37	11.65
21.14	30.53	26.13	19.21	30.46	25.95
13.87	29.07	42.88	15.58	26.95	45.24
100%	100%	100%	100%	100%	100%
44.96	44.51	54.66	44.71	45.37	55.40
55.04	55.49	45.34	55.29	54.63	44.60
100%	100%	100%	100%	100%	100%
23.61	54.51	77.57	21.63	51.28	77.57
26.32	58.18	64.48	23.75	54.89	63.05

table 3.2 for African Americans and table 3.3 for Hispanics. The sample size for Hispanics with access only in IDS 4 was too low for reliable reporting. The major demographic differences between Whites and African Americans occur for age and income.

• The youngest (16–24) age segment differentiates usage segments more for African Americans than for Whites. African American Web users are more likely to be under 25, across all three surveys. Overall, Web users are more likely to be under 46 years of age.

• Overall, Web users are more likely to have some college or a college degree, although African American Web users are more likely to have less than a high-school education than White Web users. However, our African American samples overrepresent students and some of the individuals in this group are students.

• Tables 3.1 and 3.2 may provide evidence of an education-driven digital divide. However, it is larger for African Americans than for Whites, though it appears to narrow in IDS 4. Of African Americans with no Internet access, 70.27% were high-school graduates or had less than a high-school education in IDS 2, compared with only 62.11% of Whites in the same educational categories with no Internet access. Of course, African Americans are more likely, in general, to have less education, so this result requires further study.

Similarly, of African American Web users, 56.34% had some college or college degrees in IDS 2, compared with 70.89% of White Web users. This gap also does not appear to be diminishing over time. However, to the extent that African Americans are less likely to have some college or a college degree, this result is tentative.

Occupation categories were defined as follows. The professional, homemaker, full-time student, and retired/not currently working categories were self-identified single-response. The white-collar category included those respondents who indicated their primary occupation was either technical, administrative/managerial, clerical, sales, or service worker. The blue-collar category included those respondents who indicated their primary occupation was laborer or craftsman/craftswoman. Due to its extremely low representation in the sample, respondents indicating they were in the military were excluded from analyses including the occupation variable. For this reason, the occupation column totals may not necessarily sum to 100 percent.

Web users are most likely to be professional, white collar, and students, regardless of race. The percentage of African American Web users who are blue-collar workers has more than tripled over time.

• The lowest income group (<$40K) differentiates usage segments much more for African Americans than for Whites. Of African Americans with no Internet access, 80.72% had household incomes less than $40,000 in IDS 2, compared with only 60.9% of Whites with no Internet access. Thus, within the African American group, the income-driven digital divide appears larger than for Whites. Further, it is not diminishing over time. Again, however, African Americans are more likely to have lower incomes than whites, so these results are tentative until further study.

Similarly, of African American Web users, 59.73% had household incomes above $40,000 in IDS 2, compared with 71.01% of White Web users. This gap has also not diminished over time.

This concern over an ever-widening gap within African American income segments has been identified by sociologists as a serious concern, which "will continue to grow as the Black middle class moves forward and poor Black Americans stagnate" (Beaupre and Brand-Williams 1997).

Katz and Aspden (1997) reported evidence of what Lloyd Morrisett of the Markle Foundation has termed a "digital divide," with Internet users being generally wealthier and more highly educated. Sparrow and Vedantham (1995) summarize the broader information technology situation as follows: "Information technologies include basic telephone service, personal computing, and computer networking. Although these technologies are becoming everyday conveniences for many Americans, some communities are being left out. Disparities exist in levels of access between rich and poor and between suburban and inner-city residents" (p. 19).

In summary, tables 3.1, 3.2, and 3.3 show evidence of a digital divide for both Whites and African Americans. Within both racial groups, "Web users" were most likely to be among the wealthiest individuals (those with incomes above the median of $40,000), while the "no Internet access segment" was the most likely to be composed of individuals with the lowest incomes (less than $40,000). The same holds true for education. The "Web user" segment was most likely to consist of individuals with some college or who had completed college, while the "no access" segment was most likely to be composed of those with a high-school education or less. All these effects were more pronounced for African Americans than Whites and these effects appear to persist over time.

Table 3.2
Demographic Differences over Time in Web Access and Use for African Americans

	IDS2		
	no access	access only	Web user
N	298	73	109
Age:			
<25	16.20	21.25	46.30
25–45	37.23	53.43	39.13
46–64	22.76	21.04	14.10
>64	23.80	4.28	0.47
Total	100%	100%	100%
Education:			
less than h.s.	40.52	16.09	29.45
high school grad	29.75	33.70	14.21
some college	17.71	27.45	26.04
college grad	12.03	25.58	30.30
Total	100%	100%	100%
Occupation:			
Professional	11.32	24.02	28.59
White collar	23.13	35.66	28.56
Blue collar	14.00	7.46	2.99
Homemaker	10.28	2.72	0.00
Student	7.10	17.33	30.46
Retired	33.56	9.87	8.09
Total	99.39%	97.06%	98.70%
Household Income:			
<$10K	34.28	9.02	15.62
$10K–$19,9	19.87	11.31	2.90
$20K–$29,9	17.70	22.00	10.63
$30K–$39,9	8.87	8.32	11.23
$40K–$59,9	10.94	24.28	27.43
$60K+	8.34	25.07	32.30
Total	100%	100%	100%
Gender:			
Male	38.15	53.55	55.40
Female	61.85	44.65	44.60
Total	100%	100%	100%
% or column who ...			
Owns a PC?	16.70	44.18	65.05
PC access at work?	18.74	65.39	63.54

Table 3.2 (continued)

IDS3			IDS4		
no access	access only	Web user	no access	access only	Web user
387	108	190	266	30	144
13.00	17.53	38.51	10.78	5.46	49.47
46.72	51.82	50.12	38.40	47.24	41.76
22.02	22.96	11.01	28.68	46.46	8.31
18.27	7.70	0.35	22.15	0.84	0.47
100%	100%	100%	100%	100%	100%
36.57	25.39	16.37	41.57	38.27	30.63
35.35	24.71	11.57	33.00	32.20	17.14
20.70	36.96	37.51	18.75	22.90	32.50
7.37	12.94	34.54	6.67	6.63	19.74
100%	100%	100%	100%	100%	100%
12.36	25.23	26.55	11.84	15.60	18.95
25.80	39.60	38.91	22.89	54.82	28.94
18.47	10.36	3.08	13.09	18.61	9.61
11.13	3.37	1.10	20.75	0.00	2.15
5.39	9.01	28.36	4.42	3.18	29.60
26.85	12.43	1.99	25.68	5.29	4.66
100%	100%	100%	98.67%	97.49%	93.91%
30.92	12.63	4.55	26.80	4.75	8.56
28.80	12.23	4.24	21.50	22.54	6.98
15.43	19.71	11.93	19.07	27.86	12.44
6.00	16.33	19.36	12.00	14.33	14.48
12.52	26.46	18.81	11.25	19.81	24.75
6.33	12.64	41.11	9.38	10.71	32.79
100%	100%	100%	100%	100%	100%
38.68	44.01	55.78	34.10	46.46	53.61
61.32	55.99	44.22	65.90	53.54	46.39
100%	100%	100%	100%	100%	100%
14.82	34.53	65.62	12.09	29.30	68.24
24.49	58.20	67.49	24.45	44.85	63.00

Table 3.3
Demographic Differences over Time in Web Access and Use for Hispanics

	IDS2		
	no access	access only	Web user
N	182	32	93
Age:			
<25	16.85	46.51	55.20
25–45	61.51	36.09	36.39
46–64	16.98	17.40	5.45
>64	4.67	0.00	2.96
Total	100%	100%	100%
Education:			
less than h.s.	35.00	29.67	41.20
high school grad	32.75	28.18	8.64
some college	22.58	29.98	30.62
college grad	9.67	25.78	19.55
Total	100%	100%	100%
Occupation:			
Professional	11.83	14.18	16.22
White collar	28.59	32.88	30.62
Blue collar	19.37	8.35	4.36
Homemaker	19.52	3.62	2.07
Student	5.60	40.97	38.14
Retired	14.50	0.00	7.37
Total	99.42%	100%	98.77%
Household Income:			
<$10K	10.33	3.70	12.24
$10K–$19,9	30.70	2.54	13.11
$20K–$29,9	19.09	4.50	11.65
$30K–$39,9	14.34	27.27	10.29
$40K–$59,9	15.02	25.24	18.83
$60K+	10.52	36.77	33.87
Total	100%	100%	100%
Gender:			
Male	42.93	38.91	56.35
Female	57.07	61.09	43.65
Total	100%	100%	100%
% or column who ...			
Owns a PC?	26.26	58.21	61.99
PC access at work?	24.23	0.92	49.58

Table 3.3 (continued)

IDS3			IDS4		
no access	access only	Web user	no access	access only	Web user
278	41	121	84	15	61
13.92	34.30	47.99	10.01	33.56	46.91
53.83	58.02	40.92	45.86	41.13	41.22
21.29	7.68	10.17	30.41	25.32	8.36
10.96	0.00	0.92	13.72	0.00	3.51
100%	100%	100%	100%	100%	100%
55.55	36.21	28.85	52.01	14.60	34.38
27.95	35.94	14.11	24.58	37.44	20.62
12.12	21.39	32.49	18.26	43.94	22.37
4.37	6.46	24.55	5.15	4.02	22.63
100%	100%	100%	100%	100%	100%
6.95	11.22	21.77	8.93	16.14	23.32
26.86	30.59	43.83	16.35	45.55	30.77
25.62	35.24	4.91	14.02	0.00	0.00
20.09	0.00	0.62	37.98	0.00	2.52
3.75	17.51	26.32	3.20	33.56	35.50
16.73	5.44	2.54	18.05	4.76	2.37
100%	100%	100%	98.53%	100%	94.48%
20.94	29.03	5.85	20.25	4.01	10.79
32.70	16.75	3.50	27.38	0.00	6.10
21.78	17.12	9.39	19.79	20.13	7.23
11.20	10.67	16.03	10.34	9.06	8.05
9.25	21.84	24.56	10.22	12.69	25.81
4.14	4.59	40.67	12.02	54.11	42.02
100%	100%	100%	100%	100%	100%
45.42	63.21	55.60	31.99	40.72	70.86
54.58	36.79	44.40	68.01	59.28	29.14
100%	100%	100%	100%	100%	100%
13.90	36.16	72.00	11.54	20.09	77.45
21.85	61.62	59.52	19.02	54.52	50.00

Table 3.4
Aggregate Recent Web Use over Time

	IDS2 (1996)	IDS3 (1997)	IDS4 (1998)
Raw count	1555	2305	1562
Recent Web users in millions	45.02	56.23	69.55
% recent Web users	22.5	27.8	34.4
Total number of people in millions	199.93	202.34	202.37

4   How Demographic Variables Impact Differences in Web Use among African Americans and Whites

In this section, we analyze differences among Whites, African Americans, and Hispanics in Web use in the context of key demographic variables. Each demographic analysis will first examine differences in Web use among all respondents. Then, we examine detailed Web use behavior for recent Web users only. Below we provide statistics on recent Web use for each IDS to facilitate these comparisons. (See tables 3.4 and 3.5.)

In IDS 2, 16.6% of African Americans had used the Web in the six months preceding the survey. This translated into 3.9 million African American Web users at the beginning of 1997. Thus, there is substantial support for the claim of at least one million active African American Web users, and our baseline figure of 3.9 million African Americans who had used the Web in the past six months in 1997 is considerably higher than estimates of one million African Americans with Internet access that have been reported elsewhere (*New Media Week* 1997; *Interactive Marketing News* 1997). Note that this number has been steadily increasing, so that by IDS 4, almost 22% of African Americans had ever used the Web, amounting to over 5 million African Americans in June 1998 who had used the Web in the past six months.

Race Differences over Time in Web Use
[*Portion of text omitted.*] In IDS 2, overall, Whites were more likely than African Americans to have access to the Internet, and to have ever used the Web. Whites were also more likely to own a computer, have PC access at work, and have fax, cable, and a satellite dish at home.

Table 3.5
Recent Web Use over Time by Race

	White		
	IDS2	IDS3	IDS4
Raw count	1304	2015	1368
Recent Web users in millions	35.22	48.36	60.41
% recent Web users	22.4	30.04	35.78
Total number of people in millions	157.12	160.95	168.81
	African American		
	IDS2	IDS3	IDS4
Raw count	104	151	117
Recent Web users in millions	3.9	4.04	5.21
% recent Web users	16.6	16.97	21.89
Total number of people in millions	23.5	23.8	23.8
	Hispanic		
	IDS2	IDS3	IDS4
Raw count	91	96	56
Recent Web users in millions	4.79	2.91	5.38
% recent Web users	25.2	15.16	28.02
Total number of people in millions	19.01	19.2	19.2

As table 3.6 shows, the percentages of access and use for both Whites and African Americans has increased over time, but the gaps persist. In fact, *the overall gap between Whites and African Americans in Internet access and having ever used the Internet have actually increased over time.* In IDS 2, 35.8% of Whites had Internet access, compared to 31.68% of African Americans. By IDS 4, although 49.33% of Whites had access, the percentage of African Americans with Internet access had risen only a few percentage points, to 35.54%. Similarly, in IDS 2, 24.34% of Whites had ever used the Internet, compared to 18.76% of African Americans. In IDS 4, eighteen months later, 40.37% of Whites had ever used the Internet, compared to 27.98% of African Americans.

Although Whites are still more likely to own a PC and to have PC access at work, these gaps have not increased over time. Further, the gaps in cable and satellite ownership have disappeared. In fact, satellite

Table 3.6
Race and Ethnicity Differences over Time on Key Web Usage Variables

	White		
	IDS2	IDS3	IDS4
Among All Respondents			
N	4,906	6,000	3,447
Current Access	35.84	43.25	49.33
Ever used	24.34	33.56	40.37
Own a PC	44.24	44.62	46.66
PC access at work	38.23	42.07	42.35
Home fax	14.00	13.68	14.86
Cable	68.46	72.87	74.49
Staellite	10.55	11.96	13.52
Among Recent Web Users			
N	1,304	2,015	1,368
First Used			
... in past 2 years +	16.17	33.14	49.47
... in past 1–2 years	18.41	23.95	19.99
... in past year	22.40	23.77	15.69
... in past 6 months	18.65	9.39	8.81
... in past 3 months	24.36	9.74	6.05
Last Used			
... in past 6 months	8.40	7.68	5.37
... in past 3 months	12.09	11.67	6.57
... in past month	21.95	19.38	19.30
... in past week	27.89	26.81	30.19
... in past 24 hours	29.68	34.46	38.56
Frequency of Use			
... once a day +	18.49	22.20	26.79
... few times/week	28.59	29.30	31.54
... two-four times/month	26.67	24.77	25.03
... once a month or less	26.25	23.73	16.64
Ever Used			
... at home	61.36	64.94	68.85
... at work	44.15	51.77	50.55
... at school	28.31	29.26	28.79
... at other locations	26.22	39.40	35.06

Table 3.6 (continued)

African American			Hispanic		
IDS2	IDS3	IDS4	IDS2	IDS3	IDS4
493	691	441	319	448	164
31.68	38.99	35.54	38.64	29.84	39.73
18.76	23.22	27.98	28.06	19.73	31.77
28.92	29.05	29.07	39.86	26.86	32.33
32.97	38.96	36.70	33.56	32.31	31.52
9.04	7.26	8.03	14.31	8.72	14.29
63.36	72.87	75.11	65.61	63.87	68.30
5.06	7.49	12.69	7.74	7.27	11.23
104	151	117	91	96	56
6.79	31.91	43.98	14.96	27.28	48.94
15.78	20.77	17.61	5.01	22.86	16.94
15.42	26.09	19.46	22.10	31.27	18.13
18.39	9.23	6.10	21.35	11.88	5.59
43.62	12.00	12.85	36.58	6.71	10.10
10.50	4.70	2.32	8.70	4.67	6.58
30.94	21.19	11.46	10.18	15.35	0.56
23.77	26.86	21.44	33.68	23.34	23.92
18.90	25.62	35.62	32.18	23.62	39.01
15.88	21.63	29.17	15.25	33.02	29.94
15.33	15.67	25.33	10.31	25.94	30.97
25.92	27.97	32.26	36.44	29.34	31.30
28.25	26.10	23.28	28.05	30.76	30.42
30.50	30.26	19.13	25.21	19.96	7.31
46.44	55.02	60.83	35.98	65.74	73.34
36.73	63.37	61.06	32.07	44.83	44.69
44.39	40.18	57.07	48.58	32.58	51.84
24.39	48.36	53.69	30.28	50.29	46.87

penetration has doubled among African Americans and the penetration rate in IDS 4 equals that for Whites.

Our estimate of 29% of African American households with access to a personal computer in IDS 2, 3, and 4 compares with estimates provided by Simmons Market Research Bureau (*Interactive Marketing News* 1997), which reported that 23% of African Americans owned a personal computer. The gap between Whites and African Americans in computer ownership has been cited as the key explanation for corresponding gaps in Web usage. A Yankelovich Monitor study (*Interactive Daily* 1997) "suggests that what bars entry to cyberspace among African Americans is owning a home PC, not lack of interest in the Internet." However, a Forrester Research study (Walsh 1999) cites "technology optimism" as an important predictor of technology adoption. Further research is required to understand these increasing gaps in access and usage.

A number of reasons have been provided in the popular press for the gap between Whites and African Americans in computer ownership. Price and value are often cited as explanations. For example, Malcolm CasSelle, co-founder of NetNoir, stated, "African-Americans just don't perceive the value of the Internet. Many blacks would pay $500 for a TV, and you could get a computer, though maybe not a top-of-the-line one, for not much more than that" (Holmes 1997). Similarly, Larry Irving, Assistant Secretary of Commerce, noted that WebTV® is in the under-$500 price range, and "laptop and PC prices are coming down. As that continues to happen, the Internet will become more prevalent in the African-American community" (Holmes 1997).

However, our analysis suggests that PC penetration rates are not increasing overall among African Americans. Although the percentage of Whites owning a home computer has increased slightly over time, approaching 50%, the overall percentage of African Americans who own a home computer has remained at 29%. Later we will investigate home computer ownership among different usage segments.

Overall, then, the gap in access and use is persistent and appears to be increasing. However, a different picture emerges when we examine recent Web users. In IDS 2, Whites were more frequent and more recent

Web users than African Americans. White recent Web users in IDS 2 were also more likely to have ever used the Web from home and work, while recent African American Web users were more likely to have ever used the Web from school. African Americans in IDS 2 were much more likely to be newer users, and Whites were much more likely to have been using the Web for two years or more.

But over time, it is apparent that African American Web users have made significant gains in Web use. Indeed, the gaps are diminishing rapidly. The gap in Web use at home has decreased dramatically (even as the overall PC penetration rate among African Americans stagnates) and African Americans now appear to be more likely than Whites to have ever used the Web from work, school, or other locations. Additionally, African American Web users are becoming more recent and more frequent Web users. In fact, differences between White and African American Web users in their recency and frequency of Web use have disappeared. African Americans are still among the newest users, but are now also joining the ranks of the long-term users. By IDS 4, 43.98% of African American recent Web users, compared to 49.47% of White recent Web users, had been using the Web for two years or more. This suggests that one cause of the digital divide arises from the differential lack of access.

Student Status
The differences on most indicators of Internet access and use, and also home computer ownership between Whites and African Americans is greater for students than non-students. We examine non-students first.

Non-Students   White non-students in IDS 2 were more likely to have access to the Web, to have ever used the Web, to own a PC, and have PC access at work. Additionally, White non-students were also more likely than African Americans to have a home fax, cable, and a satellite dish.

Over time, and similar to the previous analysis, overall differences between White and African American non-students actually appear to be *increasing*. Note that the percentage of White non-students who own a home computer is increasing slightly, but that the percentage of African

American non-students who own a home computer is actually *decreasing* over time. At the same time, the percentages of African American non-students who have cable or a satellite dish have increased and are now similar to the penetration rates for Whites.

Among non-student recent Web users, we see that over time African Americans are making steady gains in Web use. Since IDS 2, African Americans are increasingly likely to have been using the Web for two years or more, more likely to have ever used the Web at home, work, school, or other locations, and more likely to be more recent and frequent users of the Web.

However, White non-student recent Web users are making similar gains, and in some cases, their use still outpaces that of African Americans. For example, Whites are still more likely to be among the most recent Web users. In IDS 4, 39.96% of Whites reported using the Web in the past 24 hours, compared to 30.55% of African Americans.

On the other hand, differences in Web use frequency (a few times a week or more) between White and African American non-student recent Web users have disappeared. Additionally, African American non-students are more likely to have used the Web from work, school, or other locations. Because African American non-students are also more likely than Whites to be the newest users, we may expect increasing gains in Web use, compared to White non-students, over time.

These results point out the importance of home computer ownership and multiple access points for African Americans and other minority groups. African American non-students are significantly less likely to own a home computer than White non-students (and in fact, even less likely over time), and consequently, we believe, exhibit lower overall rates of access and usage.

Yet, among recent Web users, who by definition have access somewhere, recency and frequency usage rates for *African American respondents has over time come to mirror that of Whites.*

Students   [*Portion of text omitted.*] Overall, Web access, usage, and PC penetration rates are considerably higher for students than non-students, regardless of race. Additionally, Web access, usage, and PC penetration rates are all rising over time for *both* White and African American students. In fact, 53.83% of African American students owned a home computer in IDS 4, compared with only 25.67% of African American non-students. Eighteen months earlier, in IDS 2, the PC penetration rate was considerably lower (and similar to non-students): only 31.88% of African American students, compared with 28.66% of African American non-students, owned a home PC.

At the same time, [the data] reveals clear disparities in Internet access and use between African American and White students. For example, though both groups have higher rates over time, White students are more likely to have Web access, and to have ever used the Web, and these differences persist over time.

What might explain the persistent gap in Internet and Web access and use between African American and White students? White students are more likely to own home computers than African American students and this difference remains over time, despite the fact that home computer ownership over time among White students is flat and home computer ownership among African American students has been steadily and impressively rising.

However, the gaps in access and usage are clearly *decreasing* over time and this may in part be due to increasing rates of PC ownership among African American students. Additionally, African American students were more likely to have access to a PC at work in IDS 4. Thus, one could hypothesize that as PC ownership and PC access rates continue to rise, so will overall Web access and usage rates. Eventually, we would expect the access and usage gaps between White and African American students to disappear.

We now turn to an analysis of recent student Web users. Sample sizes are very small for African American students who are recent Web users, so results for this sub-segment must be interpreted with extreme caution. [*Portion of text omitted.*]

African American recent Web user students, like their White counterparts, are increasingly likely to be more recent and more frequent Web users. In fact, the differences between the two groups, as for non-students, have effectively disappeared. However, White students are still more likely to have ever used the Web from home, while African American students are more likely to have ever used the Web from work and school.

Home Computer Ownership

In this section, we examine the impact of home computer ownership on Web access and usage. Because there are such dramatic differences between students and non-students, we treat student status as a separate variable in this analysis. We first analyze non-students and then turn to students.

Non-Students   Table 3.7 compares Web access and usage patterns for White and African American non-students who do not own a home computer. Table 3.8 shows the same comparison for White and African American non-students who do own a home computer. First, it is quite clear that the presence of a computer in the home has a dramatic impact overall on access and usage. *Non-student respondents, regardless of race, are much more likely to have access to the Web and to have ever used the Web if they own a home computer.* Additionally, among non-students with a home computer, Whites are more likely to have access and to have ever used, but the differences are small.

Yet, there are striking gaps in access and usage among non-students without a home computer. In IDS 4, Whites were more likely than African Americans to have access to and have ever used the Web. Further, the gap in use among non-students without a home computer is *increasing* over time.

Turning to an examination of recent Web users, we first examine those non-students who do not own a home computer. Sample sizes for African Americans in this sub-segment are very small, so results must be interpreted with extreme caution. Here we notice that Whites and African Americans have similar rates of usage frequency and recency, suggesting once again that *given access, usage follows* for both groups. African Americans without a home computer are more likely than Whites to have ever used the Web at school or other locations.

Among non-students recent Web users with a home computer, both recency and frequency of Web use increase over time for both Whites

Table 3.7
Race and Ethnicity Differences in Web Access and Use by Student Status and Home Computer Ownership: Non-Students without a Home Computer

	White			African American			Hispanic		
	IDS2	IDS3	IDS4	IDS2	IDS3	IDS4	IDS2	IDS3	IDS4
N	3,258	3,134	1,733	282	421	271	158	274	94
Current access	13.91	19.35	22.87	14.23	22.77	16.91	17.65	14.39	14.35
Ever used	6.47	11.37	14.84	4.99	7.04	8.84	12.21	5.37	6.29

Table 3.8
Race and Ethnicity Differences in Web Access and Use by Student Status and Home Computer Ownership: Non-Students with a Home Computer

	White			African American			Hispanic		
	IDS2	IDS3	IDS4	IDS2	IDS3	IDS4	IDS2	IDS3	IDS4
N	2,025	2,442	1,479	140	197	116	105	130	44
Current access	58.36	66.87	74.31	59.76	66.56	69.35	50.80	59.76	74.42
Ever used	40.87	55.09	63.82	38.50	48.53	60.19	37.21	48.56	72.72

and African Americans, and differences are diminishing rapidly. By IDS 4, 73.85% of White non-students with a home computer had last used the Web within the past week, compared to 67.58% of African Americans and 64.62% of Whites had used the Web a few times a week or more, compared to 59.05% of African Americans.

Both groups enjoy similarly high percentages of having ever used the Web at home; 80.55% of Whites and 82.12% of African Americans in IDS 4 had ever used the Web at home. In IDS 4, African American non-students were more likely than their White counterparts to have ever used the Web at work, at school and at other locations.

Students Tables 3.9 and 3.10 below show the analysis for students with and without a computer in the home.

Sample sizes are much smaller for African American students when segmented by whether they have a computer at home, so the results must be interpreted with caution. Compared to tables 3.7 and 3.8, tables 3.9 and 3.10 show that students are more likely to have access to the Web and to use the Web, compared to non-students.

Regardless of race, non-students with a home computer have access and usage rates that are similar to students without a home computer. Students with a home computer enjoy the highest levels of access and use, while non-students without a home computer have the lowest levels of access and use.

Additionally, having a computer in the home leads to much higher levels of Web access and use for students of both races, but the difference is clearly more dramatic for non-students than students. That is, the differences in access and usage for non-students with and without a home computer are larger than the differences for students with and without a home computer. Presumably this is because students have more opportunities for access at school, even if they do not own a computer at home.

However, without a computer in the home, there is a much larger gap between African American and White students in terms of Web access, and the corresponding percentages of having ever used the Web are also smaller. In fact, the gap in access for students without a computer in the home appears to be *increasing*.

Table 3.9
Race and Ethnicity Differences in Web Access and Use by Student Status and Home Computer Ownership: Students without a Home Computer

	White			African American			Hispanic		
	IDS2	IDS3	IDS4	IDS2	IDS3	IDS4	IDS2	IDS3	IDS4
N	89	125	59	42	41	24	22	17	9
Current access	65.14	73.13	78.76	59.65	60.22	61.90	82.49		
Ever used	45.21	65.99	65.78	38.47	51.98	60.02	51.93		

Table 3.10
Race and Ethnicity Differences in Web Access and Use by Student Status and Home Computer Ownership: Students with a Home Computer

	White			African American			Hispanic		
	IDS2	IDS3	IDS4	IDS2	IDS3	IDS4	IDS2	IDS3	IDS4
N	247	280	159	22	27	26	33	23	17
Current access	85.59	94.40	95.30	69.06	87.61	86.19	81.49	87.63	
Ever used	69.19	83.55	90.93	53.13	67.53	83.80	57.79	64.73	

It also appears that the presence of a computer in the home is bringing African American and White students to parity in Internet access and Web use. Increasing the Internet access opportunities for students, especially African American students without home computers, may help to reduce the gaps in access and usage.

Tables 3.11–3.12 show the influence of education on Web access and usage between Whites and African Americans. In general, increasing levels of education lead to higher levels of Web access, usage, PC ownership, and PC access at work. However, these levels are higher for Whites than for African Americans and these race differences persist even after adjusting for education. In fact, *the gaps in access and usage are largest for those with a college degree.*

Less than High School and High-School Graduates   At the lowest levels of education, Whites are more likely than African Americans to have access to the Web, to have ever used the Web, and to own a computer. What is more, these differences persist over time.

Education
Among those with less than a high-school education, African Americans are gaining ground faster than Whites in Web access, use, and PC ownership over time. Overall, the gaps are smaller here. Whites are more likely to have access to a PC at work, in IDS 2 and IDS 3. By IDS 4, there is no difference between Whites and African Americans with less than a high-school education on this variable. However, students are included in this group and that could account for some of these gains.

Among high-school graduates, levels of computer ownership among both groups are stagnant, and Whites are more likely than African Americans to own a PC. African American high-school graduates are more likely to have access to a PC at work than are White high-school graduates. Additionally, the gap in access and use between Whites and African Americans is larger for high-school graduates than for those without a high-school degree.

Some College   Table 3.13 shows the results for respondents with some college, but no degree. In IDS 4, Whites were more likely to have Web

Table 3.11
Race and Ethnicity Differences over Time on Key Web Usage Variables for Respondents with Less than High-School Education

	White		
	IDS2	IDS3	IDS4
N	492	609	360
Current access	23.46	32.89	32.83
Ever used	14.93	26.45	28.26
Own a PC	28.92	31.99	32.60
PC access at work	11.26	16.72	13.28
Home fax	8.29	9.48	9.55
Cable	61.41	69.63	68.88
Satellite	10.82	13.76	13.17
	African American		
	IDS2	IDS3	IDS4
N	93	125	98
Current access	21.41	25.92	29.96
Ever used	15.46	11.85	22.40
Own a PC	15.26	10.25	20.70
PC access at work	7.64	10.09	13.73
Home fax	2.40	0.97	6.93
Cable	42.19	62.78	64.48
Satellite	3.89	8.32	16.56
	Hispanic		
	IDS2	IDS3	IDS4
N	73	130	41
Current access	40.55	19.35	27.83
Ever used	31.30	11.28	25.15
Own a PC	29.75	15.71	20.39
PC access at work	11.98	16.11	7.83
Home fax	9.60	4.90	7.35
Cable	62.51	54.41	58.62
Satellite	7.33	9.16	13.13

Table 3.12
Race Differences over Time on Key Web Usage Variables for High-School Graduates

	White		
	IDS2	IDS3	IDS4
N	1,475	1,710	998
Current access	23.09	28.13	33.35
Ever used	12.42	17.77	22.87
Own a Computer	32.31	31.18	35.30
PC access at work	30.01	32.20	31.67
Home fax	8.95	8.69	9.87
Cable	68.61	72.37	74.08
Satellite	12.34	13.72	15.20
	African American		
	IDS2	IDS3	IDS4
N	149	187	129
Current access	25.64	23.38	25.37
Ever used	9.39	9.52	16.69
Own a Computer	20.26	22.23	21.34
PC access at work	26.98	35.18	36.20
Home fax	7.87	4.30	5.66
Cable	70.69	70.86	81.44
Satellite	3.09	8.20	9.34
	Hispanic		
	IDS2	IDS3	IDS4
N	75	122	44
Current access	21.17	24.67	39.15
Ever used	9.46	10.60	26.91
Own a Computer	27.33	20.66	32.71
PC access at work	32.21	39.44	34.55
Home fax	6.86	7.59	12.02
Cable	59.29	68.13	68.03
Satellite	9.34	4.98	10.62

Table 3.13

Race and Ethnicity Differences over Time on Key Web Usage Variables for Respondents with Some College

	White		
	IDS2	IDS3	IDS4
N	1,397	1,943	1,117
Current access	42.51	50.67	58.85
Ever used	28.40	39.40	45.49
Own a computer	53.44	52.03	51.33
PC access at work	47.09	52.98	53.26
Home fax	16.65	15.79	16.60
Cable	70.09	93.24	77.22
Satellite	11.42	12.40	13.51
	African American		
	IDS2	IDS3	IDS4
N	131	242	151
Current access	41.46	53.51	47.25
Ever used	23.31	32.06	39.69
Own a computer	44.34	36.37	46.31
PC access at work	49.36	58.22	60.64
Home fax	10.62	10.19	9.99
Cable	75.10	80.42	80.03
Satellite	4.68	7.76	12.60
	Hispanic		
	IDS2	IDS3	IDS4
N	103	127	55
Current access	45.85	50.19	49.06
Ever used	31.84	37.23	31.92
Own a computer	52.07	49.03	38.34
PC access at work	47.41	54.14	55.75
Home fax	17.01	12.09	17.98
Cable	69.84	76.92	82.21
Satellite	5.97	6.01	6.11

access, to have ever used the Web, and to own a home computer. Except for access, the gaps are diminishing over time. African Americans are more likely to have PC access at work.

Larger sample sizes permitted us to examine Web usage patterns among recent Web users with some college. In IDS 2, twice as many African Americans as Whites with some college education reported using the Web for the first time (50.62% of African Americans compared to 25.25% of Whites). More than twice as many Whites as African Americans reported using the Web for two years or more (14.23% Whites compared to 5.97% African Americans). Thus, in IDS 2, Whites were more likely to be long-term users and African Americans were more likely to be newer users.

By IDS 4, similar percentages of African Americans and Whites have been using the Web for two years or more; 43.81% of Whites and 46.59% of African Americans had been using the Web for two years or more.

In IDS 2, Whites were more both recent and frequent users of the Web, compared to African Americans. Over time, however, these differences have effectively vanished, with 65.82% of Whites and 66.87% of African Americans in IDS 4 reporting using the Web within the past week. Similarly, 29.13% of Whites and 26.30% of African Americans with some college used the Web once a day or more in IDS 4, and African Americans with some college are actually more likely than Whites to have used the Web a few times a week.

In IDS 2, Whites with some college were more likely to have ever used the Web at home and work, and African Americans were more likely to have ever used the Web at school. By IDS 4, African Americans were more likely than Whites to have ever used the Web at work, school, or other locations. The percentage of African Americans who have ever used the Web at home has risen dramatically, going from 47.33% in IDS 2 to 76.52% by IDS 4.

College Graduates   Table 3.14 examines differences in access and use for college graduates. In IDS 2, Whites had higher levels of access, usage, and home computer ownership than African Americans. In IDS 3, it appeared that these differences had disappeared. But then in

Table 3.14
Race Differences over Time on Key Web Usage Variables for College Graduates

	White		
	IDS2	IDS3	IDS4
N	1,542	1,738	972
Current access	57.85	65.92	75.78
Ever used	43.37	56.50	70.18
Own a PC	64.65	66.81	70.21
PC access at work	63.21	65.52	70.86
Home fax	23.47	22.26	24.79
Cable	72.28	75.92	76.74
Satellite	6.49	7.29	11.34
	African American		
	IDS2	IDS3	IDS4
N	120	137	63
Current access	51.00	69.10	58.34
Ever used	33.09	55.09	53.49
Own a PC	54.09	70.43	43.60
PC access at work	76.40	74.16	70.09
Home fax	23.52	21.72	14.40
Cable	83.00	85.13	85.96
Satellite	6.40	3.76	7.83
	Hispanic		
	IDS2	IDS3	IDS4
N	68	69	24
Current access	53.63	64.18	70.77
Ever used	42.69	56.12	67.75
Own a PC	69.01	67.23	69.66
PC access at work	70.02	62.77	75.04
Home fax	37.22	28.03	40.18
Cable	78.11	80.86	81.17
Satellite	9.47	5.59	15.22

IDS 4, African American rates dropped, leading to dramatic differences and larger gaps. *Thus, it appears that education does not account for the digital divide in access and usage and home PC ownership.*

Interestingly, both Whites and African American college graduates have high levels of PC access at work and there is no gap on this variable. Outside of this finding, it is an interesting question to ask why there is such a large gap in access and usage between educated African Americans and Whites. Further examination of college-educated African Americans in IDS 4 is warranted.

Among recent Web users who are college graduates, we find other interesting results. Whites and African Americans report similar levels of recency and frequency of use, as with those with some college. Whites and African American college graduates are also equally likely to have ever used the Web from home, work, or school. However, there is a small tendency for African American college graduates to be more likely to have ever used the Web from other locations, and this difference has persisted over time.

Income

Tables 3.15 and 3.16 show the relationship between income and Web access and usage for Whites and African Americans. Not surprisingly, respondents whose household income is above the median income of $40,000 report higher levels of access, use, home computer ownership, and PC access at work. Below we examine race differences within income levels.

Household Income Less than $40,000   At household incomes below $40,000, Whites are more likely than African Americans to have access to the Web, to have ever used the Web, and to own a home computer. The gaps in access and use may actually be increasing, although the gap in home PC ownership appears to be improving slightly. There is no difference between Whites and African Americans in PC access at work at this income level.

Household Income of $40,000 and Above   Above the median household income of $40,000, differences between Whites and African Ameri-

Table 3.15
Race and Ethnicity Differences over Time on Key Web Usage Variables for
Respondents with Household Income below $40,000

| | White | | |
	IDS2	IDS3	IDS4
N	1,967	2,472	1,315
Current access	24.67	28.69	32.92
Ever used	14.52	20.63	24.68
Own a PC	29.49	28.45	30.52
PC access at work	26.37	30.93	28.72
Home fax	6.31	6.23	7.27
Cable	63.16	66.67	68.43
Satellite	10.90	12.14	13.42
	African American		
	IDS2	IDS3	IDS4
N	244	381	223
Current access	21.68	28.13	24.98
Ever used	10.83	13.51	17.42
Own a PC	14.39	16.26	19.81
PC access at work	19.55	30.83	30.65
Home fax	3.54	2.91	6.36
Cable	60.29	67.64	75.95
Satellite	4.96	6.02	11.30
	Hispanic		
	IDS2	IDS3	IDS4
N	164	247	69
Current access	24.98	18.73	19.45
Ever used	19.38	7.87	15.23
Own a PC	23.45	14.08	14.64
PC access at work	25.41	25.92	20.83
Home fax	5.49	4.90	6.90
Cable	60.17	62.18	57.18
Satellite	8.53	5.69	3.36

Table 3.16
Race and Ethnicity Differences over Time on Key Web Usage Variables for Respondents with Household Income $40,000 and Over

	White		
	IDS2	IDS3	IDS4
N	1,993	2,332	1,366
Current access	51.55	60.07	66.84
Ever used	35.66	47.78	56.51
Own a PC	62.31	61.24	63.60
PC access at work	57.78	61.28	63.02
Home fax	22.25	21.69	22.61
Cable	75.26	77.75	78.94
Satellite	11.05	12.22	14.33
	African American		
	IDS2	IDS3	IDS4
N	138	173	114
Current access	58.42	64.26	58.01
Ever used	35.60	44.92	50.36
Own a PC	64.95	63.61	61.26
PC access at work	75.32	72.40	60.48
Home fax	26.75	19.72	18.10
Cable	87.23	90.10	84.26
Satellite	9.27	9.80	12.96
	Hispanic		
	IDS2	IDS3	IDS4
N	108	113	54
Current access	54.12	60.03	63.80
Ever used	37.66	47.77	49.68
Own a PC	55.35	62.96	54.67
PC access at work	54.38	60.89	62.11
Home fax	23.87	21.70	27.48
Cable	72.36	86.56	87.27
Satellite	8.86	11.68	16.74

cans in access, usage, PC ownership, and PC access at work are greatly diminished compared to respondents with less household income.

We also examined recent Web users at this income category. In IDS 2, there were significant differences in the length of time that Whites and African Americans had been online. While 170.8% of Whites had used the Internet for two years or more, only 9.08% of African Americans had. In contrast, African Americans were almost twice as likely as Whites to be new users in IDS 2. By IDS 4, these gaps had disappeared with over fifty percent of both African Americans and Whites to have been Web users for two years or more. In IDS 2, 59.48% of Whites, compared to 44.21% of African Americans, were the most recent users. By IDS 4, this gap had largely disappeared, with 73.78% of Whites and 75.22% of African Americans with incomes of $40,000 and over reporting they last used the Web within the past week.

A similar result was found for frequency of use. In IDS 2, 49.69% of Whites, compared to 30.94% of African Americans, used the Internet a few times a week or more. By IDS 4, 62.86% of Whites and 59.08% of African Americans had.

Upper-income African American recent Web users are more likely than their White counterparts to have ever used the Web at other locations.

Gender

Tables 3.17 and 3.18 report the relationship between gender and Web access and use for Whites and African Americans. It is clear that overall levels of Web access and use are lower for women than men. Among recent Web users, men are more likely to have been using the Web longer, and to have used the Web more recently. Women are more likely to be newer users. While White men are more frequent users than White women, African American men are not more frequent Web users than African American women. Below we analyze differences by race for each gender.

Men   White men are more likely to have access to the Web, to have ever used the Web, and to own a PC at home than African American men and these differences have persisted over time. Interestingly, the percentage of

Table 3.17
Race and Ethnicity Differences over Time on Key Web Usage Variables for Men

	White		
	IDS2	IDS3	IDS4
N	2,045	2,465	1,402
Current access	41.97	47.05	53.85
Ever used	30.08	38.14	45.45
Own a PC	47.59	47.64	49.66
PC access at work	43.55	46.25	45.47
Home fax	16.89	15.77	16.78
Cable	68.01	73.12	74.15
Satellite	12.02	13.10	13.17
	African American		
	IDS2	IDS3	IDS4
N	192	265	151
Current access	38.94	45.74	45.72
Ever used	22.02	28.85	37.04
Own a PC	31.43	33.40	34.03
PC access at work	39.38	42.23	42.01
Home fax	12.42	9.81	10.19
Cable	64.41	77.42	78.24
Satellite	2.98	4.70	15.28
	Hispanic		
	IDS2	IDS3	IDS4
N	136	187	72
Current access	42.99	35.27	57.19
Ever used	33.51	21.66	49.51
Own a PC	41.66	27.34	42.69
PC access at work	39.43	34.01	36.61
Home fax	17.27	10.87	21.17
Cable	69.92	67.10	76.70
Satellite	7.65	7.72	14.02

Table 3.18
Race Differences over Time on Key Web Usage Variables for Women

	White		
	IDS2	IDS3	IDS4
N	2,861	3,535	2,045
Current access	30.12	39.72	44.98
Ever used	17.98	29.33	35.29
Own a PC	41.16	41.82	43.78
PC access at work	33.34	38.19	39.33
Home fax	11.35	11.74	13.02
Cable	68.87	72.65	74.82
Satellite	9.21	10.90	13.85
	African American		
	IDS2	IDS3	IDS4
N	301	426	290
Current access	26.26	33.80	28.62
Ever used	15.63	17.97	21.74
Own a PC	27.07	25.65	25.70
PC access at work	28.32	36.39	33.10
Home fax	6.56	5.28	6.57
Cable	62.58	69.31	72.98
Satellite	6.59	9.68	10.93
	Hispanic		
	IDS2	IDS3	IDS4
N	183	261	92
Current access	34.90	24.58	25.43
Ever used	22.19	16.87	16.78
Own a PC	38.33	26.39	23.67
PC access at work	28.58	20.66	27.27
Home fax	11.79	6.65	8.63
Cable	61.92	60.77	61.28
Satellite	7.82	6.83	8.88

respondents who report owning a PC at home has grown for White men, but not African American men. There is a small tendency for White men to be more likely to have PC access at work.

Among recent Web users, African American men are much more likely than White men to be newer Web users and this finding persists over time. In IDS 2, White men were more than three times as likely as African American men to have been online for two years or more (20.31% versus 6.20%). By IDS 4, over fifty percent of White and African American men had been online that long.

In IDS 2, White men were more likely than African American men to be the most recent Web users (65.46% compared to 37.04%). By IDS 4, both White and African American men were equally and highly likely to have used the Internet recently (75.03% compared to 71.37%, respectively).

White men were also more frequent Web users than African American men in IDS 2 (55.94% versus 38.9%). White men were still more likely to be more frequent Web users than African American men by IDS 4, though the difference had shrunk considerably (67.5% versus 54.65%).

Over time, the percentage of African American men ever using the Web at home, work, school, or other locations has increased considerably. In contrast, the percentage of White men who ever used the Web at school is flat, has grown only modestly for home and work, and has fallen for ever used at other locations. By IDS 4, African American men were more likely to have ever used the Web at school or at other locations, compared to White men.

Women   White women are more likely than African American women to have access to the Web, to have ever used the Web, to own a PC, and to have PC access at work, and these differences have persisted over time. As for men, the percentage of women owning PCs at home has increased over time for White women, but not African American women.

In IDS 2, African American women were much more likely than White women to be new users, but over time this difference has vanished. White women were more likely in IDS 2 than African American women to have used the Internet most recently (45.32% versus 31.75%). By IDS 4, 60.74% of White women, compared to 56.79% of African American women, had used the Internet within the past week. In contrast to previous results, African American women were more likely than White women to be the most frequent Internet users (44.38% versus 33.36% in IDS 2). By IDS 4, this gap had diminished with 49.02% of African American women, compared to 46.53% of White women having used the Web a few times a week or more. African American women were more likely to have ever used the Web at school or from other locations.

Children at Home
Tables 3.19 and 3.20 compare Web use and the presence of children in the home for Whites and African Americans. Not surprisingly, overall levels of access and usage are higher for respondents who report having children under seventeen in the household. Below we examine Web access and usage by race.

No Children under Seventeen   In IDS 4, Whites without children at home were more likely than African Americans without children at home to have access to the Web, to have ever used the Web, to own a PC, and to have PC access at work. Some of these gaps were persistent.

Among recent Web users, over fifty percent of both groups had been using the Web for two years or more by IDS 4, although African Americans without children at home were much more likely than Whites to be newer users, especially in IDS 2 and IDS 4.

By IDS 4, there were few differences in recency and frequency of Web use between Whites and African Americans. African Americans were more likely to have ever used the Web at school and other locations.

Children under Seventeen   Whites were more likely to have access to the Web, to have ever used the Web, to own a PC, and slightly more likely to have PC access at work. The percentage of respondents owning a home PC, though higher for Whites than African Americans, has remained constant over time.

Among recent Web users, Whites with children at home were more likely to be long-term Web users and to be more recent users, but not more frequent users, compared to African Americans with children at home.

Table 3.19
Race and Ethnicity Differences over Time on Key Web Usage Variables for Respondents with No Children under 17 in Household

| | White | | |
	IDS2	IDS3	IDS4
N	3,067	3,777	2,272
Current access	30.26	35.97	42.91
Ever used	20.47	28.32	35.39
Own a PC	36.36	36.82	40.59
PC access at work	34.15	37.54	39.69
Home fax	12.09	11.29	12.65
Cable	68.28	73.43	73.69
Satellite	9.56	11.27	12.62

| | African American | | |
	IDS2	IDS3	IDS4
N	256	393	236
Current access	27.71	36.94	27.04
Ever used	16.18	20.56	23.67
Own a PC	19.18	25.49	24.37
PC access at work	25.56	34.67	33.29
Home fax	7.81	5.55	5.53
Cable	61.26	71.32	73.25
Satellite	2.71	5.39	12.80

| | Hispanic | | |
	IDS2	IDS3	IDS4
N	156	203	85
Current access	34.41	22.31	43.15
Ever used	27.12	16.59	33.60
Own a PC	33.20	22.55	33.83
PC access at work	27.44	27.76	35.18
Home fax	14.31	8.99	10.80
Cable	60.31	63.75	75.42
Satellite	7.53	5.16	6.82

Table 3.20
Race Differences over Time on Key Web Usage Variables for Respondents with
Children under 17 in Household

	White		
	IDS2	IDS3	IDS4
N	1,838	2,220	1,172
Current access	44.59	54.20	59.46
Ever used	28.97	41.57	48.08
Own a PC	56.45	56.35	56.30
PC access at work	44.58	48.93	46.45
Home fax	16.93	17.25	18.32
Cable	68.76	72.00	75.73
Satellite	12.09	13.00	14.98
	African American		
	IDS2	IDS3	IDS4
N	237	297	205
Current access	36.24	41.48	45.45
Ever used	20.83	25.53	32.98
Own a PC	40.38	34.06	34.55
PC access at work	41.58	44.63	40.69
Home fax	10.49	9.64	10.96
Cable	65.81	74.90	77.29
Satellite	7.83	10.04	12.56
	Hispanic		
	IDS2	IDS3	IDS4
N	163	245	79
Current access	42.17	35.59	36.80
Ever used	27.65	21.47	29.84
Own a PC	45.35	30.14	31.01
PC access at work	38.62	35.80	28.30
Home fax	14.32	8.51	17.26
Cable	70.03	63.97	62.03
Satellite	7.91	8.89	15.11

Whites were also more likely to have ever used the Web at home, though this has diminished over time. African Americans were more likely to have ever used the Web at school and other locations.

[*Section 5, Differences in Commercial Web Usage for African American, Hispanic, and White Web Users, is omitted.*]

6   Developing a Research Agenda

Based upon the results we have presented, we raise a series of points for further discussion. We believe these issues represent the most pressing unanswered questions concerning access and the impact of the racial divide on the emerging digital economy.

Computers in the Home

While previous research has shown that inequalities in Internet access in schools persist (Educational Testing Service 1997, Sax et. al. 1998), our results suggest that inequalities in Internet access at home may be even more problematic. The role of access to the Internet at home needs to be much more clearly understood (Abrams 1997).

Whites are more likely to have access to the Internet and to have ever used the Web than African Americans and these gaps appear to be *increasing* over time. Our results are consistent with other recent research (Babb 1998; Cooper and Kimmelman 1999; McConnaughey and Lader 1998) that has explored the digital divide. However, we have probed more deeply and discovered that among recent Web users, who by definition have access, the gaps in Web use have been *decreasing* over time. By IDS 4, in most cases there were no or only slight differences between Whites and African Americans in how recently they had used the Web, how frequently, or in their length of time online.

Gaps in general Web access and use between African Americans and Whites appear to be driven by whether or not there is a computer present in the home. Access to a personal computer, whether at home, work, school, or somewhere else, is important because it is currently the dominant mechanism by which individuals can access the Internet. We have shown that access translates into usage. Overall, individuals who own a home computer are much more likely than others to use the Web. This suggests that programs that encourage home computer ownership (see, for example, Roberts 1997) and the adoption of inexpensive devices that enable Internet access over the television should be aggressively pursued, especially for African Americans.

Morrisette (1999) forecasts that by the year 2003, over half of all households in the United States will have access to the Internet, but that PC penetration could stall at 60 percent of households. Research is necessary to understand what motivates individual-level adoption of home computers and related technologies, as well Internet adoption, both within and outside the home. Additionally, research is required to understand the long-term impact of home computer ownership on Internet access and use.

Katz and Aspden (1997) investigated the role of social and work networks in introducing people to the Internet. The dominant three ways people were originally introduced to the Internet were 1) taught by friends or family, 2) learned at work, and 3) self taught. Formal coursework was the *least* often mentioned way people were introduced to the Internet. Long term Internet users were most likely to have learned at work; for recent Internet users, friends/family and self-taught were equally important. These results reinforce the importance of the presence of a computer at home, or the opportunity to access the Web from locations other than the home, in stimulating Web use.

Insight into the importance of reducing this gap in Web use between Whites and African Americans is provided by Anderson and Melchior's (1995) discussion of *information redlining*. Information redlining signifies the relegation of minorities into situations where satisfying their information needs is weighed against their economic and social worth. From the minority point of view, this is both an access issue and a form of discrimination. The new technologies of information are not simply tools of private communication as a telephone is, or tools of entertainment as a television is. They provide direct access to information sources that are essential in making social choices and keeping track of developments not only in the world at large, but also within their immediate neighborhoods. Unless the neighborhoods are properly served, there is no way out of information redlining for most of these disadvantaged groups. Research on this topic is warranted.

We found interesting differences in media use between Whites and African Americans that also deserve further probing. For example, although the rate of home PC ownership among African Americans is flat or even decreasing, the rates of cable and satellite dish penetration are increasing dramatically for African Americans. At a minimum, our results suggest that African Americans may make better immediate prospects than Whites for Internet access through cable modems and satellite technology.

Web Use outside of the Home
In addition to gaps in home computer ownership, the implications of differential Internet access at locations outside the home, including school, the workplace, and other locations needs to be clearly understood. Our research suggests that additional access points stimulate usage. Research is necessary to understand the impact of multiple access points on Web use, particularly for individuals who have no access at home.

Public-private initiatives such as Bell Atlantic's efforts in Union City and Bill Gates's announcement of a $200 million gift to provide library access to the Internet are a step in the right direction (Abrams 1997). It has also been noted that "community networks and public access terminals offer great potential for African-American communities" (Sheppard 1997). Further, the recent roll-out of E-rate funds (Schools and Libraries Corporation 1998) provides a significant opportunity for researchers to understand the factors important in stimulating Web usage among those least likely to have access.

School Web Use
The role of Web access in the schools, compared to other locations, needs to be clearly understood. Students enjoy the highest levels of Internet access and Web use, especially when there are computers in their households. However, White students are still more likely than African American students to have access and to use the Internet, and these gaps persist over time. Indeed, our findings closely parallel statistics compar-

ing student Internet use at private universities and Black public colleges (Sax et. al. 1998). As a recent report by the Educational Testing Service (1997) makes clear:

• There are major differences among schools in their access to different kinds of educational technology.
• Students attending poor and high-minority schools have less access to most types of technology than students attending other schools.
• It will cost about $15 billion, approximately $300 per student, to make all our schools "technology rich." This is five times what we currently spend on technology, but only 5% of total education spending.

Anderson and Melchior (1995) cited lack of proper education as an important barrier to technology access and adoption. Access to technology does not make much sense unless people are properly educated in using the technologies. Our data do not speak to the quality of the hardware/network connections, or the quality of information technology education that is provided by schools. As noted by the ETS report, creation of educational opportunities requires financial commitment that cannot be generated by the minority groups from within their resources.

Comparisons of All Racial/Ethnic Groups

Comparisons of Hispanics are preliminary in this working paper. Comparison among additional minority groups, in particular, Asian Americans and Native Americans, are required. Understanding the differences in Internet access and use among *all* racial and ethnic groups in the United States is required for a comprehensive understanding of technology adoption and its impact on the digital economy. Subsequent studies need to oversample members of minority groups. This is required so that there will be sufficient numbers of all minority groups to perform post-stratification adjustments to create weights that yield population-projectable results for each minority group.

Differences in Search Behavior

Reasons for the gap between African Americans and Whites in Web search behavior need to be clearly understood. Such differences could have important implications for the ultimate success of commercial efforts online. White Web users are more likely to report searching for product- or service-related information than African Americans. One possibility is that despite a range of sites such as NetNoir,[1] the African-American Financial Index[2] (Castaneda 1997), and Black Entertainment Television,[3] general-purpose search agents may not be perceived as an effective way to locate Web content that is compelling to African American users. This suggests the development of search engines and portals targeted to the interests of racial/ethnic groups.

Shopping Behavior

We found no differences between African Americans and Whites in the incidence of Web shopping. Is this because race doesn't matter for "lead users" who are most likely to shop, or is this because commercial Web content better targets racial and ethnic groups than does non-commercial Web content? Previous research (Novak, Hoffman, and Yung 1999) suggests that more skill is required to shop online than to search. However, as noted above, Whites are more likely to search for information online than are African Americans. More generally, consumer behavior in the commercial Web environment is complex and only weakly understood. Further research is needed to explore fully the differences in consumer behavior on the Web and their implications for commercialization.

Multicultural Content

Studies investigating the extent of multicultural content on the Web are needed. Another possibility for the gap between African Americans and Whites in Web search behavior is that there is insufficient content of interest to African Americans. *Interactive Marketing News* (1997) claimed that "while there are about 10 million sites on the Web, there are fewer than 500 sites targeted" to African Americans. However, others have commented on the multicultural diversity of the Web. Skriloff (1997) reported, "there are thousands of Web sites with content to appeal to Hispanics, African-Americans, Asian-Americans, and other ethnic groups ... A Web search for Latino sites, reported in the Feb./March 1997 issue of *Latina* magazine, turned up 36,000. Many of these sites are ready-for-prime time with high quality content, graphics, and strategic purpose."

Community Building

Are there different cultural identities for different parts of cyberspace? Schement (1997) notes that by the year 2020, major U.S. cities such as Los Angeles, Chicago, and New York will have increasingly divergent ethnic profiles, and will take on distinctive cultural identities. An important question is whether there are divergent ethnic profiles for areas of cyberspace. While the questions in the three IDSs do not allow us to directly address this issue, our analyses provide some preliminary evidence of divergent ethnic profiles for various Web usage situations. For example, African Americans appear to be more likely to use the Web at school and at other locations, and in some cases, are more likely to use the Web at work. How much of this is driven by the lack of a PC in the home and how much by other factors we have yet to hypothesize and investigate?

In addition to facilitating community building at the global level, the Web also facilitates neighborhood-level community building. Schwartz (1996) discusses how the Internet can be used as a vehicle for empowering communities. Anderson and Melchior (1995) raise the issue of the ways in which telecommunications can be used to strengthen communities. Thus, we should expect to find neighborhood Web sites emerging as an important aspect of cyberspace, and that these Web sites will parallel the ethnic profiles of the corresponding physical communities.

Income and Education

Income matters, but only after a certain point. Household income explains race differences in Internet access, use, home computer ownership and PC access at work. In terms of overall access and use, higher household income positively affects access to a computer. But at lower incomes, gaps in access and use between Whites and African Americans existed and were increasing. Research is necessary to determine the efforts most likely to be effective to ensure access for lower-income Americans, especially African Americans.

The situation is different with education. As with income, increasing levels of education positively influences access, Web use, PC ownership, and PC access at work. However, Whites are still more likely than African Americans to have access to and use the Internet, and own a home computer, and these gaps persist even after controlling for educational differences.

The policy implication needs to be carefully considered: To ensure the participation of all Americans in the information revolution, it is critical to improve the educational opportunities for African Americans. How this might best be achieved is an open research question.

7   Conclusion

In summary, we have presented a comprehensive analysis of the relationship of race to Internet access and usage over time. Our objective is twofold: 1) to stimulate an informed discussion among scholars and policy makers interested in the issue of diversity on the Internet, and 2) propose a research agenda that can address the many questions raised by this and related research.

Notes

1. ⟨http://www.netnoir.com⟩
2. ⟨http://nestegg.iddis.com/aaindex/dex.html⟩
3. ⟨http://www.betnetworks.com/newhome.html⟩

References

Abrams, Alan (1997), Diversity and the Internet, *Journal of Commerce*, June 26.

Atkin, C. K., B. S. Greenberg, and S. McDermott (1983), Television and Race Role Socialization, *Journalism Quarterly*, Vol. 60, 407–414.

Anderson, Teresa E. and Alan Melchior (1995), Assessing Telecommunications Technology as a Tool for Urban Community Building, *Journal of Urban Technology*, Vol. 3, No. 1, 29–44.

Babb, Stephanie F. (1998), The Internet as a Tool for Creating Economic Opportunity for Individuals and Families, unpublished doctoral dissertation, University of California, Los Angeles.

Beaupre, Becky and Oralandar Brand-Williams (1997), Sociologists Predict Chasm Between Black Middle-Class, Poor Will Grow, *The Detroit News*, February 8.

Castaneda, Laura (1997), African American Financial Index Available on Web, *The San Francisco Chronicle*, April 7.

Clinton, William J. (1997a), State of the Union Address. United States Capitol. February 4. ⟨http://www.whitehouse.gov/WH/SOU97⟩

Clinton, William J. (1997b), Remarks by the President at Education Announcement/Roundtable, The East Room, The White House, Office of the Press Secretary, April 2. ⟨http://www.iitf.nist.gov/documents/press/040297.htm⟩

Coley, Richard J., John Cradler, and Penelope K. Engel (1997), Computers and Classrooms: The Status of Technology in U.S. Schools, ETS Policy Information Report. Princeton, NJ: ETS Policy Information Center. ⟨http://www.ets.org/research/pic/compclass.html⟩

Cooper, Mark and Gene Kimmelman (1999), The Digital Divide Confronts the Telecommunications Act of 1996: Economic Reality Versus Public Policy, *The First Triennial Review*, February, Consumers Union. ⟨http://www.consunion.org/other/telecom4-0299.htm⟩

CyberAtlas (1999), As Internet Matures, So Does Its Users, April 26. ⟨http://www.cyberatlas.com/big_picture/demographics/inteco.html⟩

Educational Testing Service (1997), *Computers and Classrooms: The Status of Technology in U.S. Schools*, Policy Information Center. ⟨*http://www.ets.org/research/pic/compclass.html*⟩

eStats (1999), Net Market Size and Growth: U.S. Net Users Today, May 10. ⟨http://www.emarketer.com/estats/nmsg_ust.html⟩

Harmon, Amy (1997), Net Day Volunteers Back to Wire Schools for Internet, *New York Times*, October 25.

Hoffman, Donna L. (1996), Affidavit: ACLU v. Reno. ⟨http://www2000.ogsm.vanderbilt.edu/affidavit.html⟩

Hoffman, Donna L., Thomas P. Novak, and Patrali Chatterjee (1995), Commercial Scenarios for the Web: Opportunities and Challenges, *Journal of Computer-Mediated Communication*, Special Issue on Electronic Commerce, 1(3). ⟨http://jcmc.huji.ac.il/vol1/issue3/hoffman.html⟩

Hoffman, D. L., W. D. Kalsbeek, and T. P. Novak (1996), Internet and Web Use in the United States: Baselines for Commercial Development, Special Section on "Internet in the Home," *Communications of the ACM, 39* (December), 36–46. ⟨www2000.ogsm.vanderbilt.edu/papers/internet.demos.July9.1996.html⟩

Hoffman, D. L. and T. P. Novak (1998), Bridging the Racial Divide on the Internet, *Science*, Vol. 280, April 17, 390–391.

Hoffman, D. L. and T. P. Novak (1996), Marketing in Hypermedia Computer-Mediated Environments: Conceptual Foundations, *Journal of Marketing*, 60 (July), 50–68.

Hoffman, Donna L., Thomas P. Novak, and Alladi Venkatesh (1997), Diversity on the Internet: The Relationship of Race to Access and Usage, paper presented at the Aspen Institute's Forum on Diversity and the Media, Queenstown, Maryland, November 5–7, 1997. ⟨http://www2000.ogsm.vanderbilt.edu/papers/aspen/diversity.on.the.internet.oct24.1997.html⟩

Holmes, Tamara E. (1997), Seeing a Future With More Blacks Exploring the Internet, *USA Today*, February 20.

Interactive Daily (1997), More African-Americans Plan To Go Online, February 18.

Interactive Marketing News (1997), Web Marketers Beginning to Focus on Minority Audience, 4(9), February 28.

Katz, James and Philip Aspden (1997), Motivations for and Barriers to Internet Usage: Results of a National Public Opinion Survey, paper presented at the 24th Annual Telecommunications Policy Research Conference, Solomons, MD, October 6, 1996.

Keller, James (1996), Public Access Issues: An Introduction, in Brian Kahin and James Keller (Eds.), *Public Access to the Internet*. Cambridge, MA: The MIT Press.

Lawrence, Steve and C. Lee Giles (1998), Searching the World Wide Web, *Science*, Vol. 280, No. 5360, p. 98.

Liebling, A. J. (1960), *The New Yorker*, 36, 105, May 14.

Maraganore, Nicki and Shelley Morrisette (1998), The On-Line Gender Gap is Closing, Data Insights, *Forrester Research Reports*, 1(18), December 2.

McConnaughey, James W. and Wendy Lader (1998), Falling Through the Net II: New Data on the Digital Divide, July 28, NTIA, United States Department of Commerce. ⟨http://www.ntia.doc.gov/ntiahome/net2/falling.html⟩

Morrisette, Shelley (1999), Consumer's Digital Decade, *Forrester Report*, January, Forrester Research, Inc. ⟨http://www.forrester.com⟩

NetDay (1998). ⟨http://www.netday96.com⟩

Network Wizards (1999), Internet Domain Survey, July. ⟨http://www.nw.com/zone/WWW/report.html⟩

New Media Week (1997), BET, Microsoft Sees Potential in African-American Audience, March 3.

Nielsen Media Research (1997a), The Spring '97 CommerceNet/Nielsen Media Internet Demographic Survey, Full Report. Interviews conducted in December 1996/Jan 1997. Vols. I and II.

Nielsen Media Research (1997b), The Fall '97 CommerceNet/Nielsen Media Internet Demographic Survey, Full Report. Interviews conducted in August/September 1997. Vols. I and II.

Nielsen Media Research (1998), The Spring '98 CommerceNet/Nielsen Media Internet Demographic Survey, Full Report. Interviews conducted in May/June 1998. Vols. I and II.

Novak, T. P., D. L. Hoffman, and Y. F. Yung (1999), Modeling the Flow Construct in Online Environments: A Structural Modeling Approach, manuscript under review, *Marketing Science*.

Pew Research Center (1998), Online Newcomers More Middle-Brow, Less Work-Oriented: The Internet News Audience Goes Ordinary, The Pew Research Center for the People and the Press. ⟨http://www.people-press.og/tech98sum.htm⟩

Research Triangle Institute (1997), *SUDAAN: Software for the Statistical Analysis of Correlated Data.* ⟨http://www.rti.org/patents/sudaan/sudaan.html⟩

Roberts, Regina M. (1997), Program Lowers Costs of Going Online; Families Can Get Break on Equipment, *The Atlanta Journal-Constitution*, June 19.

Rutkowski, Anthony M. (1998), Internet Trends, February. Washington, D.C.: Center for Next Generation Internet. ⟨http://www.ngi.org/trends.htm⟩

Sax, L. J., A. W. Astin, W. S. Korn, and K. M. Mahoney (1998), The American Freshman: National Norms for Fall 1998, Higher Education Research Institute, UCLA Graduate School of Education & Information Studies. ⟨http://www.acenet.edu/news/press_release/1999/01January/freshman_survey.html⟩

Schement, Jorge Reina (1997), Thorough Americans: Minorities and the New Media, paper presented at the Aspen Institute Forum, October 1996.

Schools and Libraries Corporation (1998), First Wave of E-Rate Funding Commitment Letters Sent, November 23 news release.

Schwartz, Ed (1996), *NetActivism: How Citizens Use the Internet.* Sebastopol, CA: O'Reilly & Associates, Inc.

Sheppard, Nathanial (1997), Free-Nets Reach Out to Communities' Needs, *The Ethnic NewsWatch*, April 30.

Skriloff, Lisa (1997), Out of the Box: A Diverse Netizenry, *Brandweek*, February 17.

Sparrow, J. and A. Vedantham (1995), Inner-City Networking: Models and Opportunities, *Journal of Urban Technology*, 3(1), Fall 1995, 19–28.

Walsh, Ekaterina O. (1999), The Digital Melting Pot, *The Forrester Brief*, March 3, Forrester Research, Inc.

II

The Context: Background and Texture

The digital divide notion is really just a new label for a similar concept of the previous generation: information haves and have-nots. And this concept owes much to an even earlier construct that goes under the universal service rubric. The term "universal service" dates back at least to 1907 when Theodore Vail, President of AT&T, used the phrase to refer to his desire to interconnect the highly fragmented local telephone companies into a single nationally interconnected system. The universal service provider would be AT&T.[1] The more modern concept of universal service was that of providing telephone service for everyone. That redefinition can be traced to the Communications Act of 1934, which directed the newly created Federal Communications Commission (FCC) to "make available, so far as possible, to all people of the United States, a rapid, efficient, nationwide and world-wide wire and radio communication service with adequate facilities and reasonable charges."[2] Notions of the federal government being responsible for providing digital access to all Americans is therefore derived as an extension of the "telephone gap" of the 1930s.

Yet history suggests several bumps on the road to government solutions. The rapid adoption of radio, television, and VCRs took place without government intervention. Though radio spectrum was given out gratis by the government, the model of advertising-sponsored programming that has dominated was clearly determined by the marketplace. And the fact that most spectrum now changes ownership at substantial prices means that even that has to be paid for within a business model. The telephone-rate cross subsidies that were possible during the 70 years of regulated AT&T monopoly resulted in higher rates than needed for urban dwellers for the benefit of rural dwellers; those who needed to make long-distance calls were overcharged to subsidize local basic rates; and businesses were charged twice the rate for service as residences— costs that ultimately found their way into the prices of their goods and services. And despite such subsidies it was not until 1946 that 50% of U.S. households had telephone service (slowed, of course, by the Depression and World War II).

In recent years, there has been a big push to use taxes on telephone service (it's called the Universal Service Fund, but it's a tax) to subsidize wiring schools for the Internet. Yet the pace of technology is so relentless that this effort may be obsolete as fast as it's implemented. "The priority given by Vice President Gore and Sen. McCain to wire schools for the Internet may soon seem outdated—and to have wasted billions of dollars—if wireless technology advances sufficiently, allowing students to do Internet research without new phone or cable lines."[3]

This notion is consistent with chapter 4, which I wrote initially in 1984. Today's digital divide was yesterday's computers-in-the-schools divide (see chapter 20), the television divide of 1955, the radio divide of 1930, or the book divide of the previous half-millennium. The difference between then and now is that both the technologies and the business models seem to eliminate most of these gaps at much faster rates.

It is surprising that today there are still about 5% of households that do not have telephone service. But the reason is not purely economic. With various government subsidies that make it possible to have phone service for as low as $4 or $5 monthly, one would reason that there is little excuse not to be at 100% penetration. So the great contribution of Schement and Mueller in the research reported in chapter 5 is that at least some proportion of these non-subscribers choose not to be connected. In some cases it is because they would prefer to spend their money on the high entertainment value of a more expensive cable subscription than a telephone connection. In other cases it is because they fear that they would run up sizeable monthly long-distance bills if the phone were too convenient. Thus, some gaps may be self-imposed.

Chapter 6 must be credited to an initial insight by a former graduate student of mine, Mitchell Weinraub. In the debate over what should be included in the expanded concept of universal service, we differentiate between access to an infrastructure and access to content. For example, while cross subsidies helped make basic residential dial-tone service priced lower than real cost, no one would seriously propose that the subsidy include paying for 900 services that charge for horoscopes or sports scores. Though public funds have made books available in libraries and for many decades subsidized postal rates for magazines, society has not provided newspapers or magazine subscriptions for the less well-off economically. So in the debate of online access, what, if anything, might be subject to some sort of need-based subsidy: the hardware needed for access? The ability to connect to the Internet? The cost of services available online?

Mueller looks at the lessons of decades of cross subsidies as a means to further universal telephone service and concludes that at best it can be helpful only at the margins. Unsubsidized competition in the early 20th century had a far greater impact in building out the public telecommunications network than government programs to build exchanges in remote areas. More recently, there is strong evidence that competitive forces have been at work in providing low or even free Internet access: by 1998 only 12% of the U.S. population lived in counties with only one or no Internet Service Providers.

Thus, the sum of the historical context of these articles seems to provide a foundation for the point of view that the digital divide, though it may have existed at the moment of the surveys, may well be transitory, responsive to classic market forces, and that government policy may be best focused on filling small niches, as opposed to massive programs.

Notes

1. Thomas G. Krattenmaker, *Telecommunications Law and Policy*, 2nd ed. (Durham, NC: Carolina Academic Press, 1998), p. 350.

2. 47 U.S.C. §151 (1994).

3. Bob Davis and Gerald F. Seib, "Microsoft Case Shows New Economy Is Taxing Old Machinery Of Politics," *The Wall Street Journal*, May 1, 2000, p. 1.

4

Information Gaps: Myth or Reality?

Benjamin M. Compaine

A paper presented to a 1979 conference in the Netherlands warned: "If information bases are centralized and distribution facilities are limited, *as they will inevitably be* [emphasis added] then the concept of freedom as we know it is seriously threatened." If policy resolutions are neglected, "then the information revolution may effectively enslave rather than serve people ... We must not end up with two classes, an information rich and an information poor; a small technological elite attempting to cope with a large, semi-skilled unemployed majority."[1]

Disraeli said that "As a general rule the most successful man in life is he who has the best information."[2] The Bible,[3] numerous pundits, self-proclaimed sages, scholars and journalists have voiced similar truisms and expanded them to include groups, institutions and entire societies. Ever since the ancient Greeks told us that "knowledge itself is power," that theme has created a mini-industry of those who, today, warn that the rise of an information society will promote widening gaps between those individuals and societies that are information rich and those that are information (and usually economically) poor.

Whether these warnings are sound, or are merely good copy for the mass media, or are the creation of some academics with little tie to the real world, or are serving to further the political and social agenda of a cadre with a particular ideology is the subject of this article. There is evidence that this "information gap" theme has struck a certain intuitive, popular chord and that it has been placed on the public policy agenda to some degree. Is this topic indeed a budding issue in which the political, if not the economic, stakes might be considerable?

Is There an Issue?

The concept of an information gap is ill-defined from the start. It may refer to the access individuals have to information or the ability of individuals to have the tools—intellectual or tangible—to manipulate, analyse, and synthesize information. In a sense, it is a moving target, because as society has evolved from an agrarian to an industrial and on to an information-intensive one, the importance of having access to and know-how for using information has increased.

To a large extent, the information or knowledge gap issue has been perceived by the academic community. Former NBC newsman and current Stanford University professor, Elie Abel, predicts there will probably be less common sharing of knowledge by the advantaged and disadvantaged within society, thus eroding the common database which makes the American system of democracy possible. Looking at the increase in user-supported information services (cable, electronic databases, and so forth), Abel sees "a danger that sooner rather than later many Americans will be priced out of the market—debarred from the benefits promised by the new technologies because they cannot afford to pay for them ... The affluent would be even better informed than they are today; the lower orders could be even less well informed."[4] Herbert Schiller, on the communications faculty of the University of California and perhaps the most cited writer on this subject, expresses his concern within a broader social context: "The central questions concerning the character of, and prospects for, the new information technology are familiar criteria: *for whose benefit and under whose control will it be implemented?*"[5] This theme is picked up by others who differentiate between information and knowledge. While information technology may allow decentralization of information, they say, the real problem of knowledge monopoly is overlooked. What the modern computer enthusiasts monopolize, say Professors James Carey and John Quirk, "is not the data itself but the approved, certified, sanctioned, official mode of thought ... Rather than creating a 'new future,' modern technology invites the public to participate in a ritual of control where fascination with technology masks the underlying factors of politics and power."[6] Yet another member of academe brings the issue firmly into the "new literacy" arena.[7] Melvin Webber says that it was fairly easy to make the leap from pre-industrial to industrial status in part because the necessary skills were not difficult to acquire. His contention is that the same may not be true today: the requisite skills take longer to learn; extensive education is necessary to become competent at the information-handling jobs which tend to be cognitively difficult. Thus, there is the danger that "the spatial gap between lower-class districts and middle-class ones may become too wide and thus too difficult for the typical person to bridge." He asks, "Can we be assured that the communications media of the next decades will accomplish for the underprivileged youth of the year 2000 what the free library and the free public school did for immigrant youth of 1900?"[8]

Wilson Dizard, a former U.S. Foreign Service Officer now teaching in Washington, DC, straddles the fence. On the one hand, he believes that in democracies every person can become his or her own data collector and publisher for the price of the telephone and computer service bill. Like the Xerox machine previously, open electronic publishing allows any group or individual to offer their message on a new 'universal information grid'. Still, asks Dizard, is full information access one of our basic rights in post-industrial society, or is it simply a long range goal left to the play of economic and social forces? He adds that the degree to which "we extend our concept of education to include greater access to [computer and related] information resources" will shape the way our democracy evolves.[9]

Oliver Grey, an urban planner with the Urban Coalition, sees danger in that the 'lure of maximum profits and the action of public officials, large corporations, and new interest groups, may prevent any significant minority inroads into CATV and result in the development of a new technological elite.'[10]

Although the information gap theme is often expressed as an issue within Western society, a related subject is gaps among societies. Much of the rhetoric has been related to a "New World Information Order" and to such policy statements as UNESCO's 1978 Report of the International Commission for the Study of Communication Problems (the MacBride Commission). The problems caused by the export of films and television programmes from the West, mostly from the United States, is a topic frequently raised. Many of these critics have a political axe to grind. Kaarle Nordenstreng, who teaches mass communication courses in

Finland, notes that "A critical approach to these popular theories reveals that they contain more ideological manipulation than social science."[11]

Most authors in the field have determined that the West has for too long tried to persuade those in the developing countries which technologies were appropriate to purchase, often at a disservice to those countries that did not have a suitable degree of technical sophistication. Herbert Schiller is sceptical of such persuasive efforts, even those encouraging these countries to use communications satellites. He feels that most benefits will accrue to "our own already privileged population." Schiller asks:

Can the intolerable inequities that presently disfigure both domestic and international distribution be maintained? ... Will the television programs, films and other entertainment produced in a small number of Western factories continue to preempt world screens and stages ...? Will U.S. data banks, plus a few more in Europe and Japan, provide the patterned information on which social, political, and technological decisions will be based in Latin America, Africa, and Asia? ... In sum, will "interdependence" continue to be defined as binding relationships between unequals?[12]

If the information gap notion were simply the musings of a bunch of ivory tower noodlers, there would not be an issue. For the most part, the academic community has been the primary constituency of this idea. Nonetheless, other players have paid some attention, sometimes with far-reaching implications.

On the society-to-society level of discourse, UNESCO has gained high visibility. The MacBride Commission Report, debated at the General Conference of UNESCO in 1980, has become the primary document describing the need and blueprint for a new international information order. However, that report was viewed by the West in general and the United States and the United Kingdom in particular as a suspect document, produced by the so called non-aligned movement that placed national sovereignty above the needs of the free flow of information— commercial and news. Moreover, with the actual or proposed withdrawal of U.S. and U.K. support of UNESCO, that body is not likely to be a significant player on the international scene for the immediate future.

On the domestic scene the perceived problem, in limited form, has surfaced in the U.S. Congress. In his maiden speech to the Senate in 1983, New Jersey Senator Frank Lautenberg warned that computers threatened to create a new class of poor people, those without access to computers for learning. In this speech, Lautenberg described the "potential for new and distressing divisions in our society," based on a gap between children in wealthy school districts, where there is money to provide computers, and children in poor districts.[13] To address this perceived gap, Lautenberg introduced legislation to provide $600 million in federal funds for computer education in state schools, with half the total going to the poorest districts. With much the same end in mind, Representative Timothy Wirth proposed a bill that would have provided $3 billion over 10 years.

Concerns over local telephone rate increases after the breakup of AT&T have sometimes been couched in information-gap language. By July 1983, seven months after the breakup, 13 bills had been introduced in Congress to protect the concept of a universal telephone service. At one hearing, Representative Edward Markey said that if telephone service becomes a luxury, the USA could witness the creation of "an information aristocracy and underclass."[14]

This review of who has staked out what turf in the information gap area, meant to be suggestive rather than exhaustive, has yielded elements of fears, speculation, and arm-waving. For the most part, it has found a lack of empirical analysis or any semblance of rigour in looking at historical developments in information technology or political responses. The 'gap' proponents have said little on how they have measured or propose to measure the assumed gaps or even to provide a baseline from which to track prospective trends.

Diffusion of Technologies

Up to this point in history, all evidence indicates that technologies have been crucial factors in the spread of both access to information and the skills to use information. The original printing press was the first step in making information more widely available at lower prices. The big change came with the harnessing of the steam engine to the rotary press in the 1830s, combined with improvements in paper-making technology and the ability—via the railways—to reach wider audiences with the printed product. More recently, film and broadcasting have further broadened access to all types of information. Moreover, compared to 100 years ago, a far greater proportion of the population has the skill to make sense of the information and to learn how to seek it out. Those who raise the spectre of widening gaps therefore appear to assume a discontinuity in the historical trend, a burden which they have not overcome in their arguments.

Joseph Schumpeter was fond of noting that the achievement of technology was that it brought the price of silk stockings within the reach of every schoolgirl, as well as of a queen. Sociologist Daniel Bell adds, more to the point, that technology has not only raised the standard of living but "It has been the chief mechanism of reducing inequality within Western Society." In *The Coming of Post-Industrial Society*, Bell quotes Jean Fourtastie, who calculated that by 1948 the Chief Justice of the Court of Accounts in France earned about four and a half times as much as an office boy on an hourly basis. In 1800, this disparity was 50 to 1.

Historically, innovations do indeed start with a small vanguard of adopters who tend to be better off economically than the population at large. Commercial interests are often among the leaders. But the market created by this vanguard often starts a process which leads to greater interest, higher volume, thus lower cost, reduced skill levels needed, and ultimately mass utilization—sometimes referred to as an "S" curve of diffusion because of the shape of the graph of adoption plotted over time. In some cases specific public policies were implemented to affect the timing and direction of the diffusion, and these policies changed over time to meet new conditions. In other instances, the public policies were either indirect or non-existent.

Electricity, the automobile, telephone and television are among the technological innovations in the past century that have followed a path of starting on a small scale at a high price, used by those who saw value in the technology or who could afford to experiment with new technology. In each case, as the volume of use increased, the cost of providing the product decreased, with prices following. The rate of adoption by consumers varied, being shortest for the television and longest for the telephone.

The circumstances of the development of each are not perfectly comparable, as the nature of the product, the regulatory regime, and the requirements for infrastructures varied somewhat. Still, the following vignettes serve as a reminder that the computer and the related information technologies may have more similarities to than differences from their historical cousins.

Telephone

In the case of the telephone, the early entrepreneurs recognized that they could not afford to wire whole cities at once, so they chose first to wire affluent neighbourhoods and business districts.[15] The telephone companies in the USA swiftly found ways to reduce the cost to users, however, such as the introduction of metered service, pay phones for those who could not afford their own lines, and the building of minimal systems, sometimes laid down and maintained by farmers themselves. Meanwhile, government policy shifted from promoting unfettered competition to regulated monopoly. The combination of technological improvements and the public policies of universal service through nationwide cost averaging helped bring the monthly price of local service from the equivalent of two weeks' pay for the average worker in 1896 to about two hours' pay today.

Electrification

Electricity, too, was initially expensive. Again, the pattern was for the first users to be businesses and wealthy residences. According to a 1922 account by the Edison Company, Andrew Carnegie had an electric range installed in his house in 1896. Still, this was seen as little more "than an expensive toy for the wealthy customer."[16] By 1912, less than 4% of electricity consumption was for residential use. Railways alone accounted for 20%.[17]

However, it has been the case with many technological innovations that the vision of the inventor or early proponent of the product or service was a factor in the rate of diffusion. As with Henry Ford's automobile, Edison's aim was for low cost and durability. His early light bulbs cost $1.25 to make, but he was selling them for $0.40. In building up volume, he was able to bring down his average unit cost in there years to $0.37, and then in one year made up his previous years' deficits.[18]

The cost of generating and distributing electricity fell almost from the start of commercial applications until the 1970s. Still, in 1983, a resident of Hartford, Connecticut, paid 8.8 cents on average for a kilowatt of electricity, compared to 11 cents in 1905. Adjusting for the change in living costs, this translates into 39 minutes of work for the 1905 workers and less than one minute for those of 1983.[19] Meanwhile, the proportion of electricity consumed by residences had increased to 35%.[20]

Automobile

Once again the diffusion of the automobile in society went through stages, starting with adoption by wealthy urban groups, then the middle class, and ultimately the general population. In the process, the industry itself had to adjust to its customers, its labour force, and a changing industrial structure. The automobile was, at first, regarded as a plaything, certainly not a revolution. Yet it gradually changed from being a status symbol to being a useful product.

Henry Ford had a vision of the automobile for the average worker. His work in reducing manufacturing cost through production lines and the introduction of branch assembly plants led, among other ramifications, to:

• lower prices, which led to a broader market that spread beyond the USA's borders;
• a sharp increase in labour productivity and higher wages;
• perhaps least recognized but of substantial significance, a precipitous *decline* in the need for skilled workers and for mechanical skills among owners of automobiles.[21]

The magnitude of the decline in the price of automobiles is seen in comparing relative prices over the years. In 1908, a Buick cost about $1500, or the equivalent of more thn 2.5 years' wages for a production worker. Even after mechanization, the price never fell much below $1000. Today, a comparable wage earner must work about six months to pay for a $10,000 automobile. Used automobiles bring the price down to a level of affordability for almost anyone.

Radio and Television

In the mass media, history shows that the colonial press was structured for the educated elite. A series of cultural and technological developments which started to emerge in the 1830s created the conditions for the mass audience penny press. The spread of newspapers, like may cultural innovations, followed an "S" curve.

In the earliest days of radio, a user had to have a modest technical bent to use the medium, tinkering with the crystal set. With improvements in the technology and the development of programming, the radio spread rapidly. Instalment plans allowed households of modest means to purchase a radio. Even during the Depression the number of radio sets grew.

Television followed a similar pattern. As with other innovations, prices came down rapidly as production volume increased. In 1950 a small black and white television cost about $3000 in 1984 dollars. Today, a larger screen colour model can be had for $300 and even less.

Microcomputers in Schools

The best data on which fears such as those expressed by Senator Lautenberg can be based come from a survey conducted between December 1982 and January 1983 by the Center for Social Organization of Schools.[22] Among its many findings was that two-thirds of the schools in the wealthiest school districts in the USA had microcomputers, compared to 41% in the least wealthy districts.

This information is subject to various interpretations. Senator Lautenberg and others think the difference among districts is cause for concern. On the other hand, one could take the position that the survey was taken barely five years after the introduction of the basic Apple II microcomputer. Is it significant that so many schools have at least one microcomputer at such an early stage of its life? Given the reality that those with more money generally are the early adopters of technology, what significance should be placed on the finding that at this early date the proportion of schools in the poorest school districts with microcomputers is two-thirds that of most well-off schools?

Perhaps this says that any "gap" is moderate, that the technology is declining so rapidly in price, improving so quickly in ease of use, and is of high enough priority among educators and parents that there is no crisis and maybe not even need for concern. Or, it may be put in the broader context: poorer school districts would tend to have fewer new books, higher ratios of students to teachers, etc. The problem, if any, is not a computer hardware one.

The Role of Public Policy

Governments' assumptions of the potential for a new product or service colour the policies they adopt. Many of the early prognosticators on the telephone's future believed that its price would stay high and it would remain a luxury for the rich. Such prophecies could be self-fulfilling when held by those with power. In the United States the telegraph law was applied to telephone; thus policy, largely supportive of entrepreneurs' going into business, provided them with rights to string wires. In other countries, the United Kingdom and France among them, assumptions about the telephone's potential utility and its appropriate role were quite different. The restrictive policies adopted thus kept prices high and availability limited until recently.

In the current debate over what should be the role of government policy regarding the newer information media, two overarching lessons seem to emerge from history.

First, there is no need to act precipitously. Technology casts a long shadow. Thus, there is time for society to see how some technology or combinations of technologies move towards their natural markets and costs. Moreover, there is danger that jumping in too fast can lock in a technology that soon would be superseded by a better one. Examples of this abound.

The diffusion of the telephone might have been delayed for years if some influential body had convinced the federal government that telegraph was the personal communications medium of the future in 1860 and a massive effort had been implemented to see that every household was wired and provided with a telegraph key. A similar roadblock might have been the success of a proposal for the Post Office to gain control over telecommunications—the outcome in most of the world outside of the United States.

In the late 1940s, the U.S. Federal Communications Commission (FCC) was about to give its blessing to a standard for colour television developed by CBS that involved a cumbersome mechanical process that was incompatible with existing black and white broadcasting. The Korean War held up the final decision and by the time the FCC returned to the topic, RCA had perfected what, in retrospect, was a far more flexible and superior technology, which became the FCC's designated standard.

It may take decades before it is clear that some technologically innovative service or product has the potential to become an actual or near necessity, worthy of some government attention for regulation, subsidy, etc. The telephone and electricity (for residential use), the automobile, radio and television are examples of such technological innovations. It is not at all clear when, if ever, personal computers and/or access to electronic information services will be perceived to be of similar value.

Choice of Action

The second lesson is that the type of government action that might be taken, if any, is not consistent or obvious across technologies. Again, there are many examples.

The modern steam-driven rotary printing press and the attendant publishing ventures stimulated by this technology received virtually no direct help from government. In the 19th century the gradual spread of tax-supported public education and public libraries had a variety of indirect effects, including providing a larger body of literate customers. Near the end of the century the subsidization of postal rates for printed material in the United States was about as targeted a programme as government has enacted. (The withdrawal of these subsidies in the 1970s has had no measurable impact on magazine circulation, though some publishers had feared it would.)

The automobile was developed with virtually no direct government intervention or subsidy. However, government has played a crucial role in providing the infrastructure—the highway system—financed by taxes roughly tied to usage. In addition, rather than direct subsidy of automobile ownership, in the past three decades governments have adopted a policy of providing subsidized mass transit.

The telephone's early years were characterized by private development. The industry has passed through eras of monopoly during the time of Bell's early patents, to a period of competition, then government-approved and regulated monopoly, and now a period of regulated competition. The role of government to encourage cross-subsidies and nationwide cost averaging to promote universal service was pursued decades after telephone service began.

For broadcasting, there have been few direct economic subsidies to users. In this case, policies involved the conditions of ownership of licences, regulations covering broad areas of programming and the like.

Hand-held calculators are an example of an application of technologies that has had a widespread impact in a short period of time but with virtually no government role (save the funding of the space and defence research that lead to the development of much of the underlying technology).

There are indeed all sorts of "gaps" in and among societies. Many are related to the state of an economy. Poorer people and societies have fewer and older automobiles than the better off ones. The poor eat fewer steaks, rely more heavily on public education, are less able to afford designer jeans. They are less able to subscribe to magazines or purchase books.

The issue is not one of information or knowledge gaps, any more than it is one of a protein gap or transportation gap. If there is an issue, it is: What priorities should a society have in making decisions on what are necessities, what are frills, and what falls in a debatable middle ground? A second question is: What mechanisms can be implemented to address any problems?

The matters of books, magazines and education have been addressed by public libraries and public education. Concerns about protein have been addressed with food stamps. And nothing has been done about designer jeans for reasons that need not be dwelled on. Whether cable television should fall into the book or designer jeans category is debatable.

Fine Tuning

Clearly there is a role for public policy to fine tune areas not adjusted by themselves. The determination that telephone service should be universal —a consensus that did not spring full grown with Bell's first call—led to policies of nationwide averaging and a two-tier pricing structure, one for businesses and one for residences. That this structure may be in the process of being dismantled (it is not a certainty) with so far barely a yawn from the majority of subscribers may be an indication that telephone service has indeed become so cheap that the complex policies that were appropriate 40 years ago are no longer needed.

This then may suggest the direction for policy. There is evidence, only lightly drawn on in this article, that national economies that are growing with participation from a broad spectrum of the work force reduce or eliminate the need for targeted programmes and government subsidies. In the industrialized economies, the creation of a broad middle class has narrowed greatly the proportion of the population that *needs* subsidies (as opposed to the vast array of middle-class subsidies, such as deduction of interest from taxable income—the perks that a wealthy economy can rationalize).

As seen in the figures representing the constant dollar price of electricity, automobiles, telephone service and television sets, the combination of declining costs, thanks to improvements in technology, and a wealthier work force has lessened the difference in life style between the poorer and richer in society. Today, with many manufacturing jobs being transferred to the developing industrial nations, there are signs that a similar process is taking place on a global scale.

Notes

1. T. R. Ide, "The information revolution," in J. Bertirg, S. C. Mills and H. Wintersberger, eds, *The Socio-Economic Impact of Microelectronics*, Pergamon Press, Oxford, 1980, p. 40.

2. Benjamin Disraeli (Earl of Beaconsfield), *Endymion*, Longman, Green & Co, London, 1881, p. 155.

3. Proverbs 24:5.

4. Elie Abel, "Looking ahead from the twentieth century," in Robert W. Haigh, George Gerbner and Richard B. Byrne, eds, *Communications in the Twenty-First Century*, John Wiley & Sons, New York, 1981, p. 8.

5. Herbert I. Schiller, *The Mind Managers*, Beacon Press, Boston, 1973, pp. 174–175.

6. James W. Carey and John J. Quirk, "The history of the future," in George Gerbner, Larry P. Gross and William H. Melody, eds, *Communications Technology and Social Policy*, Wiley Interscience, New York, 1973, p. 501.

7. For a description of the notion of a new literacy, see Benjamin M. Compaine, *Information Technology and Cultural Change: Toward a New Literacy*, Program on Information Resources Policy, Harvard University, Cambridge, MA, 1984.

8. Melvin Webber, "Urbanization and communication," in Gerbner, *op cit*, Ref 6, p. 303.

9. Wilson P. Dizard, *The Coming Information Age*, Longman, New York, 1982, p. 119.

10. Oliver Grey, "Minorities and the new media: exclusion and access," in Gerbner, *op cit*, Ref 6, p. 322.

11. Kaarle Nordenstreng, "New international directions: nonaligned viewpoint," in Haigh, *op cit*, Ref 4, p. 193.

12. Herbert I. Schiller, "The free flow doctrine: will it last into the twenty-first century," in Haigh, *op cit*, Ref 4, p. 189.

13. Jane Perlez, "Computers pose a peril for poor, Lautenberg says," *The New York Times*, 8 June 1983, p. B-1.

14. David Burnham, "In Bell system breakup, small is expensive," *The New York Times*, 31 July 1983, Sec 4, p. 8.

15. Ithiel de Sola Pool, ed, *The Social Impact of the Telephone*, MIT Press, Cambridge, MA, 1977, pp. 28, 32, 142.

16. Thomas Commerford Martin, *Forty Years of Edison Service, 1882–1922*, Press of the New York Edison Company, New York, 1922, p. 78.

17. Richard B. Duboff, *Electric Power in American Manufacturing, 1889–1958*, Arno Press, New York, 1979, Table 12, p. 50.

18. John W. Oliver, *History of American Technology*, The Ronald Press Company, New York, 1956, p. 350.

19. Raymond R. Beauregard, "Memories on energy more myth than reality," *The New York Times*, 3 July 1983, Sec 11, p. 18. (Mr Beauregard is an economist with Northeast Utilities.)

20. Calculated from *U.S. Statistical Abstract, 1984*, Table 1003, p. 586.

21. James M. Laux and Patrick Fridenson, *The Automobile Revolution: The Impact of an Industry*, University of North Carolina Press, Chapel Hill, NC, 1982, p. xiv.

22. "School Uses of Computers—Reports from a National Survey," No 1, Center for Social Organization of Schools, The Johns Hopkins University, April 1983, p. 3.

5

Universal Service from the Bottom Up: A Study of Telephone Penetration in Camden, New Jersey

Milton L. Mueller and Jorge Reina Schement

The development of a new information infrastructure has added a new twist to the concept of universal service in telecommunications. The idea of universal access, once restricted to essential facilities such as the telephone, education, and electric power, is in the process of being extended to information and telecommunications services that are still in their economic infancy. In focusing attention on the diffusion of new technologies, however, the political rhetoric surrounding the national information infrastructure (NII) seems to have raced far ahead of reality. The physical infrastructure supporting voice telephone service has been in place in America for about 80 years.[1] Yet basic telephone service, still relatively cheap and ubiquitous, has not achieved complete universality. About 6% of all American households still lack telephone service. While the percentage may seem small, it represents about 5.6 million households, or 14.8 million people.[2] Moreover, the phoneless households are not randomly scattered throughout the nation. They are heavily concentrated on certain demographic groups and geographic areas. There are, for example, census tracts in the United States with telephone penetration levels around 55%.[3]

Who are the phoneless? What economic and social factors lead to or maintain their disconnection? How often is the absence of a telephone a temporary inconvenience, and how often is it a long-term or semipermanent condition? To what extent do the phoneless prefer to be phoneless? How do they adapt to the absence of telephone service in their everyday lives? What kind of substitutes are most commonly used? Most fundamentally, what difference does the presence or absence of basic telephone access make to their overall quality of life? Surprisingly, there is very little social science research on these questions. Accurate answers would nevertheless seem to be essential. Without understanding the economic forces that support or obstruct telecommunications access, or the real behavioral consequences of the presence or absence of access, policies to promote universal service are shots in the dark at best, wasteful and misguided at worst.

The report published here was one of the first to focus specifically on the phoneless and to take an ethnographic approach to the problem. The research was conducted in late 1994 as part of a consulting study for Bell Atlantic Corporation. It took place in Camden, NJ, a city where the telephone penetration level (80%) falls significantly below the national average (94%). The report's initial publication on the World Wide Web in February 1995 helped to reorient policy studies of telephone penetration.[4] A follow-up study building on its methods and replicating some of its most important conclusions has since been conducted in Texas (Horrigan & Rhodes, 1995).

The unique aspect of the study was its use of ethnographic methods and computerized maps to develop a more concrete picture of low penetration areas and households without telephone service. The authors characterize this method as the "bottom-up" approach to universal service research. By conducting extensive interviews with households in Camden, the researchers gleaned some interesting and unusual insights into the nature and causes of phonelessness.

In particular, the data gathered in Camden can be used to support the following claims:

• For the past 25 years, universal service policy has focused on the price of local access. The basic monthly rate paid by subscribers was believed to be the most important factor affecting affordability. The Camden data, however, suggest that most marginal users are driven off the network by usage-related costs, not the price of access.

• Universal service is usually perceived as an issue for rural areas, and many subsidies have been targeted at the elderly. Our data indicates that extensive pockets of low telephone penetration are found in inner cities as well as rural areas, and that the problem is associated with the young, the transient, and ethnic minorities.

• Many fear that in the transition to a new NII, low-income and minority areas will face "electronic redlining"; that is, their neighborhoods will be bypassed by the information superhighway. Camden data indicate a quite different problem: minority, low-income urban areas such as Camden consume a disproportionately high amount of advanced "intelligent network" features from the telephone company, and a disproportionately high amount of premium services from the cable television company. Electronic redlining seems less of a threat than that poor Americans will, upon exposure to the advanced features of the NII, buy services that they cannot afford.

• Telephone service has been widely assumed to be intrinsically more valuable than cable television service. Intellectuals and policy analysts value interconnectivity more than entertainment. But several inner-city subjects of our research had cable TV service and no telephone, for reasons that seemed quite rational given their specific situation.

We believe that bottom-up research into phoneless households has significant implications for universal service policy. Our findings and analysis follow.

Scholarship on Universal Service and Telephone Penetration

Studies of the history of the universal service concept show that the term originally had little to do with household telephone penetration (Mueller, 1993, 1996). When it first emerged in the early 1900s, "universal service" as a policy prescription was a response to the geographical and commercial fragmentation of telephone usage in America by competing, unconnected networks. "Universal service" in this context meant interconnecting the national telephone system into a geographically ubiquitous monopoly. The current meaning, which links "universality" to household telephone penetration, did not emerge until the 1970s.

The shift in the meaning of the term was an outgrowth of the rise of competition in the telecommunications industry, and its emergence was closely correlated with the political, economic, and technological upheavals that culminated in the breakup of AT&T. Under the old system of vertically integrated monopoly (in place from 1921 to 1984), telephone rates were regulated.[5] Advances in technology dramatically reduced the cost of providing long-distance service throughout the 1950s, 1960s, and 1970s. But state regulators, aided by the U.S. Congress, found it more congenial to keep long-distance rates artificially high and use the surplus to offset the rising costs of local line operation, installation, and maintenance (Wynns, 1984; Temin & Galambos, 1987; Crandall, 1991; Brock, 1994). The calculus underlying this preference was based more on politics than social policy: There were far more consumers of basic local service than there were major users of long distance. The telephone monopolies were willing participants in this bargain. If they could convince regulators that cross-subsidies from overpriced long-distance service played an important role in keeping local telephone service affordable, regulators would be more likely to shelter them from competition.

The AT&T divestiture destroyed this pact by officially sanctioning competitive forces in the long-distance market. With rate restructuring inevitable, regulators and academics began to take a closer look at household telephone penetration and the impact that rising local rates might have on it. Many feared that the rebalancing of local and long-distance rates would undermine universal service. Hence, the primary focus of recent policy literature has been the impact of competition on telephone rates, particularly the monthly subscription price of local telephone service. In the years immediately following the divestiture agreement, telephone companies commissioned major studies of the demand elasticity of local telephone service in an attempt to assuage congressional fears of a meltdown of the public telephone network (Perl, 1983; Booker, 1986; Larson et al., 1989). Consumer advocates and critics of industry liberalization began to attack the consequences of rising local access rates upon the poor (Gilbert, 1987; Hills, 1989; Milne, 1990). Albery (1995) contains a useful summary of the econometric models that have been created to estimate penetration rates as a function of various explanatory variables. A useful, long-range assessment of the impact of AT&T divestiture on telephone penetration can be found in Hausman et al. (1993).

Once it became clear that competition was here to stay, policy debate began to focus on how the subsidies allegedly required to keep local rates affordable could be financed in a competitive context. (Gabel, 1995; Noam, 1994; OPASTCO, 1993; Teleport Communications Group, 1994). It is not coincidental that as telecommunications sector liberalization has spread globally, so has the universal service debate (Gray, 1995; Wellenius & Stern, 1994).

To summarize thus far, the literature on universal service policy can be characterized as:

• Based on the assumption that telephone penetration levels are determined primarily by the price of a basic monthly subscription.

• Preoccupied with the issue of how large the subsidies to local access are and how to finance them in a competitive environment.

Within this framework,

• Aggregate telephone penetration levels are taken as the index of the success of universal service policy.

• Yet there is almost no analysis of actual phoneless households or of the economic and behavioral implications of the absence of telecommunications access.

Furthermore, the literature is characterized by a bias that is increasingly archaic, but seldom explicitly noted or defended:

• It focuses on the penetration of voice telephone service to the exclusion of other telecommunication capabilities, such as cable television, pagers, or computers with modems.

With respect to the last point, a new strand of literature has begun to emerge in the 1990s focusing on how universal service concepts might be applied to a new information infrastructure. Dordick and Fife argued in 1991 that "defining universal service in the era of the modern telephone with its varieties of enhanced and discretionary functions requires a much better understanding of the social uses of the telephone." Williams and Hadden (1992) and Hudson (1994) called for redefining universal service in the light of the emergence of a new information infrastructure. Schement (1995) focused on the economic and demographic characteristics of phoneless households using census data. Noting that income was the most important factor affecting household telephone penetration, Schement nevertheless proved that penetration levels vary with ethnic and other social differences even when the income variable is controlled.

In surveying this literature, the authors found themselves intrigued by the issue of phonelessness, but dissatisfied with the answers provided by existing research. A more contextual picture of telecommunications access seemed necessary. This meant examining at the behavioral level what difference the presence or absence of a telephone made in a household's ordinary life. We also wanted some understanding of the real substitution choices made by phoned and unphoned households. Telecommunications access is not really a binary variable as the penetration index implies, but a continuum. We wanted to see where inner-city residents placed themselves on that continuum, and what economic and social pressures affected their choice.

Method

Given the type of questions we wanted to answer, statistical data were not sufficient. We made a conscious decision to sacrifice the statistical validity obtained with a large sample size for the improved intuitive and interpretive validity that could be obtained from ethnographic methods.

Interviews with 14 households in Camden, NJ, were conducted in the winter of 1994. The subjects were located through the Camden Community Service Centers[6] and through the Camden public library. Respondents were interviewed in two stages. In the first stage, the researchers administered an oral questionnaire. At the conclusion of the interviews, the participants were given daily logs and asked to fill them out for a week. The logs tracked their movements and communication-related behavior. At the conclusion of the week, the logs were picked up by the researchers and the participants were interviewed about its contents. Both interviews were tape recorded with the permission of the subjects in order to obtain additional qualitative data.

Spatial and Statistical Overview of Telephone Penetration in Camden
A city of 91,000, Camden, NJ, sits on the banks of the Delaware River directly opposite Philadelphia. Once a thriving center of manufacturing, Camden's industrial base disappeared in the 1970s and 1980s. Camden's population is 53% African-American, 23% white, and 29% Hispanic.[7]

According to the 1990 Census, Camden's citywide telephone penetration rate was 80%, 14% lower than the nationwide average. If the penetration rate is broken down further, by census tract or by demographic

Figure 5.1
Population density in Camden County, based on 1990 Census figures. Each dot represents 100 households.

variables, even bigger gaps appear. In several neighborhoods only about half of the households are on the network. The maps (figures 5.1–5.3) make it abundantly clear how lower levels of telephone penetration are concentrated in particular neighborhoods. Figures 5.1 and 5.2 show Camden County, which includes the city of Camden along with several more affluent suburbs such as Cherry Hill. Figure 5.1, a dot-density map showing the total number of households, indicates that population is distributed fairly evenly throughout the County. Not so phonelessness. Figure 5.2, which maps the density of households without telephones (1 dot = 5 households), shows the concentration of phoneless households

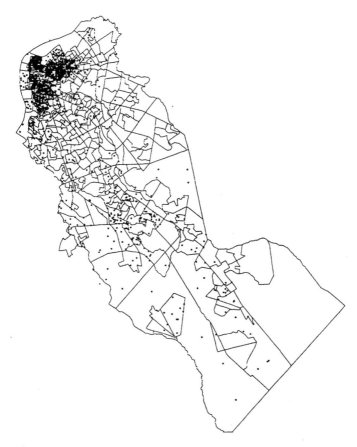

Figure 5.2
Phonelessness in Camden County. Each dot represents five phoneless households.

in Camden city and the near-total absence of them in the affluent white
suburbs.

Figure 5.3 takes a closer look at a section of central Camden city. The
map shows census tracts subdivided into block groups. One dot equals
one phoneless household (based on 1990 census data). A great deal of
the phoneless population in Camden is Hispanic. The shaded areas in
figure 5.3 indicate block groups where the population is more than 60%
Hispanic. In the lighter shaded areas, telephone penetration is between
60% and 70%. In the darker shaded areas, the telephone penetration is
less than 60%, and in some cases approaches 50%.

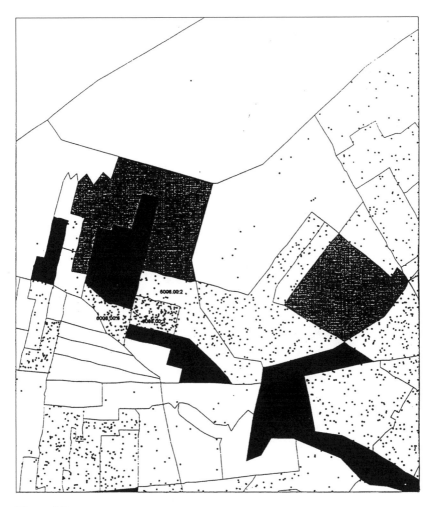

Figure 5.3
Phonelessness in central Camden city, based on 1990 Census figures. Each
dot represents one phoneless household. Shaded areas indicate block groups
where the population is more than 60% Hispanic. Lighter-shaded areas = 60%
to 70% telephone penetration; darker-shaded areas = less than 60% telephone
penetration.

Table 5.1 provides a summary of penetration data by the 22 census tracts in the city of Camden. The associated columns of data indicate how penetration is associated with other variables such as household income, homeownership, and race. The number of households of all kinds without telephone service ranges from a maximum of 43% in some tracts, to a minimum of 2% in others. The factors that account for this variation are, in order of importance:

1. Household income
2. Ownership of assets (homeowning vs. renting)
3. Age of head of household

A brief discussion of each one follows.

Household Income

There is a strong correlation between median household income within a census tract and the level of telephone penetration. If a rank-order correlation (Spearman's R) is run between median household income and penetration levels, the correlation coefficient is a high .808.

Homeownership vs. Renters

Another indication of the economic basis of low penetration is the clear distinction between penetration rates for homeowners and renters. Table 5.2 displays the pertinent data. For Camden as a whole, a little more than 91% of all homeowners have telephone service. The homeowners' penetration level ranges from a low of 76% in the poorest census tracts, to a high of 98.5% in the wealthiest sections. On the other hand, only 70% of all Camden renters have telephone service. There is also a much higher range of variation for renters. Only 43% of the renters in the lowest-penetration tract (number 6006) have telephone service. Renters in the wealthiest tracts, on the other hand, have a penetration rate of 96%.

Age of Head of Household

There is a weaker, but still significant, relationship between the age of the head of household and telephone penetration levels. Younger heads of households are less likely to have telephone service than older ones.

Even when their income levels are low, older heads of households are more likely to have service. A distinctive example is provided by census tract 6005 (see table 5.1). Although its median household income ($9016) is the lowest in Camden, 69% of the population in that tract consists of single renters over 60 years of age. The majority (78%) of these residents have telephone service. Thus, rather than falling at the bottom of the penetration ranking, as one might expect from its income, this tract falls in the middle. Table 5.3 shows the relationship between youth and decreasing penetration.

Who Are the Phoneless? Ethnographic Data

The preceding statistical profile was intended to set the stage for our interview data, which provide a deeper understanding of the specific nature of the economic barriers to telephone access, as well as some glimpses of the adaptive behavior and substitutes employed by households without service.

Reasons Cited for Losing Telephone Service

We interviewed eight households in Camden that currently had no telephone service.[8] Of the six households that did have telephone service, four had had their service disconnected at some time in the past.

The respondents' reasons for becoming disconnected from the telephone system were remarkably similar. Of the 12 families that were now or had at one time been disconnected, 8 of them had developed unusually large long-distance, credit card, or collect call bills that they were unable to pay. In several of these cases the person responsible for the account may not have been directly responsible for running up the bill. In three of these eight cases, the respondents also included the monthly rental charge for local service as a factor in keeping them off the network. In their comments, however, these respondents indicated that the telephone bill as a whole constituted an economic burden they could no longer afford. The main factor contributing to the size of the bill was usage-related consumption such as long-distance tolls or collect calls. No one checked monthly rental charges alone as a reason for disconnection.

Table 5.1
Camden City—Penetration by Census Tract

Tract #	Pop.	Male	Female	% Young hh	Medhhinc	White	Black	AmInEskAl
6040	1748	837	911	1.67%	$34,837	1716	16	1
6042	3720	1723	1997	4.59%	$33,029	3531	88	6
6020	5353	2565	2788	4.08%	$27,426	4839	366	27
6001	382	279	103	14.81%	$32,111	100	247	1
6014	5615	2529	3086	4.41%	$24,704	155	5218	32
6010	5500	2702	2798	7.80%	$24,151	1827	1712	23
6016	2685	1174	1511	6.63%	$19,092	221	2224	15
6012	6473	3102	3371	6.41%	$25,344	947	3754	19
6015	6789	3026	3763	6.26%	$19,875	846	5133	19
6017	3563	1496	2067	9.89%	$11,775	488	2792	9
6003	4106	1936	2170	6.42%	$15,792	420	2579	12
6002	2945	1328	1617	6.87%	$17,978	398	2055	12
6005	836	330	506	2.34%	$9,016	95	638	0
6004	4421	2146	2275	6.40%	$16,124	342	3068	18
6013	6604	3033	3571	9.57%	$17,170	571	4028	48
6011	10145	4667	5478	10.00%	$14,186	1746	4352	37
6019	3959	1755	2204	13.84%	$15,308	288	3261	15
6009	4607	2115	2492	10.16%	$14,003	987	1496	8
6018	2351	1116	1235	5.78%	$14,506	490	1488	11
6007	2551	1538	1013	7.39%	$15,815	405	1051	15
6008	6175	2924	3251	6.67%	$11,209	600	2599	29
6006	576	317	259	31.63%	$15,603	84	221	4
Totals/ averages	91104	42638	48466		$19,502	21196	48384	361

Table 5.1 (continued)

AsianPaci	OtherRace	TotalHisp	Household	Own_Phone	Own_Nophn	Rnt_Phone	Rnt-Nophn	% Phoneless
9	6	22	660	538	8	92	6	2.17%
51	46	101	1525	881	0	603	33	2.18%
30	91	203	2331	1654	40	614	23	2.70%
0	34	63	40	1	0	41	3	6.67%
15	195	306	1700	1055	113	451	81	11.41%
94	1844	2390	1717	954	73	551	139	12.35%
26	199	311	875	387	22	326	123	16.90%
159	1594	2128	1795	972	95	510	218	17.44%
42	749	1209	2318	998	155	97	268	18.25%
6	268	428	1143	258	27	674	201	19.66%
37	1058	1440	1183	568	106	356	153	21.89%
21	459	694	916	467	31	254	174	22.14%
0	103	136	471	55	18	300	86	22.66%
18	975	1319	1329	653	74	377	229	22.73%
54	1903	2439	1955	693	33	800	429	23.63%
515	3495	4357	3059	1007	130	1295	627	24.75%
2	393	651	1250	536	37	460	306	25.62%
32	2084	2688	1280	438	36	473	333	28.83%
44	318	596	658	228	61	170	110	30.05%
6	1074	1326	487	223	51	127	118	32.56%
8	2939	3590	1888	410	165	729	553	38.66%
11	156	201	215	54	0	73	96	43.05%
1180	19983	26598	28795	13030	1275	10173	4309	19.04%

Table 5.2
Telephone Penetration in Camden, NJ, by Census Tract: Homeowners versus Renters, 1990

Tract number(s)	Number of homeowners	Number of renters	Homeowners without phones	%	Number of renters without phones	%
6006	54	169	0	0%	96	57%
6007, 6008, 6018	1138	1807	277	24%	781	43%
6002, 6003, 6004, 6005, 6009, 6011, 6013, 6019, 6017	5167	7527	492	10%	2538	34%
6012, 6010, 6014, 6015, 6016	4824	3564	458	9%	829	23%
6001, 6020, 6040, 6042	3122	1415	48	2%	62	4%
Total	14305	14482	1275	9%	4306	30%

Table 5.3
Telephone Penetration and Age of Head of Household, Camden, NJ, 1990

	Age of head of household (yr)			
	15–59	60–64	65–74	75+
Percent without phones	23%	11%	9%	7%

The comments of interviewee 1DS are typical: "Someone took advantage of my calling card." The someone is her 18-yr-old brother, who stayed with them for a while. "He went through some problems," making "outrageous calls" to Florida, Maryland, and elsewhere. Another respondent lost service twice during the past 3 yr, both times for several weeks at a stretch. Both times it was for overdue bills, a combination of local and long-distance charges. The first time the bill reflected expenses caused by a cousin calling collect from Delaware State College. "I could not say no," she said. Respondent 6DS, a 29-yr-old mother of two who lives with her boyfriend, noted that she lost phone service in June 1993, as the bill soared from collect calls made by her boyfriend who was then living in Georgia. Respondent 5DS, a 44-yr-old woman who lives with her 2 sons, hasn't had phone service for the past 6 years due to economic hardship. "I couldn't afford it. Behind with bills. Income. Stuff like that. I know a phone is a necessity. I always wanted one." She added, "It's easy getting a phone, but it's trying to keep it on when you can't pay that bill and you got other bills, it be disconnected right there. If you got the kind of kids that's sneaking and making long distance calls to Florida, places like that, the next thing you know you get hit with this big bill and you can't pay it."

Households that have been disconnected due to large usage-related bills are faced with what is often an insurmountable barrier to their return to the network. To begin with , they must pay off the delinquent bill, which could be $100–500. In addition, they will henceforth be classified as a bad credit risk with the telephone company. Therefore they must put down a deposit to reestablish service. In New Jersey, the telephone company policy requires a deposit of at least $100.00.[9]

Only 4 of the 12 respondents did not cite excessive usage-related bills as the reason for their disconnection from the network. Three of the four said they "Don't want or need" service. Respondent K01, who claimed that she didn't want service, had disconnected telephone service in order to prevent her adolescent son's friends from calling him. Service had been discontinued for 2 years. She will get it back, she said, "when he [her son] gets his life back together ... no rush." Two of them claimed to have never had telephone service. The one remaining disconnection was a product of an oversight—the respondent forgot to pay her bill and did not respond to the telephone company disconnection notice quickly enough. In this case, service was restored relatively quickly. Thus, when users are driven off the network for economic reasons, usage-related charges are reported as the primary reason in almost all cases.

Consumption of Special Features

Despite their relatively low income levels, residents of Camden consume a much higher than average level of "intelligent network" features with their telephone service. Far from being unaware of or uninterested in advanced technology, the residents of Camden are more likely to purchase advanced services such as Return Call, voice mailbox service, 3-way Call, Call Forwarding, and Call Waiting.[10] Respondent 2DS, for example, who has twice lost phone service due to nonpayment of bills, reported having Call Waiting, voice mailbox service, and Return Call. Her monthly cable TV bill is about $50, and includes HBO, Showtime, and First Run. "They bring out so many new things," she said. "Before you know it, your bill is sky high and it's not always the long distance calls. It's what the options are." These results conform to national surveys, which show that African-American and Hispanic households spend significantly more on all types of communications services, including cable TV and long distance, than nonminority households (PNR Associates, 1994). This consumption pattern has caused controversy. Some regulators and public interest advocates have charged the telephone companies with overly aggressive marketing techniques in inner cities, implying that they prey on the uneducated by selling them large, expensive bundles of unnecessary services.

Use of Substitutes for the Home Telephone

What do phoneless households do once they have lost access to the telephone network? The logs and interviews show that phoneless people

rely heavily on pay telephones in the street and on office telephones at
their place of work. Although some of them use neighbors' phones on
occasion, this is widely perceived as a secondary, less desirable option. As
respondent 5-DS stated, "A lot of agencies I go to to take care of buiness
and what not, if you don't have a phone, they always say they would like
you to give a neighbor's phone [number], but you can't do that . . . How
do they know you get along with your neighbors? . . . I would never give
no neighbor's phone number. That got to realize it all depends on what
kind of neighbor you have. Maybe people can do that in the suburbs."
Several, generally younger, phoneless households rely on pagers as a partial substitute. Pagers, of course, must be used in conjunction with a pay
phone or some other phone. Respondent 3DS had a pager for about 6
months; "It helped, not to get a job, but to keep in touch with friends. I
just got tired of running to the phone booth so I gave it up."

More broadly, the logs reveal that phoneless users must manage their
access to telephones and that this represents a substantial demand on
their time. They develop a kind of hierarchy governing different ways of
accessing phones. Regular, predictable calls—"keeping in touch" calls to
relatives or "making appointments" calls to doctors or schools—are
made from work. Work phones are particularly useful for receiving calls.
(But of course, many of the phoneless are unemployed mothers.) Public
pay phones are used for less routine communication needs and may be
paired with shopping trips, bus rides, etc. Phoneless people know of two
or three pay phones in their vicinity and of necessity are aware of each
phone's tendency to be broken or occupied. Emergencies or inclement
weather might warrant a request to use the neighbor's phone. When
waiting for a response is necessary, the phoneless person might visit a
friend or relative. Subject K05 waited at her aunt's for 2 hours in her
quest to get a response regarding employment by a temp agency. Stories
about making trips to friends' homes only to learn that they are not
there, or of making trips to the pay phone only to find that the person
they want to call is away, are common. Half of the six households who
said they relied on pay phones for telephone service said that the pay
phones they used were frequently broken down. Two said that they were
frequently occupied. Another problem they confronted was high toll
charges associated with pay phones run by alternative operator services

(AOS). Several respondents indicated that they walked extra blocks to avoid such phones when placing toll calls.

When asked how other people stayed in touch with them, personal visits were cited most often. Respondent 6DS described her communication network as made up in large part of family members, many of whom have phones. Four of her five sisters and her brother have phone service. The brother lives in East Camden; three sisters live in Camden, and another one lives in Pennsauken. Frequent drop-by visits and family gatherings are the rule, she said. "So many of us are coming and going." The second most commonly cited method was contact at work and the relaying of messages by family members. Mail also looms larger in their lives.

When asked what is the worst thing about the absence of telephone service, the most common response was their inability to respond to emergencies. For routine life, the absence of a household telephone was approached primarily as an inconvenience. But it was perceived as a necessity in dealing with emergencies. In two cases respondents were able to describe recent events, such as break-ins or medical problems, in which they were handicapped by the absence of a household phone. According to 6DS, "Monday, Tuesday, and Wednesday I ended up having to call the police station once each day. Kids were throwing rocks and stuff through the windows. I mean, you can hit the baby. I called them [the police]. The first time I had to go shopping, so I called from the market. The other two times, I went across the street to my neighbor's house. I divide it up. If it's during the day and not too cold, I'll go to the phone booth; if it's cold or dark, I go to my neighbor's."

Thus, pay phones are probably the most important part of the public telephone network to phoneless or marginal households. America's inner cities are most affected by unexciting, basic infrastructure such as pay phones, not by a lack of access to advanced (and expensive) new services. Figure 5.4 shows that the number of pay telephones in Camden has expanded significantly in the past 4 years, by almost 50%. All of the growth in the availability of pay phones, however, has come from independent coin-operated telephones (COCOTs), that is, non–Bell Atlantic vendors. These independent pay phones are a product of competition in the marketplace, and contradict the common assumption that com-

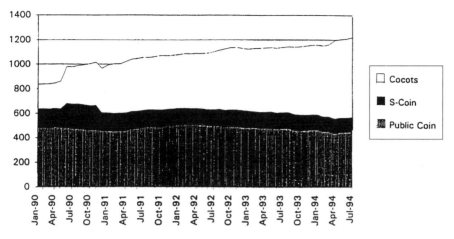

Figure 5.4
Number of pay telephones in Camden.

petition is inimical to universality. However, in their search for a market position their pricing may capitalize on user ignorance or inelastic demand. Independent pay-phone vendors are more likely to use the expensive AOS companies for long-distance service. Thus, while the growth of competition in the coin phone market has stimulated facility expansion in inner cities, the new pay phones are sometimes more expensive to use than regular pay phones.

Cable Television

Among the small group we surveyed, cable television had higher penetration than telephone service. Half of the eight households without telephone service subscribed to cable television service. (In one of those cases, we know that the respondent did not actually pay for the service but received it illegally. The others do pay for cable service.) Six of the eight had videocassette recorders (VCRs). The households had an average of three and a half televisions per family.

Respondents were asked whether TV or telephone service was more important to their quality of life, and which would be harder to give up. Half (four) of the households currently without telephone service said that cable TV was more important. Two said that telephone service was more important. Two were unable to answer. Answers were related to gender. One female respondent said that she preferred to have a telephone, but her husband preferred cable TV: "He's got to have his sports, you know ..." K01, the mother who had deliberately disconnected telephone service, viewed cable TV as a way to deal with loneliness, and as a better, safer value for her children. The entertainment programming kept them occupied, whereas the telephone exposed them to calls of friends with whom she didn't want them to associate.[11]

Computers

Although 8 of the 14 respondents said they knew how to use a computer, and 5 used them at work, only 1 of the 14 households reported having a computer in the house. Although our sample is far too small to make any statistical estimations about the population as a whole, it is apparent to anyone who visits Camden that household computers are quite rare—far more rare than current estimates of the national average, which places computers in about one-third of all households. The gap in computers is almost certainly bigger than the 14% gap in telephone penetration.

Camden's public library does not provide any public access to computer terminals. The closest Camden comes to publicly accessible computer terminals are those available to students at Camden County Community College.

Interpretation of the Findings

In this section, we provide an interpretation that draws out the policy implications of the data. Our key findings relate to:

• A new understanding of the economic barriers to telephone penetration.
• A profile of the phoneless household.
• A new approach to defining and analyzing access.

Credit-Worthiness as the Basic Economic Barrier

Making telephone service affordable to everyone has been the goal of universal service policy since the late 1960s. Traditional universal service policies focused on keeping the cost of the monthly rental charge for basic local telephone service low. Since the 1984 AT&T divestiture, policy has shifted away from this goal, at least nominally, although many such subsidies are still in place. Superficially, the strong correlation between household income and penetration levels may be interpreted as support for subsidies to local access rates. A more detailed analysis of what makes telephone service "affordable" or not, however, suggests a new and radically different conclusion.

The interview data indicate that most marginal users are driven off the network by usage-related costs rather than access-related costs. By usage-related costs we mean long-distance tolls, collect calls, credit-card calls, and optional features. Likewise, many new, younger households are kept off the telephone network by the initial deposits and charges required to get on the network, not by the ongoing cost of monthly basic service. For households that fall off the network due to unpaid bills, the problem is compounded: They will face both economic barriers (paying delinquent usage bills and high up-front deposits) at once.

This thesis ties together many of the demographic and social characteristics of phonelessness. Income, employment, and other measures of wealth or poverty are strongly related to low penetration not because the price of basic local phone service is too high, but because low-income users who run up large usage-related bills are unable to cover them. When a middle-class household runs up a $300 phone bill, paying it may cause discomfort, but it is doable. When a poor household with little disposable income is confronted with such a bill, paying it is hardly possible. Once disconnected, low-income users are also less able to afford the repayment and deposits required to get back on the network.

Credit-worthiness also explains part of the correlation between younger age and lower penetration. Potential subscribers without an established credit history face higher barriers to joining the network. They are riskier prospects for the telephone company and thus more likely to have to pay deposits. Older users are more likely to have an established credit history, either with the telephone company or with other sources of credit.

The practices of requiring deposits and of disconnecting delinquent users is not arbitrary or irrational. As things stand now, telecommunications access is the equivalent of an unlimited line of credit. In contrast to credit cards, users are not given an explicit credit limit, and individual transactions are not verified (except in advanced mobile services). As the features and capabilities of the public network increase, the risk that some consumers will spend beyond their means also increases. Under these circumstances the providers of service must protect themselves against uncollectable bills or bad credit risks in some way. The key issue in universal service policy, then, is how to maximize access while minimizing credit risk. Unfortunately, current policies toward billing and collection, credit risk minimization, and disconnection have not been formulated with universal service considerations in mind. As the analysis that follows shows, there is no simple solution to this problem.

Toll restriction, a service that is available in New Jersey and many other states, can prevent long-distance calls from being placed from a particular household or business telephone. In fact, toll restriction is an ineffective mechanism at the present time for a variety of reasons. To begin with, Bell Atlantic New Jersey charges a once-off fee of $25 and a little more than $12 per month for the privilege of toll restriction. As this option virtually doubles the cost of local phone service, a less attractive pricing scheme could hardly be imagined.[12] Aside from the unattractive pricing associated with toll restriction, its attempt to restrict the line of credit available to a telephone user is easily circumvented. Long-distance companies happily issue calling cards to any customer who wants one. Once a user possesses a credit card, long-distance networks can be accessed through 800 numbers that are not blocked by the toll restriction service. Toll restriction also does not prevent collect calls.

The leakiness of the toll billing restriction is compounded by the local telephone companies' new role as billing and collection agent for long-distance companies. Under normal business practice, failure to pay a long-distance bill should not necessarily lead to the disconnection of local service. After all, the services are offered by different companies under separate accounts. Once the local exchange companies (LECs) assume the role of billing and collection agent, however, total service disconnection is their most effective weapon in obtaining compliance. There is a tension between the LEC's dual role as primary local access provider and billing and collection service provider.

Toll billing exception is a service that flags a particular account so that the number in question cannot receive collect calls. Although the database supporting this procedure may not be used by some alternative operator services (AOS) companies and small independent telephone companies, it will catch 98–99% of all incoming calls. This service could be effective in preventing the development of uncollectable bills. The problem here is that few residential users in cities such as Camden are aware of this option. Also, our survey research indicates that there are strong social pressures on female, inner-city users to accept collect calls from family members or close friends. Such a practice may not circumvent these pressures unless they are imposed upon a household externally. Such an imposition, of course, raises other problems.

Linkup America is a program that reduces the initial payment for connection charges for customers who qualify for various government assistance programs. In New Jersey, instead of paying $40 up front, qualifying customers are charged only $20, and the $20 is recovered in their monthly bill over a 12-mo period. Although New Jersey's Linkup program does provide a small discount to its participants, two other items limit the effectiveness of Linkup as a penetration booster:

1. It does not override the telephone company's deposit policy. While reducing the initial payment by $20 may help some, it is unlikely to be decisive when the user is faced with a $100 deposit.
2. Telephone users in Camden and, we suspect, elsewhere in New Jersey are almost completely unaware of the program. Not a single respondent in our Camden survey had ever heard of the Linkup program.

According to Bell Atlantic data, only about 150 telephone users in Camden were signed up under the Linkup program. The minimal public participation in New Jersey's Linkup program is predictable given the minor contribution it makes and the lack of public awareness.

Profile of Phonelessness
What difference does it make to be phoneless? The ethnographic data indicate that the impact falls somewhere between the commonly cited extremes of total isolation and deprivation on the one hand, and a simple preference not to be on the network on the other. The absence of a household phone imposes a rather demanding regimen on users, who must manage their trips to outside phones and plan carefully in order to

be able to receive calls. The problems and limitations of phonelessness are most noticable, and most worthy of social policy attention, during emergencies. As the sophistication of communication technology increases and the information-processing capabilities of the public network expand, it may be possible to make emergency calling facilities, perhaps paging-based, available for free.

There is a clear dichotomy between residences for whom the absence of telephone service is a short-term credit problem and those for whom it is a longer term, if not permanent, condition. Five of the 8 respondents currently without telephone service had been off the network for 2 years or more. Two of them had never had telephone service. Interestingly, the short-term phoneless (i.e., households who currently have telephone service but had once been disconnected at some time in the past) spoke much more strongly about the deprivations and disadvantages of phonelessness than the long-term phoneless. One respondent noted that "after a while, you get used to it [phonelessness]." The survey also showed that some phoneless households value the capabilities and services offered by cable television more highly than access to the telephone network. This group tends to have been phoneless for a longer period of time. Based on the data obtained from the respondents' logs of their daily activities, this group tends to be more localized or less interconnected with the surrounding society. Our study only scratched the surface of this issue. More research on the long-term phoneless would be helpful.

Defining and Analyzing Access

Our decision to link cable television to the universal service issue provoked strong negative reactions when the study was first released. The critics felt that the study implied that phoneless households were really able to afford telephone service but preferred access to low-brow, mass entertainment instead. We were accused, in effect, of blaming the victims for their condition.

Upon reflection, the reasons for the harshness of this response became clear. Our approach to the analysis of affordability and access really was subversive of the traditional welfarist approach to universal service. The traditional approach hinges on designation a particular service as "essential" to a decent life. The presence or absence of this essential facility is treated as if it were a discrete variable with only two values: yes or no. Thus, those who do not have it are ipso facto deprived or victimized and in need of government support.

Our approach to the problem of inner-city access was based on radically different set of assumptions. We approached telecommunications access as a continuous variable, not a discrete one. At one extreme, there is total isolation; at the other, there is the user with a cellular phone and the full complement of answering machines, computers, and fax machines. But there are many possibilities in between: pay phones, pagers, work phones, etc. We approached affordability, too, as a matter of degree. A telephone subscription is one of many options in a household budget. Cable TV is another. Obviously, low-income families have a far more restricted range of choices than affluent families. But they do make choices about where they want to be on the continuum of access. In making these choices, inner-city consumers' preferences are not uniform. To some, the absence of a telephone represents deprivation; to others, it is just an inconvenience. To the latter group, being cut off from cable television might represent a worse form of isolation than no telephone. Taken together, this approach undermines many of the legitimizing assumptions behind the welfarist approach to universal service.

Any universal service policy that is not based on the more realistic set of assumptions just enumerated, however, is bound to be a poor one. Such a policy will end up subsidizing services that people don't want, or that don't make sense given their particular circumstances. It will paternalistically attempt to impose a specific set of choices on users. And it will send the wrong signals to the suppliers of services, who may be encouraged to expand the output of expensive traditional services to the exclusion of new possibilities, such as two-way paging, or card-based access, that may address the problems of restricted access more efficiently.

Universal service policy can no longer be focused exclusively on household telephone penetration. The growing gap in computer penetration is in some ways more disturbing than the relatively low penetration of telephone service in Camden. The importance of cable TV as a form of telecommunications access must also be recognized. The City of Santa Monica has had significant success with its PEN system, an electronic mail system in which every resident is given an account (Rogers et al., 1994). Certain aspects of the PEN model may be applicable to Camden. The adoption of paging service by many inner-city residents as an alternative to the household telephone shows the potential of wireless technologies to make telecommunications access more affordable. The most commonly cited problem with paging was of course its one-way communication nature, forcing users to run to a pay telephone to respond to a call. New service offering(s) that exploit more fully the capability of wireless to provide cheap, limited-function substitutes for basic local telephone service should be explored. Narrowband, two-way paging services have enormous potential to replace POTS (plain old telephone service) as the building block of universal service. Simple paging services could limit telephone companies' exposure to bill nonpayment while enhancing the communications access of otherwise phoneless people. Paging services are not as susceptible to overconsumption as regular telephone service.

Conclusions

While others have called for new definitions of universal service in the wake of technological change, few have examined the substitution choices and trade-offs made by users on the economic margins. The personal ecology of media usage among inner-city dwellers is more interesting and more relevant to policy than the old stereotypes would suggest. The data clearly indicate that telecommunications access is a continuum, not a binary choice, and that low-income inner-city users have varied preferences as to where they want to be located on that spectrum. Even more important, the costs of usage appear to be more powerful influences on the overall affordability of service than the monthly cost of access by itself. As the features of the public network expand, so does the risk that some consumers will spend beyond their means and be disconnected. In reformulating universal service policy, we must take account the growing heterogeneity of telecommunications access, and the vital importance of credit risk as a factor affecting public access to networks.

Notes

1. Mueller (1996) shows that 90% of the central office locations of the U.S. telephone system were established by 1912.

2. We arrived at the figure of 14.8 million individuals by multiplying the number of households (5.6 million) by 2.64, the average number of individuals per household in the United States according to the 1990 census.

3. See table 5.1 for specific examples in Camden, NJ.

4. At ⟨http://www.ba.com⟩

5. Interstate long-distance rates were not effectively regulated until 1934, after the creation of the Federal Communications Commission. But less than 3% of toll traffic was interstate at that time.

6. We gratefully acknowledge the assistance of Cathy Dunbar, Director of the Martin Luther King Community Center in Camden.

7. The "Hispanic" category overlaps with both white and black racial categories, so the percentages cited here add up to more than 100%.

8. The interviews were conducted by Duane Stolzfus and Kim Miller, PhD students at Rutgers SCILS.

9. Jean Mothena, Bell Atlantic Corporate.

10. Proprietary data from Bell Atlantic.

11. Since first releasing their study, the authors have heard FCC Commissioner Reed Hundt, Vice President Al Gore, and President Bill Clinton refer to inner-city mothers protecting their children by subscribing to cable while rejecting telephone service. In separate informal presentations, Gore and Clinton used this anecdote without attribution, and in one instance located the mother in Detroit. The mother from Camden has evidently entered the realm of metaphoric characters, doing for the Democrats what the mythical "welfare queen" did for Reagan Republicans in the 1980s.

12. This price may have been changed by the time this is published, due in no small part to pressure generated by the original study.

References

Albery, B. 1995. What level of dialtone penetration constitutes "universal service"? *Telecommun. Policy* 19(5): 365–380.

Booker, E. 1986. Lifeline and the low income customer: Who is ultimately responsible? *Telephony* 210(20): 116–132.

Brock, G. 1994. *Telecommunications policy for the information age.* Cambridge, MA: Harvard University Press.

Crandall, R. 1991. *After the breakup: U.S. telecommunications in a more competitive era.* Washington, DC: Brookings.

Dordick, H. S., and Fife, M. D. 1991. Universal service in post-divestiture USA. *Telecommun. Policy* 15(2): 119–128.

Gabel, D. 1995. Pricing voice telephony services: Who is subsidizing whom? *Telecommun. Policy* 19(6): 453–464.

Gilbert, P. 1987. Universal Service on Hold: A National Survey of Telephone Service Among Low Income Households. Washington, DC: U.S. Public Interest Research Group.

Gray, N., ed. 1995. *USO in a Competitive Telecommunications Environment: Proceedings of the Expert Symposium.* London: Analysys Publications.

Hausman, J., Tardiff, T., and Belinfante, A. 1993. The effects of the breakup of AT&T on telephone penetration in the United States. *Am. Econ. Rev.* 83(2): 178–184.

Hills, J. 1989. Universal service: Liberalization and privatization of telecommunications. *Telecommun. Policy* 13(2): 129–144.

Horrigan, J. B., and Rhodes, L. 1995. The Evolution of Universal Service in Texas. Austin, TX: LBJ School of Public Affairs (September).

Hudson, H. 1994. Universal service in the information age. *Telecommun. Policy* 18(8): 658–667.

Larson, A. C., Makarewicz, T. J., and Monson, C. S. 1989. The effect of subscriber line charges on residential telephone bills. *Telecommun. Policy* 13(4): 337–354.

Milne, C. 1990. Universal telephone service in the UK: An agenda for policy research and action. *Telecommun. Policy* 14(5): 365–371.

Mueller, M. 1993. Universal service in telephone history: A reconstruction. *Telecommun. Policy* 17(5): 352–369.

Mueller, M. 1996. *Universal service: Interconnection, competition, and monopoly in the making of the American telephone system.* Washington, DC: MIT Press/AEI Series on Telecommunications Deregulation.

Noam, E. 1994. Beyond liberalization III—Reforming universal service. *Telecommun. Policy* 18(9): 687–698.

Organization for the Protection and Advancement of Small Telephone Companies. 1994. Keeping Rural America Connected: Costs and Rates in the Competitive Era. Washington, DC: OPASTCO.

Perl, L. J. 1983. Residential Demand for Telephone Service, 1983. Washington, DC: National Economic Research Associates, Inc., for the Central Services Organization of the Bell Operating Companies.

PNR Associates. 1994. Spending and Saving on Communications Services by Minorities. Philadelphia: PNR Associates (April).

6

Universal Access to Online Services: An Examination of the Issue

Benjamin M. Compaine and Mitchell J. Weinraub

Introduction

This paper sets out to find whether there is any historical justification for expanding the traditional notion of universal telephone service to newer information services. And if so, to what? Universal service, as defined by Noam, seems straight-forward enough: "A public policy to spread telecommunications to most members of society, and to make available, directly or indirectly, the funds necessary."[1]

In the United States, universal telecommunications, if this means dial tone, has been largely achieved, with about 94% of households having telephone service.[2] This has been achieved in part through a history of cross subsidies that was possible under the regulated monopoly scheme that governed the telephone industry through most of the 20th century. Indeed, Mueller recognizes this when he writes:

A conception of universal service that centers on the wire into the home, however, is no longer meaningful.... The infrastructures of telecommunication are proliferating in number and expanding in capacity at an unprecedented rate. Furthermore, a growing body of research suggests that the rental price of the access line is not the decisive factor affecting the affordability of service. The notion that universal service hinges on regulatory subsidies to facility construction or to access line rentals seems oddly out of touch with contemporary conditions.

The most important universal service issue now and for the foreseeable future concerns how people will access and use the infrastructures that surround them.[3]

The Telecommunications Act of 1996 has apparently expanded the concept of universal service beyond that of basic dial tone. It has also codified a new regulatory regime that upsets the model of cross subsidies. Not only must the Federal Communications Commission, the state regulatory agencies and the industry players settle on a new model for a "universal service fund," as stipulated in the Act, but the notion of what is to be covered by this fund is open to question.

One of the principles which the Telecommunications Act ordered the states and federal government to consider in continuing the thrust of universal services is:

"(2) Access to advanced services: Access to advanced telecommunications and information services should be provided in all regions of the Nation."[4]

However, it remains unclear what advanced telecommunications and information services mean and which ones, if any, should be encompassed under the universal service rubric. Further, it is not clear in the Act what universal service means. It could mean nondiscriminatory "access," but no right to be connected. It could mean the right to be connected, but not the right to access "content" without payment by the user.

Nor is the mechanism for such service delineated. Are the federal or state governments expected to pick up the tab for those deemed unable to afford access or content? If there are to be subsidies, who will pay them and via what mechanism?[5]

The notion of universal service in the USA for telephone dialtone dates back at least to 1907, when AT&T first articulated its theme for the Bell System: "One System, One Policy, Universal Service." The concept of universal service was later incorporated into the Communications Act of 1934 and became essentially the quid pro quo for creating AT&T as a heavily regulated monopoly. Still, it was not until 1946 that half the households in the United States did indeed have telephone service.[6]

This paper addresses one piece of this issue: universal access to online services, including the Internet. It assumes that the reference in the 1996 Act to advanced telecommunications and information services could be interpreted to include consumer online information services, ranging from proprietary services to that which is publicly available via the World Wide Web.

With access to the Internet presumably comes access to electronic mail. Article 1, Section 8 of the U.S. Constitution specifically gives Congress the authority to establish and fund a postal system. This was the first network to reach everywhere. It was considered an essential piece of the experiment in democracy.

Yet the First Amendment also prohibits Congress from infringing in the content business (limited to literally "the press" at the time). Is access to the Internet, to a telecommunications-based mail service analogous to the post or the press? Indeed, the question may be as simply as if we address the issue of continued universal access to dialtone do we need to look further? Is access to content, in effect, a non-issue?

While cross-subsidies have made it possible for telephone companies to price dialtone in high cost-of-service rural areas close to the price of service in lower cost urban areas, telephone service providers have never had to give away their service. Nor has a government agency directly paid for telephone services for low-income households.

Similarly, while initially giving away broadcast spectrum helped keep down the cost of radio and television broadcasters, we have never incorporated into social policy subsidizing the purchase of television sets (though they cost about U.S.$3500 in 1950 converted to current dollars), VCRs, or cable connections (and despite the lack of subsidies, today more U.S. households have a television set than have telephone service).[7]

The print media have received only the most indirect—and today close to zero—subsidies in the form of postal rate discounts when they mailed their products. A general consensus that access to newspapers, magazines and books is critical for an informed populace for political decisions, decision-making, and general culture has been accommodated not by providing everyone with a subscription to *Time, Newsweek* and their local newspaper, but by promoting their availability through tax-supported libraries and schools.

So the contentious issues of today are: *to what* should we be providing access , *why, how,* and *for whom*? Ultimately the central issue of universal access is access to what: to communication or to information content?

Communications or Information?

Communications is not the same as information, although we often include "telecommunications" under the popular rubric of the "information revolution." In brief, communications is a process. Information is substance. Graphically this is illustrated by the Harvard Information Business Map that was developed in the late 1970s. In figure 6.1, the left side of the map encompasses communications services. These include mail service, in the top left hand corner, and telecommunications, at the top also on the left hand side. The horizontal axis on the map is a continuum from format on the left, to substance on the right. Telecommunications, like mail service, is primarily concerned with form. The substance—or information—is provided by what users put in envelops, say into speakers, or otherwise create and transmit using these formats. These cover the products and services on the right side of the map and include the traditional mass media.

This distinction, between the communications process and the information that is delivered may be critical to formulating policy under the "advanced telecommunications and information" wording of the U.S. act or similar wording elsewhere.

The History of Universal Service and Access

Although not measurable or concrete, the highest measure of value of any technology is whether or not society as a whole feels that every citizen will require access. Throughout history only a few technologies have been granted this highest level of concern. The questions have already been asked. Will access to advanced telecommunications and information services be required for participation in tomorrow's society, or will it just be another medium like radio and television? For those with access to the online services and the Internet, it seems that a wealth of communication, information, and interactive resources await. But what about those without access? Will the world end up, as T. R. Ide warned, with two classes, the information rich and the information poor?[8] The subject of universal access is one which must be examined as telecommunications technology spreads.

Computers and online services are not the first technologies to raise the question of universal service. Although rarely discussed in relation to older technologies such as publishing and printing (with the possible exception of literacy, if that is to be counted as a technology), universal service became an issue in older electronic communication technologies

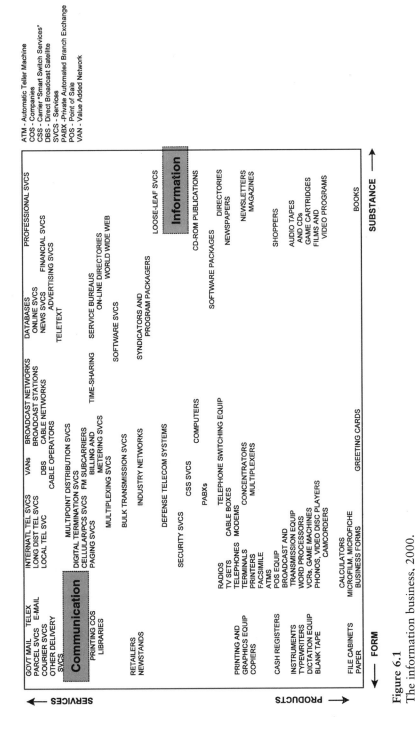

Figure 6.1
The information business, 2000.
Sources: Program on Information Resources Policy, Harvard University, 1986. Updated by Ben Compaine, 2000.

as well. This concern has been raised regarding both the telephone and teletext/videotext systems.

Universal Telephone Access

Questions concerning access to the telephone network are almost as old as the technology itself. As early as 1878, Alexander Graham Bell contemplated getting the telephone into every home. He wrote "it is conceivable that cables of telephone wires would be laid underground or suspended overhead, communicating by branch wires with private dwellings, counting houses, shops, manufacturers, etc, uniting them through the main cable with the central office."[9] When discussing automatic exchanges, he accurately foresaw that they will "so reduce the expense that the poorest man cannot afford to be without his telephone."[10] The concept of universal service was picked up by American Telephone & Telegraph from the beginning. The AT&T annual report of 1909 first included the statement: "The Bell system was founded on broad lines of 'One System, One Policy, Universal Service.'"[11]

"What is universal service?" It depends who is asked. The Organization for Economic Co-Operation and Development's (OECD) standard incorporates three subsidiary concepts to be taken into account when discussing universal service. These are:

· Universal geographic availability.
· Non-discriminatory access.
· Reasonable costs or affordability.

However, the OECD report "Universal Service and Rate Restructuring in Telecommunications" explains that "most of the debate on universal service has concentrated on the provision of a simple connection to the analog telephone network and has measured the universality of that provision in terms of penetration rates either in lines per hundred inhabitants or in percentage of households with a telephone."[12]

Why Is Universal Service for Telecommunications so Important?

Increasingly since the 1970s, there has been a persistent call for universal access to telephone service around the world.

Some commentators and scholars have couched the need in social and political terms. Pool was one of the first to report on the importance of access to the telephone. In *Social Effects of the Telephone*, Pool described how the telephone has expanded human freedom.[13]

However, most of the rationale for access to phone systems has been based on the economic advantages. Cherry described the telephone as "a wealth creating tool, by virtue of its great assistance to people's organizing powers."[14] Others have tried to quantify the economic effects. Among the most important reports describing the economic advantages gained by access to telephone systems are the International Telecommunications Union's (ITU) Maitland Commission reports, the World Bank's *Telecommunications and Economic Development*,[15] and Hardy's *The Role of the Telephone in Economic Development*.[16] The World Bank report showed that the telephone itself was by far the most important aspect for telecommunication of developing countries (accounting for 90% of telecommunication investment, traffic, and revenues). The Hardy report, a correlation study, reinforced that the telephone was an extremely important factor in economic development (stronger, in fact, than broadcast media).

Measuring the Value of Communication

If the concept of what should be included under the universal service label is to be expanded beyond POTS (Plain Old Telephone Service), then there needs to be an empirical justification beyond some intuitive assertion. Providing content is expensive. It is generally labor intensive and often requires creativity. It involves some combination of reporters, writers, editors, graphic designers and artists, producers, directors, photographers and other talents that are not likely to change regardless of the means of distribution.

Although electronic distribution saves costs compared to physical production and distribution, these costs may account for a fourth to a third of the consumer price of current media products.

If any policy is going to seriously consider providing any sort of universal access to information content, then a value must be ascribed to it. There are several approaches to try to assess a value to online communications services deriving from communications research and economic literature.

The Uses and Gratifications Model

One theoretical method for looking at the value of a communication medium is derived from the uses and gratifications approach to media consumption. According to Urban, this approach "studies not only the patterns of behavior, but also the value of the media behavior to the individual."[17] Urban says that media gratifications fall into three basic categories:

• Media are sought after to provide information or education.
• Media are used for escape from daily reality.
• Media fulfill people's need to 'belong' and 'connect' to the social group.

Media are Sought After to Provide Information or Education

Although it is too early to identify any studies applying uses and gratifications theories to consumer online media, the three categories suggest that the value (for the consumer) of these new media will be high. Online services and the Internet are already known to be popular sources of information for the millions of users of the Internet. More sources seem to be announced every day. Access to entire university libraries catalogues are already available. Access to some of the content is just starting, making an online computer the source of information and education available to virtually anyone with this minimal equipment. Indeed, most of the research for this paper was conducted via the Internet and an online computer. There were more than 1500 newspapers in North America with sites on the World Wide Web by mid-1996,[18] hundreds of magazine sponsored sites (some versions of the print product, others solely for the Web), countless academics posting their research papers, students' papers and reading lists, and tens of thousands (or more) sites by individuals with content ranging from the useful to the ephemeral. Government agencies, such as the Federal Communications Commission, were making their decisions and data available on the Web. All forms of organizations were creating sites with useful information about their products or services, giving even greater truth to the old Yellow Pages slogan, "Let Your Fingers Do the Walking."

Media are Used for Escape from Daily Reality

Urban's second category also suggests a bright and valuable future for online computer systems. With the advancements in games, audio and video, as well as features like MUDs (Multi-User Dungeons), computer users may soon be able to escape from reality as never before. Instead of just watching a film or reading a linear story, computer users are able to interact with and travel throughout other worlds. They will not only have the capability to escape from their own world but become part of another. This escapism should become a much more valuable gratification than any other current medium can provide. To those that believe current theatrical films and television provide us with more than enough escapism, this scenario might sound like good reason *not* to consider encouraging high speed online service. But it is and *will continue to be* part and parcel of the information accessing features of the Internet.

Media Fulfill People's Need to "Belong" and "Connect" to the Social Group

Although a cadre of social commentators worried that computers would have an isolating effect, that all changed with widespread use of the Usenet section of the Internet and online service discussion groups. These online forums allow the user to participate in both real time and asychronous discussions (or just watch and listen to the discussions) held by social groups which would have been very difficult to find before the online systems developed. Here users can find social groups more to their tastes than would ever have been possible if restricted to physical boundaries. From groups whose concern is alternate lifestyles, to those who only want new information on a certain type of technology, to those that focus on surviving a particular disease, these social groups provide a greater opportunity for a user to feel part of a group or "connected" than ever before. This connection feature of the online experience may, as it turns out, be the single most compelling argument for expanding the POTS rationale for universal service in some form.

Overall, if the uses and gratifications model is to be used to value this new medium, the value of online media is probably greater than any other traditional medium available to consumers today.

Economic Models

Ultimately, the value consumers place on any product or service is what they actually pay for it. Various economic models have been applied determining the value of a communication technology. Wenders spells out mathematically the value that customers place on an existing service, telecommunications. He defines the demand for telephone access as how much the subscriber would pay for the right to be connected to the network and make calls at whatever price is charged for usage.[19] From this he describes what he calls the customer surplus, or the excess of what one would be willing to pay for a certain number of units of production over what one does pay. This, however, doesn't fully explain the value of the service to the customer. He says that customers may be willing to pay more per month depending on two other factors. These factors are the value they place on *incoming* calls, and the value they place on the *option* to make and receive calls.[20]

Similarly, many feel that the value a customer places on a product or service in a free market society can be understood by the price he or she is willing to pay. Although access to computer networks has not reached what many would consider "critical mass," the value of these systems could be determined by what current users are paying. Here, we must look at the major online services and the Internet separately, as the prices and price structures are currently quite different.

All of the major online services (America Online, Prodigy, Microsoft Network, and CompuServe) initially charged their customers for the time they spend connected to the network. This pricing structure is based on the fact that all of the subscribers to these services use modems and dial phone lines to gain access. Until 1996, the popular rate was US$9.95 per month for the first 5 hours of connect time and $2.95 for each additional hour. At that time approximately 12 million Americans subscribed to these online services,[21] placing a value on access to the services of at least $120 annually.

The pricing structure for direct access to the Internet is somewhat different. Many users, those who use the Internet via universities, the government, or large corporations, pay no direct fee for their access (in the case of universities the cost can be said to be figured in to the cost of tuition or activities fees). Users with individual direct access to the Internet usually pay a monthly charge for which they are given unlimited time and access to the Web, email, Usegroups and chat. In 1996 this fee was generally about US$20 monthly.

Economic theory suggests that prices should be matched to costs. According to MacKie-Mason and Varian, there are three main areas of network costs: the cost of connecting, the cost of providing additional network capacity, and the social cost of congestion.[22] The cost of connecting is relatively easy to figure out; it's the cost of the modems, the lines, the router, and some labor effort. However, they add that charging for incremental capacity is quite difficult because it requires usage information (something not easy to acquire). They suggest that although it seems simple to just charge more for access during pre-determined peak hours, it's not really that straight-forward when computers are involved. First it is rather easy for computers to be set up to do some of their work at what would be considered off-peak hours (leading to a shifting peaks problem) as well as the fact that the Internet is global and multiple time zones would come into play. The authors do not detail a method for pricing the social cost of congestion, but suggest that it may be necessary to do so in order to prevent massive Internet congestion.

Yet another means of determining the value of a particular technology is by the choices that consumers make to allocate their resources to one technology rather than another. Mueller and Schement took the opportunity to compare access to telephone, cable television and computers among the residents of Camden, New Jersey. Camden is a relatively low socio-economic area with a large percentage of the population falling either at or below the poverty line. The importance of this fact is that some Camden residents are often forced to choose between technologies instead of having access to any technology they wish.

The study focused on telephone service, especially those residents without telephones in their homes. Of the Camden residents who did not have telephone service in their home, 50% said that they did however have cable television service. In fact, half the respondents expressed a feeling that cable television was more important to the quality of their lives than telephone service. At the time of the survey, none of the residents without telephone service had computers in their homes and the computer penetration rate in Camden was estimated at only 7%.[23] This study suggests that individuals have differing opinions on which technologies are more important to their quality of life and thus (at least on an individual basis) which technology has greater value.

Lessons Learned from Previous Consumer Data Services

Two advanced electronic technologies that have been capable of providing universal access to information are teletext and videotext. The term teletext is generally used to refer to the transmission of 'pages' of linked textual and graphic data using the excess capacity of broadcast television signals. These pages are generally compiled into "magazines" of information on a particular subject. The information is then accessed using a special decoder, or a decoder built into a television, in a progressive linear (within each magazine) fashion. Videotext, on the other hand, generally refers to a 1970s technology that used special terminals to allow interactive transactions such as email, shopping, banking, and information retrieval, usually using the television set as the terminal. In the age of the online computer, the most interesting aspect of both of these (now) 'low tech' systems is that they offered many of the same services that are now becoming available via new online computer systems.

Teletext

Teletext was attempted a number of times in the United States, never with very much success. Both CBS and NBC made major pushes to supply teletext data, and of course advertising, via the broadcast networks. "In 1986, the somewhat heralded efforts at teletext by CBS and NBC in the United States came to a crashing stop; transmissions seen by few except affiliate station engineers and convention attendees were laid to rest, without being accessible to the general public."[24] Other attempts at teletext were made by companies such as Electra, whose service was distributed by the Primestar direct broadcast satellite service. With this system, customers receiving the Primestar signals via a Scientific Atlanta satellite receiver could access dozens of pages of general, sports, and financial news as well as instruction on using the Primestar system by tuning to a particular channel. Although this service was delivered to 70,000 customers across the United States, it was never widely used and was discontinued in favor of a newer transmission system that could provide more channels of video programming in early 1994.

In other countries, teletext systems have been more successful. At the same time that the major U.S. networks were ending their teletext trials, the BBC teletext system, Ceefax, was celebrating its 10th anniversary. The British system was given government approval in 1976 and began carrying advertising in 1991. Thus, Britons now have access to four separate teletext services (on the four British broadcast television channels) with about 200 pages of information each. These pages regularly carry news, weather, sports, entertainment, and travel information. Londoners can even check on the arrival times of flights to Heathrow and Gatwick airports. Studies show that 59% of Britons with access to teletext use it for 1–10 minutes every day.[25] In 1995, 50% of British households had teletext sets.[26] In spite of the amount of information available and its reported use, little discussion can be found regarding appeals for universal access to Ceefax data.

Videotext

Videotext is another technology that failed as a consumer business everywhere it was offered. Three major U.S. organizations made attempts at videotext in the 1980s. "Keyfax," a partnership of Centel, Honeywell, and Field Enterprises, "Gateway," a Times Mirror Venture, and Knight-Ridder's "Viewtron" were all discontinued within a few years of their creation.[27] These systems provided two main services to users: transaction-based services and news. The transaction-based services were often shopping and banking. The news and information component was often very similar to the information already available via other media in the area. To the extent they offered email, it was only available to others who subscribed to the system.

Although there are many theories behind the failure of videotext in the United States, most believe it was a "chicken and egg" problem; too few users to support innovative services and no innovative services to attract users.[28] To that must be added that the technologies involved were not yet ready for prime time: slow modems, expensive proprietary hardware, and reliance on the modest display capabilities of the television set.

In Britain, videotext struggled for years as a consumer service and finally found modest success with some business applications. The British system, called Prestel, was created by British Telecom and was opened in 1979. By 1983, Prestel was the largest videotext service in the world (a dubious distinction, given the lack of competition) and in 1986 served 74,000 customers, far short of the millions that had been predicted.[29] Although it was begun as a common carrier system, Prestel was more successful with vertically integrated services and at its height the system had 1200 information providers supplying more than 270,000 pages of information. Throughout the 1980s the service was modified and eventually became a business service providing stock quotes, foreign exchange rates and travel reservations.

Attempts to start videotext services in the United States and Canada floundered for lack of consumer interest. Newspaper publishers Knight-Ridder and Times Mirror had the highest profile, and the most costly failures.

The only faintly successful application of a videotext-like service is supplied by France's Minitel. In 1978 the French government published the *Report L'Informatisation de la Societe*, which coined the term telematics and called for France to lead the computer revolution by providing a computer network for its people.[30] One outcome was Minitel. Begun shortly after the report was published, the French government, through DGT, the French state owned phone monopoly, began giving away Minitel terminals to telephone customers who wanted one. The DGT initially justified the expense by proposing to use an online telephone directory to replace the printed version. It further saw this as a way to expand its business and services using its newly upgraded infrastructure. After 4 years there were 2 million Minitel terminals in use with over 3000 different services available including home banking, shopping, weather reports, airline and hotel reservations and real-estate listings.[31] There are now over 6 million Minitel terminals in use around France.[32]

Although France is perhaps closest to achieving the goal of universal access with the limited capacity Minitel terminals, in may not be a model for the United States or the rest of the world. At the time, Neuman reasoned, "You need a trigger service or a trigger provider. The French example is plain not going to happen in the United States—the government is not going to pay for the terminals. If it happens by a provider, it's going to happen when the banks develop a standard and decide it's in their best interest to pay the cost of getting the terminals out there. You need some kind of transaction service."[33]

Moreover, in making a massive commitment to the technology and economics available when it started, French households are stuck with dumb terminals (not PCs), that do not have the graphics capability needed to get the most from today's online services. Usage studies also found that the most used feature was "adult" chat services.[34]

The Federal Government and Universal Service for Online

There are those who doubt the importance of the coming revolution in computers and communications, or the Global Information Infrastructure. In a speech delivered at the Superhighway Summit at the University of California, Alan Kay, the former chief technology guru for Apple Computer, said that the superhighway is not the answer. He called for the world's scientific community to stop looking for the information superhighway and begin looking at how to "transcend the psychological and social limitations of being human."[35] However, this seems to be a minority viewpoint. More commentators see the formation of the GII as a major change to the way the world society will function. If they are correct, the questions then become, who should have access and how will that access be provided?

The Arguments for Universal Access

Leading the U.S. government's charge for universal access was Vice-President Al Gore. At the G7 Information Summit in early 1995 and the International Telecommunication Union World Telecommunication Development Conference a few weeks later, Gore set out the position of the Clinton Administration. At the G7 summit, Gore said the Clinton Administration was committed to the goal of connecting every classroom, every library, every hospital and every clinic to the national and global information infrastructure.[36] At the ITU conference, Gore called for all nations of the world to cooperate in building the Global Information Infrastructure founded on the principles of universal access, the right to communicate, and diversity of expression.[37] Other politicians and government groups have seconded the vice-president's call.

In 1994, the National Telecommunications and Information Administration (NTIA) conducted a series of field hearings on universal access across the U.S. After claiming that the goal of universal access to POTS was still not achieved, its report called for an increase in the goal beyond basic analog voice grade service. In addition, the NTIA hearings called for government to play an active role in providing universal access. In a commentary featured in *Wired* magazine, U.S. Senator Bob Kerry (along with filmmaker George Lucas) described the importance of universal access to education. They wrote that "in the dawning of the information age—where access to information will be the currency of power and knowledge—the definition of access for educational institutions should be expanded to include multimedia technologies and service." They went on to say that "Connecting every public school classroom and library to the developing superhighway is a legitimate goal of public policy."[38] In the context of the language of the Telecommunication Act of 1996, the political front seems to have reached a consensus on the goal of universal access, but little in terms of specifics or plans to achieve this goal have been offered.

Speculations on the Importance of Being Connected

The critical role of educational institutions has been widely touted . Why access to advanced computer and information services are important to education has been explored from numerous angles. One approach is that of the development of a New Literacy that reflect the tools of communications and computers, in much the way that the technologies of printing and mechanization helped shape the need for the current version of literacy.

The New Literacy is the ability to use and work with the new computer and information systems (a skill that has become easier to master as the technology improves and will continue to get easier to use effectively). Over time, those literate in newer processes are likely to internalize fresh approaches to using the content provided by online sources.[39] In terms of education, "perhaps the time will come when spending extensive classroom hours on memorizing multiplication tables, spelling lists, and the fine point of grammar will be as unnecessary as it has become ineffective."[40] Meanwhile, educators and schools need to manage the transition in allocating budgets from traditional literacy expenditures (such as textbooks, serials, added library stacks) to the tools for the New Literacy (PCs, networks, and online services).

Papert takes this notion from a scenario to a prescription. He says that access to this advanced technology will allow students to explore and learn new information without the reading and library skills that have always been required. This will let students learn before their natural quest for knowledge is slowed by the need to learn these 'old' skills. He says "A child who has grown up with the freedom to explore provided by such machines will not sit quietly through the standard curriculum dished out in most schools today."[41]

Others have taken the importance of access in education forward to calls for action. Tom Grundner of the National Public Telecomputing Network has been credited with originating the "Free Net" concept. Grundner suggests that a nationwide system of public access computer systems be established. He imagined a free network (much like the free library system) where anyone who was interested could get controlled access to the Internet.[42]

Anderson et al. cite statistics that show that school experience with computers leads to wage advantages as well as success in the job market and increased economic productivity for entire societies. They summarize that "the overall impact of *computer access in schools* appears to have been beneficial to education."[43] In addition to stressing the importance of computers for children, they explain that this access must be provided by the schools. "Since much computer learning occurs outside of school and is therefore income dependent, it is argued that educational systems have a special obligation to compensate for this disparity."[44]

On a similar note, Yourdon describes the importance of computers in education as well. He says that "those children with access to computers and the wherewithal to use computers as an effective tool will reap social benefits, educational benefits, and (ultimately) remunerative benefits."[45] He differs from Anderson et al. in that he calls for parents to make sure that their children have this access.

One of the first studies to try to compare the performance of school students with online access in school to a similar group without such access found a substantial advantage for those with access. The online group showed higher skills in information management, communication, and presentation of ideas.[46]

Of course, children are not the only ones who benefit from access to computers and networks. Cherry focuses on the individual. He sees access to communication technology as a way for all citizens to arm themselves against the bureaucratic powers that be. He says that computers are "an example of a technology which can help to free the general public just a little from the grip of the professional expert."[47]

Taking an even more global view, Pool looked at society as a whole. He called computers and networks a "technology of freedom" in that it allows everyone to participate, communicate, and learn. He said that the "lines between publication and conversation would vanish in the egalitarian world of computer networks."[48]

Dordick took the significance of computers and networks as yet another vision that trumpets the potential importance of these technologies. After describing the importance networks will play in future society, he predicted what would happen in a technology driven future. He envisions that there will be growing public interest in the widening split between the information haves and have-nots, and that "the issue of information equality is likely to become one of some significant public concern, hence of political action."[49] In fact, Dordick said that this concern would peak in the mid-1990s.

One of the strongest arguments for universal access to online services was made in a study conducted by the RAND Corporation. Its mission was specifically to support universal access to email. Anderson and his colleagues give numerous arguments for universal access. Anderson argues that (among other benefits) email provides new opportunities for information, supports social integration of groups, provides wider resources, can facilitate citizen participation in the political process, is a catalyst to network use, and even supports global democratization.[50]

The report also looks at the current state of email access and the technical and financial consideration necessary to make universal access a reality. It found that there are some hurdles to overcome, and that true universal access will require public subsidies. However, Anderson *et al.* propose it is worth the price. They find that "use of electronic mail is valuable for individuals, for communities, for the practice and spread of democracy, and for the general development of a viable national information infrastructure. Consequently, the nation should support universal access to email through appropriate public and private policies."[51]

Almost as aggressive as RAND's call for universal access was that made by representatives of the European Commission at the G7 Information Society Conference. The commission's conference theme paper included the following passage: "Access to information is a basic right of every citizen ... The benefits of the information society should not be limited to business but should be available to society as a whole.... All citizens, wherever they live, can benefit from essential information at an affordable price."[52]

At the end, the commitment by the G7 countries was not quite as strong. The G7 did, however, commit to promoting universal service.

Should There Be Universal Access as a National or Global Policy?

The call for universal access is far from universal. In fact, there are many reasons favoring a go slow policy that involves economics, the rate of technological change, and political reality.

The "Go Slow" Position

Economic Concerns   The questions of who will pay, and how much, are important questions being raised by many investigating the possibility of universal access. These arguments are more than just a simple "we can't afford it." Most agree that the money could be found if necessary, but question the effect this will have on government, network providers and the users. If universal access to the GII were to follow the plan set forth by the United States phone system, the question becomes: who will pay?

If one group (presumably the poor and the rural) is going to get network service at or below cost, somebody else has to pay more than their share. Browning reminds us, "So to encourage one group's use is to discourage others—and the greater the encouragement, the greater the corresponding discouragement. History shows that the discouragements can become very large indeed."[53]

If the decision of who will pay more is decided, he says that fiddling with rates is impossible without an AT&T-like monopoly. A very large service base would be required in order to subsidize those in need.

Another economic argument put forth by Browning is that a mandated system of universal access would require a great deal of political involvement in GII network pricing and probably include a government subsidy. In this case there is the danger that the services would be subject to political control. He says, "By pushing companies to offer network services at something like the cost of providing them ... regulators can put networks on a sound financial footing, and so make them independent of the whims of politics and subsidy."[54]

Noam, however, has proposed a mechanism for maintaining universal service within a fully competitive environment that he believes is politically neutral and "friendly." He calls this the Net Transmission Account System, based loosely on a value added tax approach. Its highlight is that it can accommodate "universal" to any degree—that is, providing anywhere from a very basic level of dial tone on a universal basis to any sort of advanced service that may fall within some definition of universally-desirable service.[55]

Bad Timing   Another reason to go slow is the argument that the technology may not yet be in the best form for universal distribution. There is danger, writes Compaine, "that jumping in too fast can lock in a technology that soon would be superseded by a better one."[56] Disaster would have occurred if the government had mandated universal access to the telegraph (with Morse code required teaching in the schools), if the FCC had accepted the first color television standard, or if DC electric current had been chosen for distribution to every household, before the AC method we currently use was devised. It may take decades "before it is clear that some technologically innovative service or product has the potential to become an actual or near necessity, worthy of some government attention for regulation, subsidy, etc."[57] France's Minitel is a case study in bad timing. The rate of change that has come about since its inception was not foreseen. To upgrade now under the same terms as the original government subsidies is impossible. According to Sutherland, Minitel "faces being absorbed into Internet access, a market dominated by companies based in the United States of America."[58]

Harm to Network   Not only might a mandated rush to implementation of universal access be difficult at this time, but it would hurt the networks and those who would use them. Some feel that the network would be harmed if it were forced to cater to the least common denominator. Following the information superhighway metaphor, Meyers warns, "One problem with universal access is the implication that the network should accommodate every potential user, regardless of the level of driving skill."[59] He feels that it would require massive resources to attempt to make the networks accessible to all; a waste of funds on a project that can never be solved. "No matter how wide the road," he says, "there will always be bystanders."[60] Browning seconds this argument that any attempt at government-ordered universal service now would hurt the network. He writes that although universal access may provide equality, it would also deliver fewer choices and fewer but larger providers. "It could, in fact, derail the entire information economy."[61] Metcalfe adds that not only would universal access hurt the networks, in the long run it would hurt the users it was intended to help. He feels that burdening the information highway by providing access to all would bring the entire network down to a level where it couldn't help the so-called information have-nots.[62]

Setting Priorities   There is a point of view that suggests that there are other aspects of society that are just more important than universal access. All kinds of gaps already exist but are rarely discussed in these terms. Most of these gaps are related to economics. "The issue," says Compaine, "is not one of information or knowledge gaps, any more than it is one of a protein gap or a transportation gap."[63] We don't read op-ed articles proposing to close the steak gap or the automobile gap. Societies need to examine what is really important and then attempt to figure out how to provide it. Similarly, Browning argues that it is not universal access that is necessary for the GII to become important. He advocates open access. Although he says that the distinction is subtle, it is an important one. While universal access requires government to determine what services every citizen needs and how much they should pay, open access protects people's ability to decide for themselves.[64]

Schrange voices a similar argument. He feels that calls for universal access are misguided. First, he points out that fully half of American adults are close to functionally illiterate. He asks "what does network access mean to them?" He also points out that access to the latest media technology is nowhere near as important as access to the latest health-care technology. He too mentions that the lack of subsidy for radios, televisions, and VCRs hasn't created a communications rich and poor. He concludes that "The real problem isn't access; it's some pundits' insistence that issues of social equity and economic opportunity are better shaped by investing in technology than in people. That's a bad idea and it leads to bad policy."[65]

Not Needed   A final argument for putting off a policy of universal access for online connections is that it is simply not necessary in today's society. One way to look at this argument is to say that people just don't want it anyway. Sandfort and Frissell argue that there are already relatively inexpensive ways to get on to the Internet but very few take advantage of it. They write that many Internet functions can be accomplished with a used Commodore 64, a black and white television, and a 300 baud modem totalling $55. They argue that "the real problem is that most people don't yet know that they want to be wired."[66]

Browning argues that the idea (or what he calls the moral bargain) underlying universal service was predicated on the concept of scarcity. For this reason, monopolies were formed creating a public resource. Since most would agree that scarcity and public resources are no longer problems (telephone companies, cable companies, direct broadcast satellite, and even utility companies are all competing to provide access over private networks), then why call for universal access? Browning says that "If the resources are not scarce, then the moral duties owed the community by telecom providers are no greater than those owed by other firms."[67]

Others agree that universal access is not necessary, but for different reasons. For example, all new technologies are first picked up by a group of early adopters. These early users tend to be more well-off financially than the population at large. However, this does not necessitate a call for universal access. Most of the technologies in question eventually become cheaper and easier to use allowing mass utilization.

Moving toward Universal Access without a National Policy

In the United States there has been mostly talk regarding universal access. The Telecommunications Act of 1996 is the closest that there has been to formulating policy. Some of the subsequent rulings by the Federal Communications Commission and the States' commissions will further shape universal access policy.

Most of the action, however, has been in the private sector. Ameritech, one of the regional Bell operating companies has proposed doing for the GII exactly what the old AT&T did for analog phone service. In its "Customers First: The Advanced Universal Access Plan," Ameritech offered to bring advanced 21st century telecommunications services to its customers in the Midwest. However, in order to accomplish this goal, the RBOC proposed that the federal government lessen a number of restrictions that have been placed on the RBOC business.[68]

AT&T itself has announced its own plan to eliminate one barrier to universal access to the Internet. In 1996 AT&T offered limited free nationwide high speed (28.8 k bps) access to the Internet via dial-up local exchange numbers and to provide low-cost modems to its customers.[69] Several competitors matched AT&T's plan. Meanwhile, a group of industry leaders representing cable television, telephone, and other communication technologies gathered in California to express their support for universal service. Although no plan was announced, Spencer Kaitz of the California Cable Television Association said that "I don't know of anyplace that is so poor that we won't all be there with wires."[70]

Numerous forces have been working at creating better technology for access. The U.S. unit of Japan's Nintendo announced Internet plans. Nintendo has reportedly been talking to the leading World Wide Web server and browser provider, Netscape, about developing Internet connections for its next generation 64-bit video game machine called Ultra 64.[71] This plan, if brought to fruition, would provide cheaper access to many, presumably younger, Americans. Older Americans are not being left out of the mix, however. An affinity group called Prime Life, which offers specialized information and discounts to Americans between 40 and 65, has announced plans to provide tailored Internet access to the more mature crowd.[72] Announcements come almost daily about products or services that, driven by technology, are newer, better and cheaper than what was available six months earlier. Typical was the announcement by semiconductor producer LSI Logic Corporation of a new single chip capable of providing Internet access without a full personal computer. This technology paves the way for smaller cheaper devices which can access the Internet, or even allow televisions to provide the same access.[73]

In 1996 two start-up firms began offering free Internet email accounts. They were supported by advertising messages added to each message and to the screens viewed by the sender.[74] Users still had to have a PC, modem, and phone line for access. Still, this was similar to the free broadcast TV and radio model—the user buys the hardware, the content and network access are "free."

Conclusion

There are many ways to assess the value of any new technology or telecommunications service. This paper addressed some of them. Although many of these methods may be able to express value in economic or comparative terms, they can at best only be surrogates for the true value of the technology to members of the society. Because it conveys a public question of equality, the highest measure of societal value of any technology is when it is elevated by the political process to the status deserving of universal access. This has happened rarely in our society. The authors of the U.S. Constitution perceived a need and mandate to provide for a universal postal service. And in 1934, the political process, in the context of the trauma of the Great Depression, saw universal telephone service as the next needed ubiquity.

If members of a society are willing to make public arguments for and even commit scarce public resources to providing universal access, then the technology in question might have the highest value and be of the highest concern. This kind of commitment places access to the technology one step away from a legally guaranteed right.

Other resources have been judged important to society, yet calls for universal access have been limited. Although most would agree to the importance of transportation, there is scant evidence that commentators, policymakers, or even industrialists (except possibly Henry Ford) felt the need to establish a national agenda supporting a car for every citizen. Instead, most governments have chosen to provide a system of public transportation utilizing buses and trains, as well as tax-supported highways in order to provide this basic need to everyone. Likewise, throughout the last few decades (at least prior to the widespread use of home computers) an encyclopedia has been a necessary resource for elementary through high school students, yet interest groups have not formed to lobby government to provide a full set of encyclopedias for each student. Instead government has provided funds to school and public libraries where students can equitably access the same information. Although news about the society around them is considered by many to be vital to every voting citizen in a democratic society, here too there has never been a serious movement to subsidize a newspaper on every doorstep or a radio on every kitchen table. In this case, most societies have chosen to post the daily newspaper in a public place, either in the town center or the public library.

The question remains: What is the difference, whether concrete or in people's minds, between the encyclopedia and newspaper on the one hand, and the telephone and postal service on the other?

The answer is that the former are primarily information resources while the latter are primarily communication resources, the right side vs the left side of the Information Business Map. If there is a basic need, it is a need to be connected.

In general, Western society appears to have put a much higher value on access to communication than to information. Information seems to be a resource that is provided with somewhat more limited public access, such as through public libraries, schools and public postings of news, while communication is delivered directly to individuals. We are willing to go to great lengths to make sure that every citizen has the right to express his or her basic opinions and needs, but we are not as committed that citizens get access at home to information.

Perhaps this is due, in the United States at least, to the sensitivity to the principles of the First Amendment when it comes to information providers. But more likely it is the sense that providing access for *information* outside of the home is sufficient, while access to that most basic process, *communication*, must be provided to the last mile.

The digitization of society is creating a new resource that can serve both as a source of information and a means to communicate. Before a decision can be reached on universal access to the Information Highway, policymakers will need to address whether its value is primarily as an information resource or a basic means of communication. This should dictate the level of service, if any, that must be provided to every household or citizen. The information resource aspect is enormous, in fact almost unlimited. Writings already point to the vast store of scholarly work, news, sports, and financial market information available. Future prospects include entire university library collections and full motion, even live, video. Here, the average citizen has access to information that would be almost impossible to access elsewhere.

On the communication side, the prospects are no less spectacular. A large amount of the traffic on the Internet (outside of the World Wide Web) concerns email and chat groups. Communication is obviously an important aspect of the online future. In the industrialized nations, for the most part the needed basic communication infrastructure is already in place, if measured by the percentage of households with connectivity to the current telecommunications networks.

A view of the near future would seem to show that personal communication without the Internet will continue as we know it. We will continue being served by the traditional mail service and we will still meet in person in order to discuss the most vital issues. With that in mind, online communication will likely continue to be a faster means to accomplish what can already be done with other methods. If this holds true, the value of online, at least for the near future, is more salient as an information resource than as communication resource. As discussed above, precedent suggests that information content is valued by society a notch below communication and is usually not considered worthy of the extraordinary costs for universal service.

If in the more distant future, the Information Highway does indeed become the dominant means of communication among citizens of the world and is proven as important as the RAND study on email suggests, then it will be judged to be of the highest value to society and may necessitate a more encompassing government policy for universal access. Of course, if this scenario plays out, it may be no more needed for governments to mandate universal access for communication than it was for broadcasting; the high value and decreasing cost virtually took care of universal service on its own.

For the time being it would seem that forbearance by government bodies is an equitable and economic course of action.

Notes

1. Noam, E M. "Beyond liberalization III: Reforming universal service," *Telecommunications Policy* 1994 18(9): 687.

2. *Statistical Abstract of the United States, 1996*, US Bureau of the Census, Table 897.

3. Mueller, M. "Telecommunications access in the age of electronic commerce: toward a third-generation universal service policy" 24th Annual Telecommunications Policy Research Conference, Solomons, Maryland, USA, 6 October, 1996. At http://www.scils.rutgers.edu/people/faculty/CARD–ACC.HTM.

4. 47 US Code Sec 254 (b)(2).

5. Both Noam and Mueller, among others, indeed make proposals that respond to these questions.

6. US Bureau of the Census, *Historical Statistics of the United States, Colonial Times to 1970*, Part 2 Series R 1–12 783.

7. *The Kagan Media Index*, 31 August, 1996 (114): 8.

8. Ide, T R. "The information revolution" in B M Compaine (ed.), *Issues in New Information Technology*, Ablex, Norwood, NJ (1988), p. 179.

9. Pool, I D. *Forecasting the Telephone: A Retrospective Technology Assessment*, Ablex Norwood, NJ (1983), p. 21.

10. Pool, *Ibid.*

11. Organization for Economic Co-Operation and Development *Universal Service and Rate Restructuring in Telecommunications* OECD, Paris (1991), p. 27.

12. *Ibid.*

13. *Op cit* Ref 9.

14. Cherry, C (compiled by W Edmondson). *The Age of Access: Information Technology and Social Revolution*, Croom Helm, London (1985), p. 64.

15. Saunders, R J, Wafford, J J and Wellenius, B. *Telecommunications and Economic Development*, World Bank, Washington (1983). The international monetary organizations such as the World Bank and IMF have recognized the importance of telecommunications infrastructure, but at the same time are pressing for privatization and cost-based pricing. In the short-term, at least, these measures may run counter to increasing widespread telephone access.

16. Hardy, A P. "The role of the telephone in economic development," *Telecommunications Policy* 1980 4(4).

17. Urban, C. "Factors influencing media consumption: a survey of the literature," in B M Compaine (ed.) *Understanding New Media*, Ballinger Publishing, Cambridge, Mass (1984), p. 239.

18. Outing, S. "A little something for everyone," 12–13 August, 1996. At http://www.mediainfocom/ephome/news/newshtm/stop/stophtm.

19. Wenders, J T. *The Economics of Telecommunications: Theory and Policy,* Ballinger Publishing, Cambridge, Mass. (1987), pp. 47–48.

20. *Ibid*, p. 48.

21. The actual number is hard to pin down. The largest, America Online, claimed 6 million in September 1996. CompuServe may have had 3 million, Prodigy 1 million. The number of users of the World Wide Web, though the subject of surveys by AC Neilsen and others, may be 10 to 20 million world wide, depending on how the question is asked. What is not disputed is that based on subscriptions to Interest Service Providers, domain registrations, servers connected and "hits" on server pages, the use of electronic information services was growing dramatically in 1996.

22. MacKie-Mason, J and Varian, H. *Economic FAQs about the Internet, 1995.* At World Wide Web FTP://gophereconlsaumichedu/FAQs/FAQsAllhtml.

23. Mueller, M and Schement, J R. *A Profile of Telecommunication Access in Camden, NJ*, Rutgers University Project on Information Policy, New Brunswick, NJ. See chapter 5 of this volume.

24. Greenberg, B S. "Teletext in the United Kingdom: patterns, attitudes, and behaviors of users" J L Salvaggio and J Bryant (eds) *Media Use in the Information Age: Emerging Patterns of Adoption and Consumer Use,* Lawrence Erlbaum Associates, Hillsdale, NJ (1989), p. 87.

25. *Ibid*, p. 95.

26. Central Office of Information. *Britain 1995: An Official Handbook*, HMSO, London (1995) p. 468. All new television sets in Great Britain must include the

chipset that decodes the teletext signal. It reportedly adds about $350 to the cost of manufacturing the set.

27. Krasnow, E and Stern, J A. "The new regulatory identity crisis," in B Compaine (ed.) *Issues in New Information Technology,* Ablex Publishing, Norwood, NJ (1988), p. 111.

28. Ettema, J S. "Interactive electronic text in the United States: can Videotext ever go home again?" in J L Salvaggio and J Bryant (ed.) *Media Use in the Information Age: Emerging Patterns of Adoption and Consumer Use,* Lawrence Erlbaum Associates, Hillsdale, NJ (1989), p. 111.

29. Hooper, R. "Prestel, Escher, Bach: Changes within changes—lessons of a Videotex pioneer," B M Compaine (ed.) *Issues in New Information Technology* Ablex, Norwood, NJ (1988), p. 16.

30. Nora, S and Minc, A. *The Computerization of Society: A Report to the President of France,* The MIT Press, Cambridge, Mass (1978), pp. 3–7.

31. Brand, S. *The Media Lab: Inventing the Future at MIT,* Viking, New York (1983), p. 25.

32. Sutherland, E. "Developing French videotex," *Minitel—the Resistible Rise of French Videotex,* at http://stargate.acs.lamp.ac.uk/~ewan/minitel/developing.html (1995).

33. *Op cit* Ref 31, p. 26.

34. Ghesquirere G. *French Minitel: Strategic Lessons for Videotext in the US Market* Communications, Trends/Samara Associates, Larchmont, NY (1989).

35. Kay, A. "The Infobahn is not the answer," *Wired* 1995 **2**(05). At http://www.hotwired.com/wired/2.05/departments/idees.fortes/infobahn.not.html.

36. Gore, A. "The GII: conditions for success," *Intermedia* 1995 **23**(2): 48.

37. Tarjanne, P. "The GII: moving towards implementation," *Telecommunications* 1995 **29**(5) ABI/Inform Abstracts.

38. Lucas, G and Kerrey, B. "Access to education," *Wired* 1994 **2**(09). At http://www.hotwired.com/wired/2.09/departments/idees.fortes/access.ed.html.

39. Compaine, B M. "Information technology and cultural change: toward a new literacy?" in Benjamin M Compaine (ed.) *Issues in New Information Technology,* Ablex Norwood (1988), p. 155.

40. *Ibid,* p. 172.

41. Papert, S. "Obsolete skill set: the 3 Rs," *Wired,* 1993 **1**(2). At http://www.hotwired.com/wired/1.2/departments/idees.fortes/papert.html.

42. Cisler, S. "Access issues for the national research and education network" in C Huff and T Finholt (eds) *Social Issues in Computing: Putting Computing in Its Place,* McGraw-Hill, New York (1984) p. 391.

43. Anderson, R E. "Equity in computing" in C Huff and Thomas Finholt (ed.) *Social Issues in Computing: Putting Computing in Its Place,* McGraw-Hill, New York (1984), p. 353.

44. *Ibid*, p. 352.

45. Yourdon, E. *Nations at Risk: The Impact of the Computer Revolution,* Yourdon Press, New York (1986), p. 133.

46. "The role of online communications in schools: a national study" Center for Applied Special Technology, Peabody, Mass., USA 01960 (1966). At http://www.cast.org/downloads/OnlineRep.RTF.

47. *Op cit* Ref 14, p. 68.

48. Pool, I D. *Technologies of Freedom* Harvard University Press, Cambridge (1983), p. 231.

49. Dordick, H S. *The Emerging Network Marketplace* Ablex, Norwood (1981), p. 238.

50. Anderson, R et al. *Universal Access to E-mail: Feasibility and Societal Implications* RAND Corporation, Santa Monica, Calif. (1995). See chapter 11, p. 252.

51. *Ibid.*

52. Berendt, A. "Universal service: what is it, and how?" *Intermedia* 1995 **23**(2): 42. There is a certain paradox in the EC's position, as its members have long maintained the tight controls over the state-owned telephone and postal monopolies, charging rates for access and service far higher than in the United States. Broadcasting has also been controlled by the governments, offering far less choice in programming than in the US as well.

53. Browning, J. "Universal access (an idea whose time has passed)," *Wired* 1994 **2**(09). At http://www.hotwired.com/wired/2.09/features/universal.access.html.

54. *Ibid.*

55. Noam, E M. "Beyond liberalization III: reforming universal service," *Telecommunications Policy* 1995 **18**(9): 695.

56. Compaine, B M. "Information gaps: myth or reality" in Benjamin M Compaine (ed.) *Issues in New Information Technology* Ablex, Norwood, NJ (1988), p. 187.

57. *Ibid.*

58. Sutherland, E. "Minitel—the resistible rise of French videotex." At http://www.bf.rmit.edu.au/~ewan/minitel/conclusion.html.

59. Meyers, S J. "Universal access? Take the high road," *Data Communications* 1994 **23**(9) ABI/Inform Abstracts.

60. *Ibid.*

61. *Op cit* Ref 53.

62. Metcalfe, B. "Beware of mandated access for solving the problem of information have-nots," *Infoworld* 1995 **17**(20): 49, ABI/Inform Abstracts.

63. *Op cit* Ref 39, p. 189.

64. *Op cit* Ref 53.

65. Schrage, M. "Let them read books," Los Angeles Times Syndicate, Los Angeles 1994 http://wwwvirtualschooledu/moz/Academia/ShragueLetThem ReadBookshtml.

66. Sandfort, S and Frissell, D. "The big lie of universal access subsidies," *Wired*, 1995 3(05). At http://www.hotwired.com/wired/3.05/departments/access.if.html.

67. *Op cit* Ref 53.

68. Weiss, W. "The power behind a radical proposal," *Rural Telecommunications* 1994 13(1) ABI/Inform Abstracts.

69. Verity, J W. "Everyone's rushing the Net," *Business Week* 5 Jun 1995.

70. Avalos, G. "Communication executives vow to serve all economic segments," *Contra Costa Times*, 18 April 1996, via America Online.

71. "Nintendo in talks with Netscape," *Simba Media Daily*, 27 November 1995.

72. "Concentric and prime life team to offer the Net to the 40-plus set," *Simba Media Daily*, 27 November 1995.

73. "LSI logic, Netscape announcements propel tech stocks," *Simba Media Daily*, 4 December 1995.

74. See Freemark Communications at http://wwwfremarkcom and Juno at http://wwwjunocom.

7

Universal Service Policies as Wealth Redistribution

Milton L. Mueller

This article, which offers a critical reassessment of the underlying rationale for universal service policies, argues that public policies designed to promote universal telecommunications access are simply a form of wealth redistribution. By reconceptualizing universal service subsidies in this way, one can obtain a more realistic assessment of the proper scope and limits of universal service policies. Universal service policies, at best, can play a supplementary role. Economic reforms that encourage investment and promote robust competition are more fundamental to the development of a ubiquitous infrastructure than government subsidies. The redistribution of wealth via telecommunications can ameliorate inequalities, but it cannot eliminate their causes, and advocates should stop pretending that it can. Furthermore, universal service advocates must become more aware of the political and economic risks and pitfalls that are inherent in the process of wealth redistribution.

The purpose of this article is to encourage individuals, stakeholder groups, and interested organizations to scale down the rhetoric and expectations associated with universal service policy. Universal service policies refer to those regulatory and fiscal measures that governments undertake to make sure that as many people as possible are connected to the telecommunications infrastructure.

The article makes two essential arguments. First, universal service policy is about redistributing wealth. At best, redistribution consists of taking money away from those who can easily afford it, and giving it to those who would fare really badly without wealth—hopefully, without undermining the basic incentive structure of society. At worst, the money can flow in the opposite direction or create perverse and counterproductive incentives. At any rate, redistributing wealth to promote more universal access is not a substitute for the kind of economic growth that can finance the construction of a ubiquitous infrastructure. This is not a way of fostering the growth of an information society. It is not an economic development plan, nor is it a way of altering the basic opportunity structure of society. It is simply a way of making things slightly more balanced. Public discourse about universal service policy will become more focused and rational when its advocates explicitly accept this fact.

The second argument is to call attention to the fact that wealth redistribution is a political process. Universal service advocates need to become a bit more sophisticated about the constraints and limits of politically mandated wealth redistribution. Once the essential nature of universal service policy as a form of wealth redistribution is accepted, some fairly clear guidelines emerge about what universal service policies can reasonably be expected to do—and not to do—and what pitfalls to avoid.

Wealth and Telecommunications Access

The subject of wealth and its relationship to telecommunications penetration is a good beginning point from which to launch the article. The strong positive correlation between per capita wealth and the geographic and social penetration of telecommunication and information services has been evident for decades.[1] Rich societies have the highest levels of telephone penetration and poor societies have the lowest. Wealth causes penetration levels to approach universal levels, not the other way around. Although some econometric studies suggest that economic growth and telecommunications growth are related in a cycle of mutual causation,[2] that statistical relationship only exists in historical data of already-developed economies such as the United States. The data suggest that a society with an expanding economy also needs to expand its telecommunications infrastructure, and that if the infrastructure expansion does not keep pace with the growth of the economy, growth and wealth-creation will be impeded.

It is implausible, to say the least, to propose that it is possible to reverse the causal direction. Haiti or Burma cannot transform themselves into wealthy societies simply by building an extensive, universal telecommunications network. Where would the countries get the capital to build it? Even if some generous international agency simply donated the billions of dollars required (a not very realistic scenario), the mere presence of an advanced physical infrastructure would mean little. The infrastructure must be efficiently and organically related to the economic and social needs of the country. The investments put into the infrastructure must generate a payback quickly enough to generate a self-sustaining cycle of growth. The residents of the country must know how to operate, use, and maintain the services in a way that actively contributes to their competitive advantage in the domestic and global economy. Otherwise, the infrastructure is nothing but an inert mass of wires, plastic, and metal.

In short, the most broadly effective universal service policies are simply to grow household wealth and to build an open, competitive economy that is able to supply information goods and services efficiently at prices that are affordable to ever larger numbers of people. Everything else is secondary.

Redistribution

Most universal service advocates would not be content to let growing household wealth produce higher aggregate levels of technology diffusion, however. They would point out that, even in advanced economies with high levels of penetration, there are major inequalities in the distribution of information goods and services.[3] Quite apart from household income disparities, there are also major differences in the cost of extending a network to different geographic areas of a country. Left to its own devices, a market economy would probably reflect those cost disparities, to the detriment of the people living there. Nearly every advanced economy, and most developing ones, engage in some form of hidden cross subsidy or explicit wealth redistribution in order to reduce or eliminate the cost disparity between rural and urban areas.

The above discussion reveals that contemporary universal service policies are really about the proper scope of the redistribution of wealth. Such policies are designed to reduce or eliminate the cost disparities among different groups in the same society. Why belabor this point? Because all too often, universal service advocates are unwilling to acknowledge this simple fact and understand its implications. Rather, they:

• Concoct elaborate and inflated claims for universal service policies: for example, that they will magically ameliorate the differences between rich and poor or stem the economic decline of rural areas.
• Invent woefully inaccurate historical myths about the contribution of government policies to infrastructure development.
• Ignore persistently the fact that, throughout the world, most of the work of extending new communications technologies to the broad population has been done by commercial investors, not by redistributionist policies.

The above lead to the second part of the argument. By explicitly identifying universal service policy as a form of wealth redistribution, a much clearer mental framework is created for the definition and assessment of universal service policies. That framework is summarized as follows:

• First, universal service policies, as forms of wealth redistribution, can only make marginal contributions to the distribution of telecom resources;
• Second, major wealth redistribution policies must be based on political bargains that reflect the perceived self-interest of major social powers;
• Third, wealth redistribution is most effective when it is narrow and targeted, and most fair when its costs are not hidden; and
• Fourth, it makes no sense to apply universal service policies to new or emerging technologies.

Redistribution Policies Are Only Relevant at the Margin

Universal service policies can only ameliorate inequalities at the margin. Employed as a supplement to normal commercial development, they may increase penetration by a few percentage points or extend geographic distribution a bit more than it would have been otherwise. No society has ever built an entire infrastructure on the basis of redistributionist policies, however. Universal service policies can be used to supplement a market-oriented, business-driven infrastructure development strategy, but the real work of development is going to be done by commercial interests and follow commercial imperatives. This was certainly the case in the United States. The Rural Electrification Administration helped to finance telephone exchanges in remote areas, but its overall impact on rural America was small compared to the massive, unsubsidized extension of the public network that took place in the early 1900s because of the competitive struggle between independent telephone companies and the Bell system.[4] The regulatory cross subsidies that kept residential telephone rates artificially low from 1965 on also had a marginal impact on the overall rate of telephone penetration. They coincide in time with the growth of household penetration from 85% to 92%. But penetration was growing rapidly before they were instituted and continued to grow as the Federal Communications Commission (FCC) phased them out.[5]

The same is true of Internet access. Five years ago, some of the more aggressive advocates of universal service–oriented intervention were eager to include Internet access in a list of subsidized services. Since then, the commercial Internet Service Provider (ISP) industry in the United States, driven entirely by normal business incentives, has done an impressive job of delivering toll-free dial-up Internet access to almost every area in the United States. An extensive study by Shane Greenstein showed that only 12 percent of the U.S. population lives in counties with only one or no ISP.[6] It remains to be seen whether this progress will continue or whether there will be some residual pockets of the country that require some sort of subsidy. Either way, the contribution of universal service policy to the spread of the Internet will be marginal compared to the impetus given by industry.

Wealth Redistribution Is Based on Political Bargains

Even when redistribution of wealth seems to be justified, it is wise to keep in mind its limitations. One of those limitations is the important fact that wealth redistribution by the state is never a pure expression of altruism, but emerges from a political process. In order to utilize the government's power to reshuffle money, political coalitions must be formed and bargains made. Such political processes are no more exempt from self-interest than the pursuit of profit in the commercial world. Granted, political processes structure self-interested interactions in a very different way than do market transactions, but one is still dealing with self-interest. Any universal service program of a significant scale is going to bear the imprints of local telephone monopolies, long-distance companies, educational institutions, rural politicians, and all the other "usual suspect" lobbying groups. That point has been made by Harmeet Sawhney in an essay comparing the development of universalistic objectives in education to universal service in telecommunications.[7] Sawhney showed that the concept of universal public education was little more than that—a concept—until a coalition of societal groups with very different interests converged around the idea. Some of the objectives of the coalition, such as the idea of "Americanizing" immigrants and the need to keep children out of the labor market, no longer seem so noble, but they were essential to the realization of the program.

Another constraint on policy is that the political bargains that underlay redistribution can be difficult for a society to extricate itself from. The political bargains that sustain the program can survive long after the need for the program has gone away.

Wealth Redistribution Should Be Explicit, Targeted, and Competitively Neutral

Politically mandated wealth redistribution is usually a zero-sum game. Such policies do not create wealth; they simply take it away from some people and give it to others. In many instances, they destroy wealth by re-allocating it in ways that are manifestly inefficient. For that reason, it makes sense to limit the scope of such programs carefully. Subsidies should be narrow and targeted, not broad and all encompassing. The public has a right to know exactly how much money it is paying for the program.

For example, telephone "lifeline" programs, which offer lower-priced telephone access to poor households and require some form of means-testing to qualify, have had a major impact on telephone penetration in low-income households. In terms of its effects, its cost, and general considerations of social justice, the Lifeline programs compare very favorably to the pre-AT&T divestiture "universal service" cross subsidies, which used long-distance revenue to lower the price of local access on a blanket basis. The latter approach to subsidies generated massive distortions in the structure of the industry and huge economic inefficiencies. It was also a hidden subsidy, and it was almost impossible to know who, aside from the telephone companies, was a net beneficiary of it and why.

Do Not Impose Universal Service Goals on New or Emerging Media Forms

If universal service policy is understood to be a form of wealth distribution, it makes little sense to impose universal service goals on new or emerging media forms. One can equalize access only to well-established goods and services, after a mass market has developed and service levels have been standardized. No matter how egalitarian one's sentiments, there is simply no way around the fact that new technologies must originate somewhere and gradually diffuse to the rest of society.

To insist that every time a new technology appears it must instantly be subject to universal service obligations would impose insurmountable social costs upon governments and private industry. Even worse, it would hinder the process of reducing the cost and redefining the form of a technology in ways designed to penetrate larger markets. (Imagine what would have happened had the government decided to subsidize the distribution of PCs around, say, 1982?)

To return to the Greenstein study of Internet service development, perhaps in a few years it will be possible to determine that the market for Internet access has equilibrated at a point where 5 percent of the most remote rural areas simply are not being served by ISPs. Then, given the importance of Internet access to participation in society and the economy, it may make sense for government to redistribute wealth to subsidize ISP access in those areas, but it is also possible that such policies will prove to be unnecessary. Rural ISPs may spread into almost every area of the country, or the development of Low Earth Orbiting Satellite Systems may create competing broadband wireless infrastructures that provide affordable access everywhere. In that case, a universal service policy designed to extend access to rural areas is simply a waste of money or, worse than that, a way to create a class of beneficiaries who will lobby ferociously to maintain the subsidies long after they are needed.

Conclusion

The academic and policy literature on universal service in telecommunications has proliferated to such a degree that the topic seems to have lost its moorings. The redistribution of wealth has some manifest positive and negative aspects. It can help to ameliorate some glaring social inequalities and improve the living standards of those on the lower rungs of the social hierarchy. However, if it is taken too far it can destroy individual initiative and freeze economic progress in its tracks. Such subsidies in support of universal service, in and of themselves, are not objectionable, but such wealth redistribution is best confined to a minor role as a supplement to the overall workings of the market economy, and deployed in a carefully targeted manner. Whatever subsidies exist should be visible to those who have to pay for them, and the burden of subsidies should not tilt the competitive playing field in favor of one supplier or class of suppliers over another.

Notes

1. A. Jipp, Wealth of Nations and Telephone Destiny, *Telecommunications Journal* (July 1963); for a more contemporary analysis of the same issue, see International Telecommunications Union, *World Telecommunication Development Report* (Geneva, Switzerland: ITU 1998), which focuses on universal access.

2. Francis Cronin et al., *The Contribution of Telecommunications Infrastructure to Aggregate and Sectoral Efficiency* (Lexington, MA: DRI McGraw-Hill, 1991).

3. See U.S. National Telecommunications and Information Administration, *Falling through the Net II: New Data on the Digital Divide* (Washington, D.C.: Department of Commerce, 1998); see also Milton Mueller & Jorge R. Schement, Universal Service from the Bottom up: A Profile of Telecommunications Access in Camden, New Jersey. *The Information Society,* 12 (August 1996): 273.

4. See Milton Mueller, *Universal Service, Competition, Interconnection, and Monopoly in the Making of the American Telephone System* (Cambridge, MA: MIT Press, 1997): chapters 5–7.

5. Ibid. chapter 13; see also the Federal Communications Commission, Common Carrier Bureau, Industry Analysis Division, *Trends in Telephone Service*

(Washington, DC, 1998) for data on telephone penetration from 1984 to the present.

6. Shane Greenstein, Universal Service in the Digital Age: The Commercialization and Geography of U.S. Internet Access. Paper presented at the conference, "The Impact of the Internet on Communications Policy," Harvard Information Infrastructure Project. JFK School of Government, Harvard University, Cambridge, MA, December 3–4, 1997.

7. Harmeet Sawhney, Universal Service: Prosaic Motives and Great Ideals, *Journal of Broadcasting and Electronic Media*, 38 (1994): 375.

III

The Advocates: Raising the Stakes

There would be no "issues" if no one cared about outcomes and if there were no substantial differences of opinion about the subject. The salience of an issue is further determined by the stakes involved. The theological question, "How many angels can fit on the head of a pin?" is not very high on the issue scale because the stakes are not very high on the outcome, despite the fact that there may be heated debate in some quarters on the topic.

The digital divide, by contrast, does rise to the level of an issue: there are differences of opinion as to what the divide is, whether there is a true gap, what, if anything, public policy should be toward it, and what, if anything, could be done about it.

That there is a digital divide that requires some sort of policy agenda has been accepted almost without question. Perhaps it is the success of the high profile of the NTIA surveys and the simpatico of the mass media in promoting it without much scrutiny. In part it may be due to the rationality of such a phenomenon: to be told that some proportion of the population cannot afford to buy computers that until recent years still cost in the low thousands of dollars, and Internet access that costs about $20 per month does not seem to require much of a leap of faith. With information technologies moving so fast, it is not surprising that the journalists who cover these stories, yet alone the public who consumes them, are hard pressed to be aware of the historical context, as shown in part II, or the current developments: low-cost Internet appliances such as WebTV® or free marketplace Internet access options.

As chairman of the Federal Communications Commission in 2000, William Kennard was at ground zero of the digital divide policy debate. It was the FCC that was mandated to implement the universal service fund provisions of the Telecommunications Act of 1996. In chapter 8, Kennard extends the digital divide concept to encompass "unequal access to opportunities to participate in the ownership and management of these vital companies." Thus, Kennard includes minority ownership of broadcast stations—an issue that predates personal computers—as a digital divide issue, confirming (as if such was needed) the political component of the digital divide issue.

More typical of the ideological component to the issue is chapter 9, "The Digital Divide Confronts the Telecommunications Act of 1996."

Typically any advocacy group claims to speak for some vague "public interest," which happens to coincide with the interests of the group that is paying for the research or making a claim. Groups with "consumer" in the title tend to lay claim to representing consumers, which includes everyone. Clearly that cannot be, as different consumers have different interests. In this chapter, the authors claim that the Telecommunications Act of 1996 has not lived up to expectations that various interests may have stipulated as desired outcomes. One of the most widely held expectations was that the Act would help stimulate competition in the telecommunications industry, particularly in local exchange telephone service. Their data shows that for certain users, telephone rates have increased, as have monthly cable rates. The anticipated competition between cable companies and telephone companies for each other's customers had not yet emerged by 1999.

But, as advocates, they tend not to see the other side of the pancake. The base rate for interexchange calling may have shot up, but anyone who watches TV has been bombarded by advertisements for various discount plans. Some, of course, are aimed at high-volume users. But many do not require monthly minimums to earn some discount. What do we know about subscribers who have not signed up for any plan? Do they only make $2 or $3 of long-distance calls per month, so that even a 25% savings would not be worth the effort to change plans? I don't know the answer, but consumers are usually pretty good about acting in their economic self-interest when the stakes are high enough.

Cable rates have gone up as well. But the cable operators will argue in their defense—and with some merit—that at the same time they have increased by two or three times the number of channels subscribers get for the price, so the cost per channel is lower. That may not please those viewers who are happy to watch the same four channels all the time, but cable is supposed to be about diversity, and the upgraded cable systems supply that, even if folks choose not to take advantage of it. There is another conundrum facing the cable companies: if they are to fulfill the dream of the consumer advocates to offer competing services for local exchange telephony or for broadband Internet service, they must spend billions of dollars to improve their facilities. That has to be recouped. The issues are, to be sure, not as simplistic as this brief rejoinder suggests. The point is that research from advocates is, almost by definition, just a piece of a mosaic.

The Benton Foundation report of four case studies of the E-rate is a soft-sell approach to advocacy: communicating the experience of four school districts with the largess of the grants from the Universal Service Fund surcharge, which presumably helps politically legitimize the tax. But such reporting really begs the larger policy question: are we justified in earmarking billions of dollars for hardware and infrastructure improvements to our schools in absence of a validated plan for its use? It may be putting the cart before the horse. The report does address what the cities are doing in the instructional area. Chicago and Cleveland are using it to enhance professional development of teachers. Detroit admits that it really had no plan, but is hopeful that parents and community members will find a use for the $110 million they expect to draw and spend from the fund. Building "stuff" is easier than determining what the "stuff" will be used for. With many teachers still at a loss on how to bring computers and the Internet into their classroom in a meaningful way, the multi-billion commitment of funds from the E-rate may be a leap of faith: Build it and hopefully they will come (before it gets obsolete).

Chapter 11, advocating including email under the rubric of universal service, is a serious policy paper that makes a reasonable, though still debatable, proposition. It argues that, just as a universal postal service was critical in forging a nation, and a universal telephone service was deemed an appropriate national goal, electronic mail access rises to the same threshold of importance and salience. Accepting that proposition, perhaps the major lesson learned is how much of what the RAND paper proposed has been accomplished. It was written in 1994 and published in 1995, thus recognizing the broadly useful societal role email would play at a time when relatively few people had—or thought they needed—this capability. But in another sense their timing was just off. The Internet was still on the periphery of their vision: the focus of the authors was on the then still-dominant proprietary online services and corporate mail networks. Among the chief concerns of the study was making sure that various email systems would be compatible, so that email could be exchanged among systems (i.e., AOL, CompuServe, ccMail, etc.) and among global systems as well. The marketplace took care of this before the ink on the book was dry: network externalities quickly convinced all players that the value of each of their systems was enhanced by the number of others who could be contacted. Before long such standards as POP3 and SMTP became universal based on marketplace forces.

The RAND authors were concerned about the costs: they called for "creative ways to make terminals cheaper." The marketplace responded without the need for national debate and policy making. WebTV® offered terminals for as little as $100 in 2000. A company called Netpliance offered a full-fledged stand-alone video screen and keyboard with Internet and email capability for $300. Both of these required monthly subscriptions of $21.95. But for those who spent $500 for a full-fledged PC with modem could get full Web access with email at no cost other than being exposed to some banner ads at the top of their browser. Yet another enterprise was selling dedicated email terminals, also for $100, with monthly service for about $8.30. Thus, the policy recommendations of the RAND group were rendered mostly moot within five years of its publication, though it was on target about email's popularity.

The section ends with a brief news article about a federal program to address the digital divide.

8

Equality in the Information Age

William E. Kennard

Anatole France once observed, "the law, in its majestic equality, forbids all men to sleep under bridges ... the rich as well as the poor." Such a stunted idea of equality neither served those who slept under bridges in the early twentieth century nor will it serve those children and communities stranded on the roadside of the Information Highway in the next century. Just as the railroads and interstates were the backbone of commerce, job growth, and prosperity in this century, the networks of information form the backbone of the next. We are enjoying the longest peacetime expansion of our economy, and this prosperity is directly linked to the rise of the information technology sector. Indeed, it is estimated that one-quarter of our economic growth has come from this sector of our economy.

Yet the technologies, skills, and infrastructure underpinning this growth have not yet reached all Americans. There exists a "digital divide," separating the technological haves and have-nots, dividing those with on-ramps onto the Information Highway from those forced to live in its shadows. This digital divide is defined not only by inequality in access to technology but also unequal access to opportunities to participate in the ownership and management of these vital companies. As technology restructures our economy for the Information Age, we must find ways to ensure that technology is a force that unites and uplifts us as a nation, rather than a force that divides. That is why I believe that the contributions in this issue of the *Federal Communications Law Journal* are so important and timely.

I   Access to the Tools of Learning

The issues discussed on the pages of this journal principally concern the lives of those not yet old enough to read it: children—the first citizens of the new millennium. The issue of access to new technology will also determine the steps of every worker on each rung of the socioeconomic ladder. It is clear that in the next century, those who are literate in computer languages and familiar with new technologies will succeed, and those who are not, will not.

The high-skilled, well-paid jobs of tomorrow demand the ability to use computers and telecommunications. By next year, it is estimated that 60 percent of all jobs will require technical skills that most Americans do not have, and the workers in these jobs earn wages that are on average 10 to 15 percent more than those of other workers. In the New Economy, every child without access to the Internet and without technology skills inherits a lifetime of missed opportunity.

Yet a lack of basic access to these technologies persists. Recently, the National Telecommunications and Information Administration (NTIA) at the Department of Commerce issued a report, entitled "Falling through the Net II," which found that many more people own computers and have access to online services than three years ago, but there is still disparity by race and income. For instance, the number of home PCs has increased by more than 50 percent since 1994, and the number of households using email has nearly quadrupled. However, the study also found that families in households earning more than $75,000 a year were seven times more likely to own a computer than those in households earning $5,000 to $10,000. White households were twice as likely to own a computer as Black households.

Other studies show that 78 percent of the schools in affluent communities have Internet access—but only half the schools in low-income areas have access. Children from low-income households and neighborhoods do not have Internet access at home or at school, and as many as three-quarters of Black high-school and college students do not have a PC. Finally, in terms of their practical ability to get services, inner-city areas are as technologically isolated as most parts of rural America. Clearly the digital divide is both a rural and an urban problem.

To bridge this gap, Congress gave the Federal Communications Commission (FCC or Commission) an important way to ensure that all of America's children have access to the learning tools they will need in the Information Age. The Telecommunications Act of 1996 directed the Commission to implement a funding mechanism to bring advanced technology to our nation's schools and libraries, a project known as the E-rate. After one year, this initiative has invested over $1.7 billion to bring technology to over 80,000 schools and libraries across the country. According to a recent study by Forrester Research, the E-rate has had a significant impact on bridging the digital divide. This year, it is estimated that African American access to the Internet will rise 42 percent, and Hispanic access will increase by 20 percent. The gap is closing, and if we continue our commitment, I am confident that we can close it.

II Access to the Tools of Prosperity

The communications and information sectors are creating unprecedented economic growth and wealth in our country. The phenomenal growth of Internet-based businesses offers tremendous potential for entrepreneurship in an exciting growth industry where entry barriers still remain relatively low.

Information technology has not only created exciting entrepreneurial opportunities, but also important new outlets for expression. Chat rooms and online campaigns hold the promise of vastly expanding the town hall of yesteryear to include a far greater number of voices and views.

But in our excitement for new technologies, we should not forget that most Americans still rely on broadcasting as their principal source of news and information. Given the power of this medium, it is striking that less than 3 percent of broadcast stations are owned by minorities. I therefore welcome the discussion of ways to remedy the severe underrepresentation of minorities as owners of broadcast stations in our country.

There are at least three steps that should be taken to increase minority ownership in broadcasting. First, Congress should restore the tax certificate. The tax certificate was the most effective means of promoting minority ownership in broadcasting. I am looking forward to working with industry, members of Congress, and my colleagues to bring back a new and improved tax incentive program.

Second, the FCC recently adopted rules to auction broadcast licenses. The new rules allow the use of "new entrant bidding credits." To fulfill our statutory duty to ensure participation by small businesses, and businesses owned by minorities and women, the Commission adopted a bidding credit for applicants with no, or very few, media interests.

Third, there is truth to the adage that the best way to deal with a business problem is to develop a business solution. Since becoming chairman, I have called on industry leaders to create employee training and managerial development programs that will open opportunities for more women and minorities and others who have not yet been positioned to reap the benefits of the New Economy. I have also encouraged industry leaders to join together to create venture capital funds that will further stimulate the economic growth of small, minority- and woman-owned businesses. By using the full breadth and depth of our human resources and potential, we can meet private needs in a way that delivers public benefits.

In the final analysis, ensuring that all Americans have access to the Information Highway and that there is greater diversity in broadcast ownership is not a minority issue or even a majority problem, but rather a profound expression of American democratic values. Our society is not represented by a chat among a homogenous few, but rather a democratic chorus of many different voices and divergent views. Achieving broadcast diversity by every constitutionally permissible means is an aspiration that calls for precisely the kind of sober analysis and critical thinking that is regularly recorded on these pages.

9

The Digital Divide Confronts the Telecommunications Act of 1996: Economic Reality versus Public Policy

The First Triennial Review, 1999

Mark Cooper and Gene Kimmelman

I   A Review of the First Three Years of the Telecommunications Act of 1996

A   It Is Time to Take Stock

The theory behind the Telecommunications Act of 1996[1] (hereafter "Telecom Act" or "Act") was that opening markets to competition, including for the provision of local phone service to consumers, would prevent abuse of infrastructure bottlenecks and monopoly power and ensure broad-based competition. Telephone services—more broadly defined to include advanced telecommunications and information services (e.g., wireless, data transmission, and Internet services)—would expand in all markets to all users (with a universal service safety net for essential services). New entrants in the multichannel video market (i.e., cable, satellite—hereafter "TV services" market) would challenge the cable industry's monopoly, bringing consumers more video choices at lower prices.

Unfortunately, the Act and its implementation are contributing to a digital divide. In the emerging digital world, the majority of consumers face price increases for many essential telephone and TV services (hereafter referred to as telecommunications services) offered under monopolistic conditions. Only a small group of premier, intensive telecom users enjoy price breaks and competitive options. The sad, unintended consequence of the Telecom Act is the growth of a costly division between telecommunications haves and have-nots. These market developments threaten to destroy the very goal many of the Act's supporters claimed to embrace: the opportunity to harness enormous technological advancements for the social and economic benefit of all citizens.

It is now time to review market developments since passage of the Act, to determine whether the Act is beginning to achieve its goal of broad-based competition across all telecommunications markets. When the old Bell System monopoly was broken up through settlement of the federal government's antitrust case against AT&T (the Modification of Final Judgment), the parties agreed that this dynamic industry should be reviewed every three years to evaluate the need for policy adjustments. The first "triennial review" led to modification of the original Bell System break-up and ultimately passage of the Telecom Act. Why shouldn't the Telecom Act be subject to the same scrutiny? This paper presents a consumer-oriented evaluation of the first three years of the Telecommunications Act of 1996.

B   Success Is Nowhere in Sight

Today's economic reality calls into question the fundamental premises and assumptions underlying the Act. The lofty public policy goals embraced by the Act have not been accomplished:

• Instead of becoming vigorously competitive, the telecommunications and cable industries have become highly concentrated.
• Instead of significant declines in prices, we have sharp increases in cable and in-state long-distance, and stagnation in local phone and inter-state long-distance rates.
• Instead of rapid deployment of advanced technologies from increased private-sector investment, we have a growing "digital divide" between those who make intensive use of the telecommunications network and those who do not.

While competition and its fruits may some day develop to serve the mass market, it is clear that at this point in time the Act has been a total failure for most consumers. The reason for this lack of success is straightforward: the fundamental assumptions applied to the industry in the Telecom Act have proven incorrect. Neither the demand-side nor the supply-side of the telecommunications industry has performed anything like Congress anticipated or hoped for.

In simple terms, Congress treated the demand-side of the consumer market as a single, homogenous market (except for basic local phone service provided to high-cost territories and low-income consumers) in the determination of what mechanical changes were necessary to promote competition for residential services. While the supply-side of the market was required to initiate fourteen specific "market opening" measures, the Act did not require the existence of effective competition before deregulation of price or ownership limits took place. Congress assumed markets would open and competition would follow, quickly penetrating all facets of the market. In reality, neither the demand-side nor the supply-side assumptions have proven correct.

On the demand side, the consumer market is not, and has never been, homogenous. It is differentiated in similar fashion for virtually all telecommunications and TV services. For services that are not absolutely essential to function in our society, there are distinct consumer sub-markets defined primarily by income (which dominates other demographic factors, like age, level of education, cultural background, etc.) and separated by volume of usage and general orientation to the value of high-tech devices. Most important, people in identifiable market segments tend to have similar usage patterns for numerous telecommunications and TV services and devices.

On the supply side, the Telecom Act's excessive reliance on undeveloped market forces to replace price and ownership/structural regulation has resulted in industry concentration through mergers, rather than an eruption of competition. The urge to merge rather than compete has engulfed virtually all facets of telecommunications, leaving consumers paying inflated prices for the services of monopolies that are becoming more, not less entrenched.

This paper explores the two fissures that have developed in the telecommunications industry since passage of the Act:

• The economic basis of the business models that are developing in the industries will not produce the ubiquitous national information superhighway that legislators promised.

• The market concentration that has overtaken the industries will doom the development of competition and the consumer benefit of lower prices and more choice that legislators promised.

Consumers experience these fault-lines first as the failure to deliver the broadly declining prices and expanding choices that were promised by the Act, but the impact goes further. These fault-lines demand careful attention from policy makers, lest they produce an earthquake that undermines the vibrancy of a critical sector for the 21st-century economy. The transformation of our society from reliance on manufacturing to dependence on information and service sectors makes the digital divide between modest/middle-American families and premier technophiles a basis for dangerous tension and unfairness between the haves and have-nots.

C   The Public Policy Implications of the Digital Divide

Thus, the continuous debate since the passage of the 1996 Telecom Act over the need to deploy infrastructure to eliminate the digital divide has been significantly misplaced. That expression has been used to refer to the possibility that some groups of consumers would be cut off from the expanding possibilities of the information age because of a failure of private-sector firms to deploy the necessary infrastructure. This paper shows a digital divide from a vastly different perspective.

We present evidence that the market activities of the firms in the industry are creating a divide not on the basis of infrastructure, but on the basis of economics. The current infrastructure is more than adequate to generate a very high stream of revenue and meet the needs of virtually all consumers. The companies appear to be interested in competing for the business of a small segment of the market—intensive users of numerous telecommunications and TV services. The group of consumers who are attractive to companies is quite small. The drive to expand the infrastructure serves the needs of this small group and leaves the rest behind.

If policy makers allow the debate over the high-end markets to drive public decisions about infrastructure deployment, the digital divide will grow, not be reduced. The availability of more infrastructure will expand economic opportunity at the top of the market and reduce the likelihood that companies will have to work their way down the market to increase their economic rewards. Profit maximizers will simply exploit the demand for more service in the upper end of the market more intensely.

This fundamental economic observation is crucial to developing sound public policy. Massive industry consolidation under a law that fails to differentiate areas of likely competitive opportunity from areas of persistent monopoly is leading to a new era of telecommunications haves and have-nots as described below.

D Time to Adjust Public Policy

It is time for policy makers to stop pretending that competition is right around the corner. It is unrealistic and possibly duplicitous to pooh-pooh today's price hikes as nothing more than a short-term setback or to blame the failure of competition and the absence of promised price reductions on regulators standing in the way. Policies must be adjusted to reflect the reality that the core telecommunications and TV services that are consumed in modest quantities by average consumers—individually and as a package—are and will be provided under monopolistic conditions for the foreseeable future.

Protecting Consumers against the Failure of Competition   The Telecom Act must therefore be adjusted to provide consumer protections against the abuses that result from the failure to achieve mass market competition.

1. Reflecting the lack of competition to local cable companies, responsible public constraint of monopoly pricing practices must be reimposed.

2. Continued price regulation of local telephone services must be maintained for each segment of the local market that does not have effective competitive alternatives to the incumbent local phone company.

3. New pricing protections for low-volume long-distance users must be established to ensure that this segment of the market is not discriminated against with price increases that do not reflect real costs.

Taking Steps to Promote Effective Competition   In addition, the Act's legitimate pro-competitive elements should be bolstered.

4. The conditions necessary to open local telephone markets to competition must be strictly enforced. It is clear that the economic and business forces driving the industry will not deliver ubiquitous competition to the vast majority of residential consumers. The local network is clearly a bottleneck for the bulk of residential and small business customers and access to it must be insured or competition will never expand.

5. Until local competition develops throughout the consumer market, local phone monopolies must be required to allow potential competi-

tors to connect to their networks at prices that facilitate competition and reflect only efficient costs for telecommunications equipment and services.

6. Efforts to create loopholes in the competitive regime under the guise of accelerating deployment of infrastructure should be rebuffed, since it is clear that such deployment will only meet the needs of an elite few.

7. Impediments to TV service competition should be removed by making local over-the-air network programming available to satellite and other distributors, and by preventing cable companies from expanding their monopolies to include high-speed Internet access.

Taking Steps to Prevent Anticompetitive Concentration

8. Mergers among potential or likely competitors in markets that are not vibrantly competitive (e.g., the SBC/Ameritech and Bell Atlantic/GTE mergers) should be blocked.

9. Mergers that will lead to cross subsidies that drive up prices for low-volume telecom/TV users (e.g., the AT&T/TCI merger) should be constrained by conditions that protect captive ratepayers of basic services.

10. Mergers and joint ventures that reinforce or extend bottleneck control over access to information services (e.g., private gatekeeping of access to the set-top box or the digital line) should be rejected in favor of an open access paradigm.

[*Section E, Outline, is omitted.*]

II Prices

A The Premise and the Promise

In anticipation of growing competition in all telecommunications/TV service markets, Congress sunset cable regulation (except for a basic tier that includes local broadcast channels) in March 1999, and called for modification of telephone pricing to reflect real "costs" (consolidating subsidies in a universal service program to ensure affordable basic telephone services for low-income consumers, high-cost rural areas, and a new program to wire schools and libraries for Internet access). The overall deregulatory thrust of the Act made it clear that regulators should do as little regulating as possible because competition was just around the corner.

The results have been quite to the contrary. This section looks at the level of prices and documents the failure of the Act to deliver price cuts, as well as the price discrimination against the have-nots that is coming to typify the digital divide.

B   Cable Rates

Since passage of the Telecom Act in February 1996, the cumulative rise in the overall consumer price index has been about 6 percent (about 1.6 percent per year).[2] Cable rates have risen about 21 percent, almost four times faster than inflation.[3] In the few communities that have head-to-head competition between two cable companies, prices are more than 10 percent lower than where there is only one cable company.[4] If the Federal Communications Commission (FCC) had continued regulating cable rates to mirror a competitive market, the average consumer's $31 monthly bill would drop to about $28, saving consumers about $3 billion per year.[5]

The history of pricing in the cable industry leaves no doubt that an unregulated monopolist will abuse its market power (see figure 9.1). During the two periods when rates have not been constrained by regulation (1986–1992 and 1996–present), prices have increased at more than three times the rate of inflation. During the short period of effective regulation in the early 1990s and prior to deregulation in 1984, price increases just matched general inflation.

The cable price increases are made all the more troubling because of price discrimination and bundling that have typified the industry (see figure 9.2). Leveraging monopoly power at the point of sale, the industry has increased the basic-service bundles, requiring consumers to buy more and more channels of less and less value. While basic-service rates have skyrocketed, premium-service prices have been stable. Those with discretionary income are spared, while the customers of the most popular bundled programming are whacked.

C   Long-Distance Rates

Long-distance companies saved more than $1 billion in 1998 by adding new monthly fees on consumers' bills.[6] They enjoyed an additional cut in their costs in July of $700 million due to reduced access charges. This

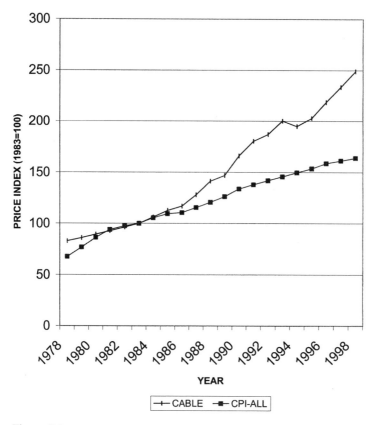

Figure 9.1
Cable prices compared to inflation.
Source: Bureau of Labor Statistics, Consumer Price Index.

comes atop access-charge reductions from prior years. In spite of these substantial reductions in costs and shifting of costs into monthly charges, the consumer price index for interstate long-distance has been flat since the passage of the Act.[7] In fact, long-distance companies have been increasing basic-service rates, which may be paid by as many as one-half of all residential ratepayers. To the extent that discounts have been offered, they have gone to high-volume users and those able to make purchases through the Internet. If the FCC does not require long-distance companies to pass along regulatory cost savings proportionately to all customers, consumers will pay more than $3 billion in monthly fees in 1999 that are not offset by per-minute rate reductions.

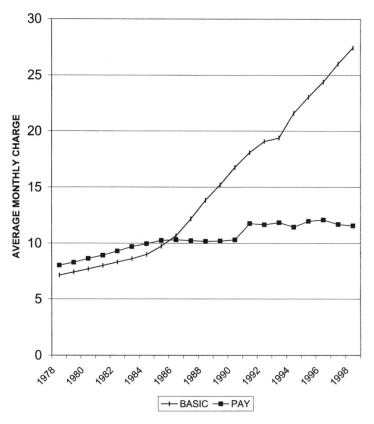

Figure 9.2
Basic versus pay cable rates.
Source: Kogan, *History of Cable TV Subscribers and Revenues.*

Figure 9.3 shows the very sharp difference in the price treatment afforded low-volume and high-volume users. Even in the residential sector, high-volume users are paying about 40 percent less than low-volume users. This price discrimination is one of the elements of the digital divide that will be discussed in the next section.

The digital divide has become deeply embedded in long-distance pricing. Rates for Internet-billed long-distance service are less than one-half the charges that basic-service customers face. By Internet-billed service we mean long-distance service that is provided over the traditional telephone network, but which is ordered over the Internet and paid for by credit card. The long-distance companies have stumbled upon a price

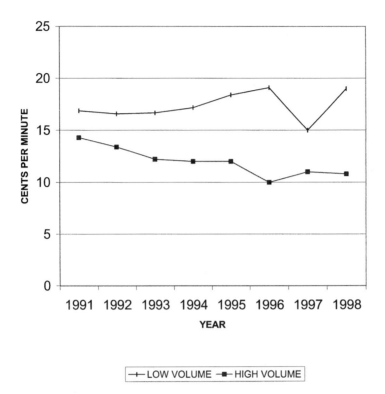

Figure 9.3
Price discrimination between low- and high-volume long-distance users.
Source: FCC, Reference Book of Rates, table 2.4.

discrimination mechanism akin to the Saturday night stay in the airline industry. Someone who uses the Internet is likely to be a high-volume consumer and, by accepting credit card billing, is low cost to serve.

Figure 9.4 shows paper-billed and Internet-billed rates for three major national long-distance companies—AT&T, MCI, and GTE. GTE is included since it is a local exchange company that has been allowed into the long-distance industry and it has a national presence. The analysis is based on national average calling patterns with the average rates calculated by the TRAC, Webpricer software. AT&T's basic rates are over twice as high as MCI's Internet-billed rates. Moreover, for both AT&T and MCI, Internet-billed rates are about 20 percent lower than paper-billed discounts. GTE's rates are substantially higher than the traditional long-distance company discounts at virtually all levels of usage. This

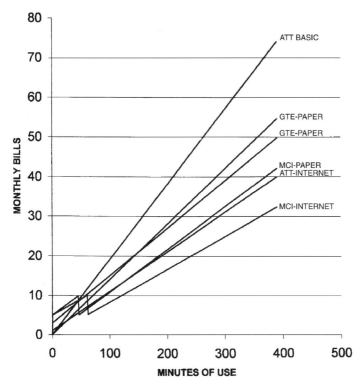

Figure 9.4
Long-distance bills with various option plans.
Notes: Plan prices are from TRAC webpricer. Usage distribution is national average: 34% weekday, 31% off-peak, 16% Saturday, 20% Sunday.

clearly shows that letting local companies into long-distance will not dramatically increase competition.

D Local Telephone Rates

Local rates have risen 3 percent since the passage of the Telecom Act[8] and remain subject to full regulation by state public service commissions. However, local phone companies keep claiming that rates should rise substantially in a more competitive environment—as much as a doubling of local rates in some instances: "In Florida, the local telephone, long-distance and cable TV industries have joined hands in a common pursuit: They've helped lawmakers draft legislation that would increase local phone bills in the state by 50 percent to 100 percent, on the theory that higher rates will make the business attractive enough to inspire competition."[9] Eleven states have raised basic rates by an average of $1.00 to $3.50. The states deciding to raise local rates exceed those that have rejected such increases by two to one. Rate rebalancing is pending in many others and is a high priority of telephone companies throughout the nation. Congress's promise to lower rates is failing badly in the realm of basic local service.

Rates for intrastate, intraLATA long-distance calls have risen about 10 percent since the passage of the Act.[10] This is an area in which local companies dominate and have significant pricing flexibility. It is also an area in which the Act closed the door on increasing competition until after the local market was opened. Freezing competition in intraLATA long-distance had the effect of reversing the trend of declining intraLATA prices, as shown in figure 9.5. Ironically, Congress gave local companies an extra incentive to resist competition by freezing intraLATA competition. The longer they keep their local markets closed, the longer they preserve their pricing power in intraLATA service.

E   Other Telecommunications Services

While prices for these basic services have been rising, prices for many of the less essential, or previously luxury telecommunications devices and services are declining (see figure 9.6). For example, competition has been driving down prices for computers (the overwhelmingly dominant customer-premise equipment necessary for Internet access), wireless phones/service, and (as noted) large-volume long-distance usage.

These new "bargains" are for higher-priced, less-used items that the majority of consumers cannot afford, have no desire to use, or are precluded from taking advantage of by price discrimination. This pricing pattern contributes to a world in which intensive telecom users are winners—the haves—and modest telecom users pay higher bills—the have-nots.

III   The Digital Divide: Consumer Usage Patterns and Business Models

A careful analysis of which groups of consumers use differing amounts of the key telecom and TV services demonstrates the substantial dividing

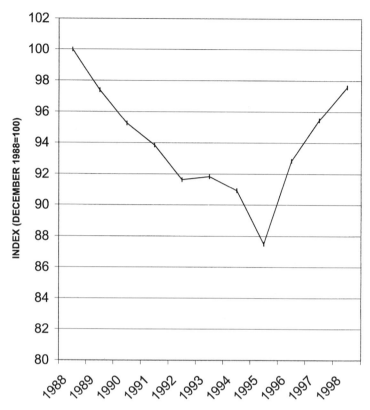

Figure 9.5
Intrastate rates.
Source: Bureau of Labor Statistics, Consumer Price Index.

line between winners and losers under the market conditions unfolding as a result of the Telecom Act.

A   Fundamental Dividing Lines
Based on data from a detailed public questionnaire in Florida, other surveys, and corresponding usage data gathered from the FCC, consumers fit into one of four groups (see table 9.1 and appendix A [*omitted here*] for a more detailed discussion of the identification of these groups).

In order to identify market segments, we used three primary discretionary telecommunications services—second line, Internet, and cellular (see table 9.1). We believe that these are driving the business models of the market participants.

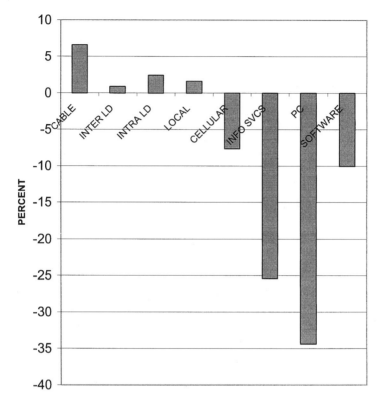

Figure 9.6
1997–1998 price changes: Various communications components.
Source: Bureau of Labor Statistics, CPI.

First, we identified the group of customers who had only one telephone line, no Internet usage, and no cellular phone. These are the items
that identify customer groups for business purposes. In order to take a
second line or have Internet access or a cellular phone, the consumer is
committing to a monthly expenditure of at least $20. The group that
does not make one of these expenditures is called the *modest* group. This
groups accounts for 45 percent of all respondents.

This first cut at the data also revealed a second group. Approximately
16 percent of respondents had a single line and no Internet, but had
taken cellular service. After reviewing the other characteristics of this
group, we called them *mobile*. This group has resources to buy an expensive discretionary service, but has only added mobile communications.

Table 9.1
Characteristics of Market Segments

	Modest	Mobile	Transi-tional	Premier	
Demographics					
% of Population	45%	16%	15%	24%	
Median Income (000)	$22.5	$41.2	$35.8	$53.8	
Segment Defining Services					
2nd Line	No	No	50%	70%	Three
Internet	No	No	62	87	of
Cellular	No	100	10	91	these
3+Enhanced Services	28%	44%	53	70	four
Usage Patterns					
Long Distance Bill	30% Below Avg.	20% Below Avg.	5% Above Avg.	60% Above Avg.	
% with TV Services	63	76	74	86	
% with Fax	5	10	28	50	

Source: See appendix A [of original paper].

In order to differentiate the top forty percent of the market, we added consideration of vertical services (e.g., call-waiting, caller-ID). We identified consumers who take three or more vertical services as making another major purchase. Three or more vertical services tend to come in packages costing around $10 per month. Thus, for the top market segment we use four discretionary purchases—second phone line, cellular, Internet, or a large package of vertical services. Respondents who had three of these four discretionary services are considered to be *premier*.[11] This group accounted for 24 percent of the respondents.

The remainder of the respondents is called *transitional*. They had one of the major discretionary services and two of the four in total. They were quite likely to have Internet. They represented 15 percent of the respondents. Thus, without fracturing the percentages too much, we can talk of a market segmented as follows:

Bottom of the market = 60% split between modest (45%); mobile (16%).

Top of the market = 40% split between transitional (15%); premier (24%).

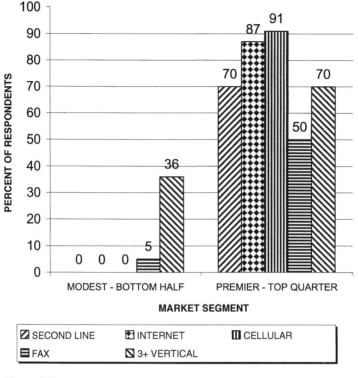

Figure 9.7
The digital divide: Services used in the past month.
Source: Florida PSC Survey.

In both consumption patterns and business strategies, the digital divide is best comprehended by the contrast between the modest segment at the bottom and the premier segment at the top.

B   Consumption of Telecommunications Services

Although we used the joint probability of consuming big-ticket items to define the market segments, the consumption patterns we observe across a broad range of telecommunications services reinforce the basic pattern (see figure 9.7).

On one side of the divide we have modest households. Almost one-half (45 percent) of households tend to be modest users of telecom and TV services. Their average monthly bill for all telecom and TV services is about $60 (based on both the frequency and size of purchases). Typically, they have the following characteristics. As noted, they have only one phone line, do not own a cellular phone, and do not have Internet access.

• They tend to buy one "vertical service" (most often call waiting or caller-ID).

• They do not do a lot of long-distance calling (about 20 percent make no long-distance calls and the typical bill is about 30 percent below the national average).

• About two-thirds purchase cable TV, but most do not buy lots of add-ons like pay channels or pay-per-view. Their cable bill is about 20 percent below the average.

• Only 5 percent have a fax machine.

On the other side of the divide we have premier households. About one-quarter (24 percent) of households are heavy users of most telecom and TV services. Their monthly bill for all telecom and TV services is about $200. They have the following characteristics. As noted, 70 percent have a second phone line. Almost all of these consumers have Internet access (87 percent) and a cellular phone (91 percent).

• 70 percent purchase at least three vertical services.

• Their long-distance bill is about 60 percent above the national average.

• 86 percent purchase cable TV and their average bill is about 30 percent above the national average.

• 50 percent own a fax machine.

In between, we find households split between mobile and transitional households. About 30 percent of consumers are beginning to use telecom and TV services more intensely but it remains unclear whether they will move into the premier group. The mobile group spends about $110 per month, with very little expenditure on discretionary wireline telecommunications services. As noted, they do not have a second line or Internet access, but all have a cellular phone.

• Just under half (44 percent) have three or more vertical services.

• Their long-distance bill is slightly below the national average.

• Three-quarters subscribe to TV services and those that do pay a bill that is slightly below the national average.

• Only 10 percent have a fax machine.

Table 9.2
Typical Monthly Telecommunications Bill

		Modest	Mobile	Transi-tional	Premier
% of Population		45%	16%	15%	24%
Local		$20	$25	$40	$50
Long Distance		20	25	30	50
Telephone Total		40	50	70	100
Internet		0	0	20	25
Wireline Total		40	50 ⟷	90	125
Cellular		0	30	5	35
Cable	30	20	30	30	40
Telecom Act Total	110	60	110	125 ⟷	200

Source: See appendix A [of original paper].

The transitional group spends about $125 per month, with a lot of that on discretionary wireline telecommunications services. They have this higher expenditure in spite of somewhat lower income than the mobile group.

· Half have a second line.
· A majority has Internet (62 percent).
· Very few have a cellular phone (10 percent).
· Just over half (53 percent) have three or more vertical services.
· Three-quarters subscribe to TV services and their bill is above the national average.
· Their long-distance bill is slightly above the national average.
· Just over one-quarter have a fax machine.

C Expenditures on Telecommunications Services

Expenditure differences are critical to the digital divide. Combining the subjective reports of expenditures with national data for expenditures, we estimate the typical bills as depicted in table 9.2. The average bills identified in the table reflect both the frequency of the bill and the amount of the bill. For example, two-thirds of the modest segment is assumed to have a cable bill of $30, so the segment average is $20. They are not intended as precise, to the penny estimates, but order-of-magnitude estimates, consistent with industry analyses. We observe dramatic differences in the expenditures in the market segments.

For telecommunications service we estimate a monthly bill of $20 for local service for the modest group. We include an average of less than one vertical service for the modest segment. The long-distance (intraLATA and InterLATA) is estimated at $20 for the modest segment. The total telephone bill is $40 for the modest segment. To this we add only $20 for cable. The average total telecommunications bill for all households in this segment is $60.

For the mobile segment we estimate a local bill (basic plus vertical) of $25. Long-distance is estimated at $25. The total telecommunications bill is $50. To this we add $30 for cellular and $30 for cable. The total bill is $110. We now jump across the divide to the transitional group. The transitional group spends about twice as much on wireline services. The higher bill is driven by the second line and Internet, but not long-distance. The much higher wireline expenditure in this group leads us to distinguish it from the mobile segment. The total bill is about $125 per month.

In the premier segment the bill is much larger. Because this segment consumes telecommunications services intensively, all parts of the bill are much higher. Local service is about $50 per month, driven up by the prevalence of second lines and vertical services. Long-distance is estimated at $50 per month, driven up by higher levels of usage. The telephone bill is estimated at $100 per month, while the total wireline bill is about $125 per month. This is about three times as high as the modest group and over twice as high as the mobile group. The addition of Internet, cellular, and high cable expenditures drives the bill up to about $200 per month.

D   Economic Resources in the Market Segments

These spending differences are driven by vast differences in income. The modest segment is made up of lower-income households (see figure 9.8). Two-thirds report annual income below $30,000. Four-fifths report annual income below $40,000. The median annual income in the modest segment is $22,500. In contrast, for the premier segment, three-quarters report annual income above $40,000 and 45 percent report annual in-

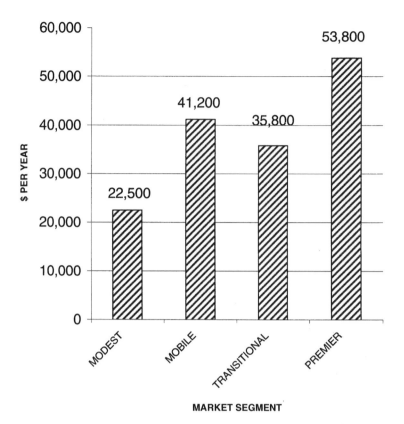

Figure 9.8
The digital divide: Median annual income.
Source: Florida PSC Survey.

come above $60,000. In the premier segment it is about $54,000. The mobile group has a median income of just over $41,000. The transitional group has slightly lower income, $35,800.

Moreover, it is important to point out that race, ethnicity, and age are not the key factors that affect the decision to take most services. Income is the most important factor. The digital divide is first and foremost an economic divide.

To conduct this analysis, variables were created based on the presence of a service in the household and the demographic characteristics of the household—race (Black), ethnicity (Hispanic), age (presence of at least one household member over 65), and income. These variables were assessed to determine the importance of these factors in explaining the presence of the services in the home in terms of the simple correlation coefficient and the amount of variance explained by each variable in a multiple regression approach.

In all cases except one, income is positively related to consumption and far outweighs the other factors. Income is always directly related to consumption and significant in all cases, except for vertical services. [*Portion of text omitted.*] The one exception where income is not significant and where other factors are more important is vertical services. Here Blacks are more likely to take the services, and households with at least one older member are less likely.

To elaborate on this observation, a cross-tabulation of Internet use, income, and race was prepared (see figure 9.9). Internet was chosen, since it is frequently the focal point of public policy debates about the digital divide. At the top and the bottom of the income distribution there is little difference between the races.

We observe that among upper-income households (Black and White) just over half of all households have Internet services. Above $50,000 the difference between Blacks and Whites is no more than 5 percentage points. Even in the $40,000 to $50,000 category, the difference is only 7 percentage points. Among very low-income households (income below $10,000), virtually no one has Internet access. Blacks (98 percent) and Whites (96 percent) lack access.

We observe that lower-middle-income Blacks lag behind in Internet access. The largest difference occurs at incomes between $10,000 and $40,000. On average, the difference is about 15 percentage points. In this range it can be said that Whites are about twice as likely to have access. Thus, there is certainly an important public policy issue for this population segment, but it should be placed in the context of the overwhelming importance of income as a determinant of access.

The presence of children in households was also considered. The presence of children increases the consumption of telephone services, but not enough to alter the earlier economic analysis. In the modest segment, households with children have bills about 25 percent higher than those without. This raises their bills just to the national average. The effect of children is smaller as the level of consumption rises. The presence of

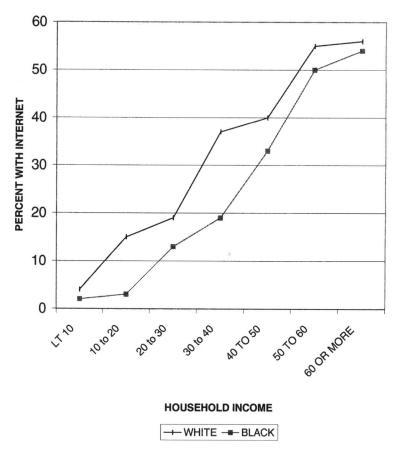

Figure 9.9
Income, race, and Internet usage.
Source: Florida PSC Survey.

children affects the percentage of households in the groups with cellular. Households with children are less likely to have Internet access. This analysis leads to the conclusion that bill differences are what drive business strategies and the likelihood of competitive entry. Income is what drives the willingness and ability to spend on these services.

[*Sections IV and V are omitted. Section IV shows "how the business models applied in the industries contribute to the existence of the divide and are endeavoring to exploit it," and Section V discusses "the severe problem of market concentration that has typified the industries since the passage of the Act, arguing that the resulting market power makes it all the more likely that the divide will become a permanent feature of the telecommunications industry."*]

Notes

1. Pub. L. No. 104-104, 110 Stat. 56 (47 U.S.C.).

2. Bureau of Labor Statistics (BLS) Consumer Price Index–Urban (CPI-U).

3. BLS, Cable Consumer Price Index.

4. In the Matter of Annual Assessment of the Status of Competition in Markets for the delivery of Video Programming, *Fifth Annual Report*, CS Dkt. No. 98-102, Dec. 23, 1998, at F-4, footnote 18 (hereafter, *Fifth Annual Report*).

5. *Fifth Annual Report*, op. cit., at appendixes C and D.

6. Although different long-distance companies have recovered these costs in different ways (per line, on a percent of bill) the charges generally are just under $1/mo. for "federal access" and another $1/mo. for "universal service."

7. BLS Intrastate and Interstate Indexes.

8. BLS local phone index.

9. Staff draft, *Report of the Florida Public Service Commission on the Relationship Among the Costs and Charges Associated with Providing Basic Local Service, Intrastate Access, and Other Services provided by Local Exchange Companies in Compliance with Chapter 98-2777, Section 2(1), Laws of Florida* and *The Conclusion of the Florida Public Service Commission as to the Fair and Reasonable Florida Residential Basic Local Telecommunications Service Rate, In Compliance with Chapter 98-277, Section 2(2)(A), Laws of Florida*, February 15, 1999, p. 12.

10. BLS Intrastate and Interstate Indexes.

11. As noted, this is the term U.S. West uses to refer to this segment.

10

The E-rate in America: A Tale of Four Cities

Andy Carvin, editor, with Chris Conte and Allen Gilbert

E-rate 101: How the Program Works

The E-rate is a federally managed program that provides significant discounts on telecommunications technologies to schools and libraries in the United States. Discounts range from 20 percent to 90 percent and are based on the percentage of students participating in the federal school lunch program who are served by the school or library. The E-rate is administered by the Universal Service Administrative Company (USAC), a private, not-for-profit corporation that is responsible for ensuring universal service to telecommunications services throughout the country. USAC's Schools and Libraries Division (SLD) is specifically responsible for providing telecommunications discounts to America's schools and libraries.

The E-rate is funded by money from the Universal Service Fund (USF), which was created in 1993 to ensure that all Americans could afford telephone services. With the passage of the Telecommunications Act of 1996 and the Federal Comminications Commission's subsequent implementation of the E-rate, the fund was expanded in 1997 to support telecommunications services at schools and libraries. Local and long-distance telephone companies are required to contribute to the fund.

Services covered by the E-rate include Internet access, videoconferencing services, high-speed data connections, phone service, and certain types of internal wiring and network equipment. Computer hardware, electrical upgrades, and many other services are not covered by the program.

Schools can apply for E-rate funding individually or in groups (such as districts or statewide consortia). The application process includes several steps:

• Prepare and submit a technology plan that meets specific SLD criteria, including a clear technical and educational strategy for implementation of telecommunications services.
• Submit Form 470, describing the specific services being sought.
• Collect bids from local vendors for these services and select vendors during a mandatory 28-day competitive bidding period.
• Submit Form 471, notifying the SLD of the contracted vendors and the specific costs involved.
• Receive notification from the SLD of those services that have been approved for discounts.
• Begin implementing services. Once services are completed, discounts are disbursed directly to vendors. These discounts appear on the bills submitted to the school or library.

The E-rate has thus far been structured as a series of funding-year cycles, with each cycle offering an application window ranging from 75 to 90 days during which institutions can submit Form 470 and begin the application process. Funding decisions are then made in waves, beginning with those institutions receiving the highest discounts and with the most basic services (such as telephone service and Internet access). Waves of funding continue to be made until all requests are met or until the budget is depleted.

E-rate Policy: Universal Service in Education and Communications

The E-rate represents a vital national commitment to equal educational opportunity, as well as a significant step forward in deploying high-speed communications networks. Because it resides at the intersection of our education and telecommunications systems, the E-rate has profound importance in each of these two spheres.

When Congress laid the foundation for the E-rate by enacting the Telecommunications Act of 1996, policy makers cited several justifications for making such a substantial investment in bringing advanced telecommunications to schools:

• *Economic.* Availing students of access to computers and the Internet prepares them for an economy in which three out of five jobs require a working knowledge of information technology;

• *Educational.* Students gain access to a greater breadth and depth of up-to-date educational resources, and quality educational services are delivered more efficiently;

• *Community Infrastructure Development.* Building technology capacity in underserved communities diminishes the competitive disadvantage faced by certain areas, especially inner cities and rural parts of the country.

These reasons tell much of the story, but there is an even more important one. American leaders since the time of the founding fathers have recognized that a nation comes closest to achieving true democracy when all its citizens have access to information about their government, the knowledge to imagine new possibilities, and the opportunity to participate in political discourse. Whether we debate the future of education or debate who shall have access to essential telecommunications services, we should ask the question: How do these proposals advance a democratic way of life? In recent years, however, the meaning of our democratic heritage has been up for grabs. Much as Alexis de Tocqueville predicted in the 19th century, Americans have been wrestling with a tension between two cherished values we associate with democracy: liberty and equality.

This conflict has taken center stage in education policy since at least the *Brown v. Board of Education* decision in 1954. Our tradition of public education open to all students reflects our commitment to equality. Indeed, many state constitutions uphold education as a fundamental right; New Jersey, for instance, guarantees all children a "thorough and efficient education." Some parents and concerned citizens have argued that lack of resources in impoverished districts effectively means that children are being denied equal educational opportunity. "Unless we get equal resources and funding to the poorest schools, there will never be equal education," notes Gary Orfield, a professor at Harvard University's Graduate School of Education. "Even with those resources for all schools, there will be some inequalities."

Courts have found such arguments persuasive, prodding policy makers to seek resource parity or educational "adequacy" across school systems.

However, the pendulum in education reform has swung in recent years away from this emphasis on equality. Schools should be held accountable for meeting certain standards, the newer thinking goes, and in districts where schools are perceived to be failing, parents should have the freedom to send their children elsewhere. But while choice may be good for individual children and families, it risks sidestepping the problem of underachieving schools.

Policies addressing communications technology also have been in flux. Just as we developed a system of universal education, we traditionally have sought to establish a system of universal service in telecommunications. In particular, policy makers have concentrated over the past half-century on ensuring that all Americans can avail themselves of telephone service. Universal service policies have been remarkably successful; currently, more Americans are connected to the telephone network than ever before, due in part to regulations that reduce the cost to poor households of both installing telephones and using them to make calls.

But just as some would have us turn away from equality in education, telecommunications policy appeared a few years ago to be shifting toward a greater emphasis on liberty. The Telecommunications Act of 1996 sought to spur the deployment of advanced telecommunications technologies primarily by enhancing industry competition. In other words, lawmakers looked first and foremost to a competitive market to provide affordable and ubiquitous services.

Within this pro-deregulation atmosphere, however, an idea began to take root: access to high-speed connections (ones much faster than standard telephone lines) is fundamental to our democracy. We have previously acknowledged telephone service as essential so that people can communicate with the outside world, dial emergency services, and seek information. Today, the idea gaining currency is that advanced information and telecommunications services also are necessary because they allow us to engage in activities that palpably affect our quality of life, such as distance learning and electronic commerce. Perhaps most important, we increasingly understand that high-speed networks could revolutionize education—and indeed are already beginning to do so in schools fortunate enough to have access to them.

The growing recognition of the importance of new telecommunications technologies came at a time of growing concern over the digital divide separating individuals and communities that have access to these tools from those that do not. Although Congress was not ready in 1996 to include advanced services to the home as a key component of universal service, lawmakers did see public access to these tools in schools and libraries as a stepping stone to developing a modern communications infrastructure in communities. Faced with the likelihood that the latest information and communications tools probably would not reach our public schools and local libraries for a long time, policy makers felt compelled to take steps to meet the infrastructure needs of these institutions.

Congress sent a clear message in crafting the E-rate. It acknowledged that the market would not deliver ubiquitous service to poor communities—at least not as fast as the belief in democracy and equal opportunity required. And by designing the E-rate so that it would provide the greatest benefit to the poorest communities and rural populations, Congress committed the nation to leveling the playing field in a society in which rapidly changing technology exacerbates inequalities. As an indication of just how far the pendulum could be swinging toward equality in telecommunications policy, former Department of Commerce Assistant Secretary Larry Irving suggested in July 1999 that Internet access is fast becoming a civil right. Of course, naming something a right does not guarantee everyone access to these tools. However, it does shift the debate, since civil rights demand appropriate public action to ensure that they work in practice and not just exist in principle. Thus, if the primary mode of delivering high-speed connections to Internet-based applications through the market is a civil right, then new policies are necessary to protect it and ensure its effectiveness. Creation of the E-rate also sent an important policy signal concerning education. By singling out schools and libraries, Congress also renewed the national commitment to equal opportunity in education.

There is, of course, no easy remedy to inequality in a free society, since policy makers can in part control the floors but not the ceilings relative to educational and technological advantage. Thus, governments cannot and should not discourage college-bound youth from taking advanced placement courses, despite the fact that these classes may not be offered in high schools in less well-to-do parts of town. Rather, policy makers should try to equalize access to these classes. Similarly, the authorities cannot wrestle computers and modems from the hands of affluent children because others cannot afford them. Instead, if telecommunications access is considered essential to the learning process, it ought to be as available as possible in schools and public access centers. Every child should be offered a fair shake in gaining access to a wealth of resources, opportunities for communication, and tools for personal expression.

Moving equity issues back to the front burner of educational reform will require a concerted effort among local, state, and federal policy makers. But the E-rate is a significant start. Educational equity expert Marilyn Gittell, professor of political science at the Graduate School of the City University of New York, has suggested that "a school reform agenda for the 21st century requires recognition that school reform, like schools, cannot be separated from other community reform efforts." A commitment to revitalize institutions will happen as programs like the E-rate are viewed in terms of giving all Americans—particularly our children—the resources and opportunities they deserve.

[*The following section, E-rate Politics: A Brief History, is omitted.*]

The E-rate in Practice: Research Findings in Four Midwestern Cities

To assess the impact of the E-rate, the Benton Foundation commissioned researchers from the EDC/Center for Children and Technology to visit four large, urban school districts during the fall semester of the 1999–2000 school year: Chicago, Illinois; Cleveland, Ohio; Detroit, Michigan; and Milwaukee, Wisconsin. These four districts serve approximately 800,000 students, most of whom live in poverty.

Common Themes
While each of the districts has pursued its own path through the process of planning, applying for, and using E-rate funding, several common themes emerge from their experiences:

Network infrastructure deployment accelerated, and Internet access improved dramatically. The E-rate initiative has made it possible for these districts to create robust, high-quality networks that would never have been put in place without E-rate funding. The E-rate has had an especially high impact for several reasons: the funding it provides was not capped at a certain level; it requires intensive planning and implementation; and it encourages leveraging of multiple funding sources. Several district administrators said E-rate funding enabled them to make a quantum leap in their districts.

E-rate funding has enabled school districts to leverage existing financial resources. Resources freed up by E-rate funding, as well as money from state-level initiatives, are now being used to pay for elements of technology programs that are not covered by the E-rate. For example: because of E-rate subsidies, Detroit has been able to combine money from a state-level program with funds saved at the district level to pay for much of its electrical upgrades.

Professional development needs are increasing geometrically. Schools must provide adequate professional development to help teachers learn how to use these newly accessible tools. Otherwise, the gap between technologically sophisticated and technologically weak schools will grow wider. Even though the need for training will only grow, departments often must support these efforts on insecure or inadequate funding. District leaders must be convinced of the importance of continuing to emphasize sustained, creative professional development for teachers around the use of these new tools.

School districts are highly dependent on E-rate funding, even though the advances they are making are highly vulnerable to changes in the political environment. Although the E-rate is enabling school districts to leverage important resources, it is not generating significant local expenditures for technology infrastructure. On the contrary, district budgets often rely on the E-rate to ensure that they will be able to sustain their newly established networks. Several district administrators expressed concern that the SLD is not yet emphasizing to schools and districts the need to plan how they will meet ongoing costs. For example, as schools make the transition to conducting districtwide administrative business online, telecommunications bills will be high; meeting them will require continuing discounts via the E-rate program.

The E-rate has led to changes in school district planning practices. The E-rate has forced school administrators to acquire new knowledge and to learn new forms of collaboration. The result has been better planning, new lines of communication, and improvements in billing and accounting practices. In some cases, staff members from educational technology departments have gained significant influence in other departments such as information technology or operations departments. Improved coordination—particularly among curriculum and instruction, educational technology, and information technology departments—will be crucial to ensuring that the E-rate leads to long-term improvements in teaching and learning at the classroom level.

The current E-rate process taxes relationships with vendors. In every district, the E-rate has stretched relationships with vendors to their limits. Many factors complicate the bidding, including payment and reimbursement processes required by the SLD; the SLD's requirement that districts have in hand the full (pre-discount) cost of the services they request; delays in receiving reimbursements from vendors; the strain placed on vendors' inventories and labor supplies by bidding and awarding processes (described as "hurry up and wait" by some); and the time constraints placed on implementation of annual plans. Implementation phases were so intense that in each of the four cities delays were caused when contractors ran out of qualified labor. As an administrator explained, "We were using every electrician in the city of Chicago. They had to bring people in from downstate to get all of the jobs done."

"Building basics" delay the deployment of information technology. These school districts faced an acute need for at least two important resources that the E-rate program does not support: electrical upgrades and hardware. In several of the districts, state grant programs were crucial to creating plans for electrical upgrades. But hardware purchasing is largely the responsibility of individual schools in these districts. District administrators should be careful to track whether individual schools increase their investments in hardware in order to take advantage of the networks that have been brought into their classrooms.

High-level school administrators and community stakeholders need to be made aware of the impact of the E-rate. In some districts, though not all, high-ranking administrators were initially dubious that the E-rate was a "real" program that would produce actual funding. Even now, administrators in some districts report that their superiors are not fully aware of the impact of this program. In order to realize the maximum benefit from the E-rate program, community members and administrative leaders in these districts need to be better informed about this program and about the work that it is supporting at the local level.

Case Studies

In this section, the impact of two full years of E-rate funding on the four school districts studied is summarized. Each site visit included meetings with district-level administrators, principals, technology coordinators, and teachers. Interviews focused on four sets of issues:

1. *The planning process.* Past technology planning efforts; planning for E-rate funding; plans for the future.

2. *The application process.* The challenges and opportunities afforded by the application process; the complexities of working with vendors within the constraints of the E-rate process; the impact of the application process on administrative procedures within the district.

3. *Impact of the E-rate program.* Impact on technology infrastructure; on financial planning for technology; on instructional programs; on professional development programs.

4. *School/district relationships.* How the district offices communicated with individual schools about the E-rate process; how new infrastructure supports or changes school/district communication; how school-level input is included in the design and deployment of the networking infrastructure.

The four districts are among the 50 largest school districts in the United States ranging from Chicago, the third largest, to Cleveland, which ranks 40th. Large urban districts such as these have a particularly great need for the E-rate, but they also face major hurdles in taking advantage of it.

The most obvious challenge is the scale of investment needed to bring modern technology into their schools. The four districts each operate between 100 and 600 individual school buildings and thousands of classrooms. Undertaking any systematic capital improvement in such districts is especially daunting because funds are rarely available to support intensive investment. State funding arrangements rarely account for the disproportionate size of large districts. One recent state-level funding program is TEACH—Technology for Educational ACHievement—in Wisconsin ⟨http://www.teachwi.state.wi.us⟩. Since 1997, the governor and state legislature have committed up to $100 million per year in order to support investment in educational technology and telecommunications access for schools, libraries and colleges. This program intentionally complements E-rate funding in some areas and allows some assistance with electrical service upgrades. However, the financial burden on the local school district is still substantial. The district still bears at least 75 percent of the full cost for internal electrical and network infrastructure.

Even if scale were not an issue, large urban schools are more likely than other districts to face large capital challenges. Their school buildings are more likely to be very old (over 100 years old in many cases), as well as to have inadequate electrical wiring and widespread asbestos problems. The most consistent criticism of the E-rate program in these districts is that the program does not cover the cost of electrical upgrades. However, these districts have been able to re-allocate other funds to meet—partially or entirely—the need for electrical upgrades.

Three of the four school districts studied (as well as many others) have gone through significant transformations in their systems of governance within the past two to five years. These changes include the takeover and reconstitution of the Chicago Board of Education by Mayor Richard M. Daley in 1995, a move followed by similar actions in Cleveland and Detroit in 1998. These shifts have led to substantial changes in the business practices, educational policies, and instructional emphases of these districts. But they have placed burdens on administrators, complicating efforts to undertake long-term planning required if schools are to make the most effective use of the E-rate program. Many administrators also suggest that the challenge of applying for E-rate funding has led to changes in planning and budgeting processes that otherwise would not have been nearly as high a priority.

Large urban school districts also face persistent challenges in attracting and retaining highly qualified teachers. The E-rate program may seem far removed from such issues, but administrators say that installing modern information technology has significantly helped them overcome this problem. Technology gives schools an opportunity to transform the day-to-day communication and information-sharing practices of teachers and administrators in the district and beyond. It enables school administrators to reconceptualize how professional development activities are delivered, sustained, and extended into the classroom. Technology also helps attract new teachers, often from outside of the district, because it offers them access to up-to-date resources.

Chicago

The Chicago Public School District includes about 578 schools and serves approximately 430,000 students, 84 percent of whom receive free or reduced-price lunches. Many school buildings in the district are over 100 years old, but the district has undertaken a major capital improvement program funded by a bond issue of over $1.9 billion. In the past two years, 15 new schools have been built and 12 more are under construction. Almost all schools have received capital improvements over the past two years, focused largely on upgrading their electrical capacities in anticipation of the installation of E-rate-funded networks. The budget for the capital improvement program includes significant funding for electrical upgrades.

Before receiving E-rate funding, the district had developed a plan for a wide-area network (WAN), but it never secured adequate funding to support full implementation. Individual schools pursued their own networking on an ad-hoc basis. A few schools had sophisticated networks, while others had partial networks or connections to the Internet. But the large majority of schools did not have Internet access or networking within their buildings.

Every school in Chicago has a Local School Council (LSC) that wields significant control over discretionary funds, makes some curricular and instructional decisions, and manages the physical plant of the school. These schools were able to apply for E-rate funds independent of the district-wide application submitted by the district administration. Information reported here reflects the outcomes of the district-level E-rate investment, and does not include the work of those individual schools that have applied for or received E-rate funding.

Impact of E-rate   In the first year of the E-rate, Chicago received $27 million. As of November 1999, Chicago had received over $74 million in E-rate funding, making it the second largest beneficiary of the program. Only New York City received a higher E-rate subsidy.

Chicago's plan for E-rate-funded networking included two major components. First, it established a WAN for both administrative and classroom use (an initiative known as the ShortScope program). This network was completed in September 1999, with T1 lines running to administrative drops in every school. Second, during the second year of the E-rate program the district moved to establish a "Local School Education Network." This $57 million initiative is intended to complement local school investments in internal wiring. The district estimates that approximately 260 of its schools have received some E-rate funding, including a total of approximately $40 million for individual school local area networks. The Local School Education Network funds will be used to ensure that all schools meet a minimal technology standard, with a goal of networking at least 10 classrooms, as well as libraries and computer labs, in every school. Coordinating the district's investments with the plans and applications of individual schools to create a single, uniform district-wide infrastructure has been a complex challenge. For Year Three, the Department of Learning Technologies has asked individual schools in the district to identify their needs for further E-rate funding and to forward them to the district. They will then submit a single E-rate application for the entire district, which should streamline the coordination process. E-rate funding has also generated significant savings in other parts of the district budget, and those savings are being funneled into professional development, educational intranet development efforts, and electrical upgrades for the schools.

Challenges of Pursuing E-rate Funding   The primary challenge administrators faced in pursuing E-rate funding was designing and coordinating their application so it was integrated with the capital improvement program, the ShortScope wide area network and individual schools' own networking efforts. The administrators described the E-rate program as a "cross-functional project" because it requires an unusual level of collaboration among many departments that are rarely required to coordinate with one another around an individual project. Submitting successful applications to the Schools and Libraries Division has required pulling people from many different departments (such as legal, purchasing, information technology, and school operations) into the same room. Many of these departments are rarely asked so explicitly to coordinate their work, and the unusual requirements of the E-rate application process challenged many of the normal business practices of the district. As one interview subject said, "E-rate gets into everybody's business."

Instructional Issues The primary focus of Chicago's Department of Learning Technologies is supporting the professional development of teachers. This group has been devoting significant resources to developing tools and resources that will be made available to teachers over the intranet network. A districtwide curriculum resource, organized around the state and city standards and the Chicago structured curriculum, already is available and is growing rapidly. The schools are also rolling out a "Curriculum Wizard" designed to support teachers in writing technology-rich and standards-based curricula.

Chicago has had a district technology plan since 1997, as well as standards and guidelines for technology infrastructures within schools since 1994. Schools are not required to follow these specifications but cannot receive technical support from the district if they do not follow them. The district office also supports 28 former teachers as a "Technology Resource Network" of consultants responsible for helping the schools develop their infrastructure and improve their use of technology.

Cleveland

The Cleveland Municipal School District includes approximately 118 schools and serves 77,000 students, 75 percent of whom are eligible for free or reduced-price lunches. Until 1996, little educational technology was available in the Cleveland schools, and what was available was concentrated in specialized magnet schools. The district had no history of investing local funds in instructional technology other than a network for administrative functions.

The Ohio SchoolNet project gave Cleveland's educational technology infrastructure a major push in 1996. This project made $500 million available to network every elementary-school classroom in the state. Cleveland did not apply for the program initially because it was run on a cost-reimbursement basis and the district did not have adequate funding available to cover costs up-front. This requirement was later changed, and Cleveland eventually participated in the program. Another initial obstacle was that SchoolNet did not originally supply computers, but this changed as well. As a result, all K–4 classrooms in Cleveland have now been wired, with each possessing four SchoolNet computers.

Anticipating the introduction of the E-rate program, Paul Karlin, manager of the district's Educational Technology Office, brought together a cross-departmental group of administrators and teachers in 1997 to develop a technology plan for the district. This effort did not stimulate new funding from the district budget, but the school board set aside $20 million for a new administrative network, which was seen as necessary primarily because of Y2K concerns. At the time, the existing administrative network—which ran over 9600-baud dial-up lines—was still the only inter-school network in the district. The instructional technology staff developed plans to coordinate the upgrading of the administrative network with the implementation of an educational network that would reach into classrooms as well.

Impact of E-rate   Cleveland received $26 million in E-rate funding in the first year of the program—the third largest commitment in the country, behind New York City and Chicago. These funds were dedicated to supporting the implementation of a wide-area network for the district as well as for internal wiring in all schools not already wired under the SchoolNet project. Some $12.5 million in Year 2 E-rate funding will support various enhancements to the network.

The district is establishing the largest and most robust school-networking system in Ohio. A T1 network runs throughout the district, and multiple T1 lines run from the district data center to the state Internet provider agency. In addition, all classrooms in the Cleveland public schools are now wired for internal communications and Internet access.

Challenges of Pursuing E-rate Funding Applying for E-rate funds was an intensive and collaborative process, involving administrative staff from many parts of the district. The process required a high level of co-ordination across the departments. Going forward with the implementation process is becoming increasingly burdensome because the district continues to pay for the administration and management of its Educational Technology Office exclusively through grants. Schools, therefore, can only seek support from the district for parts of their programs that are supported by specific grants.

Limited access to hardware in the district's 23 middle schools and 16 high schools also constrains implementation of E-rate funding in Cleveland. Additionally, the cost of electrical upgrades—met partially but not adequately by state and federal programs—is being addressed incrementally. In the meantime, this problem continues to impede full utilization of the networks the E-rate program has made available.

Instructional Issues Besides coordinating development of the E-rate-funded technology, the Educational Technology Office is placing a strong focus on supporting professional development opportunities for teachers. The district is participating in several grant-supported professional development initiatives including the Alliance Program, funded by the Joyce Foundation, and the Savvy CyberTeacher Program led by the Stevens Institute of Technology. The district aims to use a U.S. Department of Education Challenge Grant to train every elementary teacher in the program over five years. The technology office, which oversees these programs, is emphasizing the Savvy CyberTeacher training as a mechanism to familiarize teachers with the Web-based resources that are now available to them in their classrooms.

The efforts of Cleveland's Educational Technology Office are not fully coordinated with the programs of its Curriculum and Instruction Department. This disconnect has limited the influence of the instructional technology group on district-level planning for the use of technology. At the same time, technology initiatives originating in other parts of the district have not been coordinated with the networking initiatives of the

Educational Technology Office. For example, the district has invested in test preparation and integrated learning systems (mostly free-standing) and is considering increasing their presence throughout the district. These are technological investments that do not leverage or take advantage of the E-rate-funded networking infrastructure that has been put into place over the past two years.

Detroit

The Detroit Public School District includes approximately 250 schools and serves about 175,000 students, 84 percent of whom receive free or reduced-price lunches. Previously organized into six regions of 43 schools each, the district has been reorganized into clusters of elementary and middle schools feeding individual high schools. The average age of a Detroit school building is 66 years, and 20 of the district's 250 schools were built in the 1890s. Some schools are still burning coal for heat.

Before 1996, only a handful of schools in Detroit were connected to the Internet. The district was running an administrative network that supported only dial-up connections. Very few classrooms had Internet access. In 1996, the district received $500,000 from the state of Michigan to support school networking, part of a settlement Ameritech was required to pay as a reimbursement for overcharging customers. The district used funds as seed money to begin the process of establishing prototype networking projects in several high schools. Although some schools were beginning to use Title I funds to purchase computers, the vast majority of Detroit schools had little or no technology in place. The central administration had yet to define standards for technology purchases, its resources were extremely limited, and there was no coordinated plan in place for the distribution and deployment of technology. While efforts like NetDay were important catalysts for introducing network technology into some schools, Detroit was not ready to contemplate establishing a robust networking infrastructure that could support instructional practices at the classroom level.

Impact of E-rate   Detroit Public Schools received $18 million in the first year of E-rate funding. Their initial goal was to wire half of the schools in the district—all the high schools and middle schools, along with a select group of elementary schools—and to begin establishing a wide-area network. In the second year of the E-rate, Detroit received just under $18 million. This money will support continuation of the wiring program and completion of the wide-area network. The schools aim to have every building wired and the wide-area network in place by the spring of 2000. During the third year they will focus on getting every classroom wired.

Jim Davis, director of information systems management for the district, described the E-rate program as "a godsend." Previous efforts to design and implement a systematic networking structure never had adequate funding behind them. Even now, he reported, the district's technology efforts would come to a "complete standstill" if the E-rate program were canceled. The E-rate program has also generated at least $6 million in savings for the Detroit Public Schools. Davis anticipates that these savings will be transferred to the instructional technology department and used to support professional development programs.

Challenges of Pursuing E-rate Funding   Other than the E-rate, the major source of funding for infrastructure in Detroit is a portion of a large bond that was approved in 1995. Eventually this will provide as much as $110 million for technology-related resources, but the money is not yet in hand and it is unclear when it will arrive. Electrical upgrades are a problem in Detroit as in the other districts, but this problem has been effectively addressed through a state-level fund that was established to make up for past underspending on special education. This resource, called the Durant Fund, has provided $12 million for electrical upgrades in the Detroit schools, largely solving the district's electrical upgrade problem.

Instructional Issues   Unlike the other districts in this study, where departments responsible for educational technology have managed the E-rate program, the Detroit E-rate program has been managed within the Office of Information Systems Management. The district's instructional technology program falls within the curriculum and instruction department and has not been involved in E-rate planning or implementation.

Parents and community members have brought significant pressure to bring technology into the district's instructional program. In order to meet this need and to make use of the infrastructure now in place, principals are beginning to spend significant portions of Title I funds—most of which are controlled at the school level—to purchase new computers.

Compounding the challenges of providing technology-related professional development in Detroit is the fact that a large portion of the teaching staff is nearing retirement age. Most teachers in the district are either very experienced or brand new, making the task of designing appropriate professional development activities difficult. No new professional development planning has yet taken place in connection with the increased access being made available by the E-rate.

There is also a strong local emphasis on developing community technology centers and keeping schools open at night for neighborhood use. District contributions and an $8 million grant from the Annenberg/CPB Projects are supporting 15 new community technology centers, five of which are now in place. IBM and Compaq are also providing hardware for these sites.

Milwaukee

The Milwaukee Public School District includes approximately 160 schools serving 113,000 students, 80 percent of whom are eligible for free or reduced-price lunches. Some 70 of the district's schools were built before 1930, and 20 were built in the 19th century. Five new schools were built in 1991.

In 1995, the district had few computers and almost no networking infrastructure. In order to spur investment in educational technology, a group of teachers, principals, university-based collaborators and district administrators came together to develop a districtwide technology plan that articulated an overall vision for using technology to support teaching and learning. The price tag associated with the plan was around $300 million. The school board supported the plan in principle, but provided little funding to help move it forward.

Over the next three years, the district's Department of Technology pursued other funding sources, including grants from private foundations and federal and state programs. The department also worked with individual schools in allocating their individual budgets. By the fall of 1998, some important components of the plan were in place, including the beginnings of a wide-area network and internal wiring in some school buildings.

The statewide TEACH program has also been a key point of financial leverage for the district. This project partially pays for electrical up-grades, which are not eligible for E-rate funding, as well as other kinds of infrastructure investments.

Impact of E-rate   In the first year of the E-rate, Milwaukee received $23.4 million, the fourth highest allocation funds, after New York, Chicago, and Cleveland. As of October 1999, approximately half of all district classrooms were wired with fiber-optic cable and had a minimum of 12 drops each. As a result of the first two years of the E-rate, the district expects to complete a fiber-based wide-area network. They hope to have all classrooms fully wired by December 2000. The district is installing in-school wiring in high schools first, followed by middle and elementary schools. District administrators report that the technical infrastructure outlined in the original 1996 technology plan is now 80 percent realized; this result is largely because of the E-rate program. While the vision articulated in that plan continues to guide the district's technology investments, a revised technology plan is now being developed. This plan will reflect the rapid progress the district has made, as well as help guide new phases of development.

Challenges of Pursuing E-rate Funding   Leadership for technology development in Milwaukee is strong. The superintendent and the director of technology both have long histories within the district, and they share a commitment to using technology to support teaching and learning.

The administrators in Milwaukee who have managed the E-rate process have a variety of backgrounds—some are educators and some are primarily business or technical people. They have collaborated intensively on the E-rate application process, which they described as highly challenging. In particular, administrators cited difficulties in seeking appropriate bids from vendors, coordinating electrical upgrades with wiring efforts, and finding adequate funding to guarantee contracts with vendors who sometimes were unwilling to sign agreements unless the district had money in hand. Administrators had trouble finding enough skilled labor, a problem other districts reported having as well. Vendors also faced problems; there were often time lags between when they signed legal contracts and when the district actually secured its E-rate funding. Only then could the district authorize vendor work to begin.

In spite of these challenges, the process of applying for the E-rate has led to new types of relationships among district departments, between the district and local businesses and universities, as well as between the district's central office and individual schools.

Instructional Issues   The Milwaukee school district is committed to providing professional development, instructional resources, and additional support to ensure the integration of new technology into classroom teaching. For example, the district has developed an intranet site that provides an environment of resources and communication tools where teachers can collaboratively develop a standards-based curriculum. Bob Nelson, director of the district's Department of Technology, describes his ultimate goal as having students using the technology frequently and taking the lead in helping teachers learn to use the technology. He wants every student to have email and to use these resources frequently. The district also provides teachers with free email but requires them to take a 12-hour training course in order to have their accounts activated. More than 8,000 of the district's approximately 11,000 staff members have taken this course so far.

The growing availability of network resources at the classroom level is raising many new challenges for principals, such as revising curricula to take advantage of the new resources, changing in-school communication practices, setting security and acceptable use policies and providing adequate technical support and professional development for teachers. But one administrator described these challenges as "pleasurable problems" that will require the district to figure out how to maintain and expand the infrastructure—and, more important, how to use it on a regular basis to support real progress in day-to-day teaching and learning.

[Section V, An Educator's Toolkit: Planning an Evaluation of the Impact of the E-rate Program, and appendixes A and B are omitted.]

11

Universal Access to Email: Feasibility and Societal Implications

Robert H. Anderson, Tora K. Bikson, Sally Ann Law, and
Bridger M. Mitchell

Introduction

Over the last 15 years [i.e., between 1980 and 1995] the burgeoning use
of personal computers has popularized a number of new information
services, including in particular electronic mail or "email." Email is a
form of information interchange in which messages are sent from one
personal computer (or computer terminal) to another via modems and a
telecommunications system. The use of email began on the ARPAnet[1]
(the precursor of the Internet) in the 1960s and 1970s in the United
States, gradually spread along with the use of mainframe- and minicom-
puter-based local nets in the 1970s, and "exploded" along with the rapid
growth of personal computers (PCs) and the Internet in the 1980s. Email
began as a means of information interchange for small, select groups; its
use has spread to encompass millions of people in the United States and
all over the world. Email has given rise to the formation of many "virtual communities"—groups of individuals, often widely separated geographically, who share common interests. The interpersonal linkages
and loyalties associated with these virtual communities can be real and
powerful.

Email has unique properties that distinguish it from other forms of
communication; for example, it supports true interactive communication among many participants. For the first time in human history, we
would assert, the means of "broadcasting" or "narrowcasting" are not
confined to the few with printing presses, TV stations, money to buy
access to those scarce resources, and the like. Email is also, unlike telephone calls (with the exception of voice mail and answering machines),

asynchronous, so that communication does not depend on the simultaneous availability and attention of sender and recipient. Generalizing greatly, email increases the power of individuals, permitting them to be active participants in a dialog extended in both time and space, rather than passive recipients of "canned" programming and prepackaged information.[2] These characteristics give rise to the question: Can email's novel properties address society's most compelling problems? If so, by what means?

Problem Statement

It is now possible to imagine the arrangement or construction of systems in which nearly universal access to email within the United States could become feasible within a decade—indeed, that is one aspiration of the U.S. National Information Infrastructure (NII)[3] initiative. Since email use is growing rapidly (e.g., within individual corporations, CompuServe, America Online, Internet, and Bitnet systems and on numerous dial-in electronic bulletin boards), the question may be asked: "Why bother? It's happening anyway." Three important answers to this question are: (1) In spite of the growth of these email systems, the majority of U.S. residents probably will continue to lack access to email well into the next century without societal intervention; (2) there is today a significant lack of active participation by many citizens in the dialog that forms the basis for the U.S. democratic process;[4] and (3) some citizens, such as inner-city minorities and the rural poor, are relatively disenfranchised and constitute groups that will be the last to be reached by commercial email systems that evolve in private markets. Because the properties of email allow individuals to engage in an active civic dialog, with informative and affiliative dimensions, universal email might provide significant benefits in creating interactive communication among U.S. citizens and residents.

The problem, then, is achieving active, responsive citizen participation in our national dialog for all citizens—participation not only in national politics but in local affairs, job markets, educational systems, health and welfare systems, international discourse, and all other aspects of our society.

There are hints that the distinctive properties of electronic mail systems (including access to, and ability to post and retrieve messages from, various electronic bulletin boards) may well be relevant to this re-enfranchisement of all citizens. The civic networks discussed in chapter 5 of this report [*not included here*] exemplify these opportunities.

It is also clear that widespread citizen access to an email system could have profound economic implications that might provide new sources of business and revenue to entrepreneurs providing new services; for example, installation of the French Programme Télétel system resulted in a flourishing of electronic services available to virtually all French citizens (and, for that matter, many visitors—through terminals available in hotel rooms and public sites).

It is important to note, however, that the Minitel terminal used by Télétel was not originally conceived of as access to an email system but rather as an "electronic telephone directory." As is often the case, when some facility for communication becomes possible within a system (e.g., ARPAnet, Télétel, and to a growing extent the Dialog system within the United States), its convenience and empowerment of individuals quickly cause email to become an important form of usage. Lack of true email capabilities may be a major contributor to the failure of other electronic service ventures such as teletext experiments, although too many factors may be involved to confirm this assessment.

Universal Email

The initial forays into widespread availability of electronic mail, such as the ARPAnet (and now Internet) experience, Télétel, and growing Prodigy, CompuServe, and America Online usage, lead to an intriguing question: What about "universal email?" What about providing all residents of the United States with access to email service, just as they now all (or almost all) have access to telephone service and postal service? What would be involved in such an undertaking? What are the pros and cons? What are the advantages and disadvantages? Could this have beneficial effects for U.S. society? Greater cohesion? Reduced alienation? Increased participation in the political process? Influence national security? What about beneficial effects for the U.S. economy? Or other productive side effects? And who would pay for the infrastructure and its usage?

More specific questions arise immediately regarding the services and functions to be provided by a universal email system: the required degree of access to such a "universal" service; the provision of privacy; alternative system architectures and implementation schemes; the cost of such a system/service and the method of payment; the likely social and international effect of universal email; and finally, public versus private roles in creating and operating such a service. This report describes our initial study of these and related issues over a two-year period and presents the results of our analyses.

The issue of providing universal email cannot be considered in isolation. As mentioned above, it is part of a larger national debate on a "national information infrastructure" and "global information infrastructure" that is gaining momentum. We hope this report contributes to discussion of the policy and social issues arising from attempts to provide such a service, in addition to technical options regarding implementation of the supporting infrastructure per se, because of these issues' importance in the public policy debate.

Some Definitions

Electronic Mail

For the purposes of this report, we have adopted a definition of electronic mail provided in an earlier RAND report (Anderson et al., 1989):

An electronic mail system:

1. Permits the asynchronous electronic interchange of information between persons, groups of persons, and functional units of an organization; and

2. Provides mechanisms supporting the creation, distribution, consumption, processing, and storage of this information. [*Portion of text is omitted.*]

The words in this definition all have significance. Key among them are the following:

- *Asynchronous.* One defining attribute of email is the ability to send a message when the recipient is not at that moment logged in; the message is placed in an "inbox" for later inspection by the recipient at his or her convenience.
- *Electronic.* The message travels over telecommunication systems at the speed of electricity in copper, of light in a fiberoptic cable, or of microwave or a satellite link (plus additional switching delays). Although some system "gateways" buffer messages for periodic transmission, the result still has a dynamic fundamentally different from postal mail, newspapers, and other traditional media.
- *Interchange of information.* Anyone within the system can send as well as receive messages.
- *Between persons, groups of persons, and functional units of an organization.* Messages may be sent to "mailboxes" representing individuals or groups; "aliases" may be established representing a number of individual addresses, so that a message may be sent to a group of individuals in one action; mailboxes such as purchasing@abc.com or president@whitehouse.gov may be established that represent a function, to be used by whomever is presently handling that function.
- *Mechanisms supporting creation, distribution, consumption, processing, and storage.* It must be possible to create messages, send and receive them, store them for future inspection and re-use, and "process" them (e.g., copy portions and paste them into later messages, forward them to others, modify their contents, and reuse them in other applications).

By the above definition, multipart messages containing embedded formatted word-processing documents, video clips, bitmapped pictures, sound clips, and the like are certainly email. Faxes sent from one dedicated fax machine to another, appearing only on output paper, are not (because they are not processable in a useful manner), but a "fax" sent from one PC to another meets the definition (because it may be stored for later retransmission, and its contents may be "processed"—e.g., by character recognition or graphics enhancement programs; in fact, some recipients may never get it in paper form). Similarly, using a personal computer to interact with "chat" groups and MUDs[5] usually qualifies as a form of email, because most communication programs through which this interaction is carried out allow the transcript of the interaction to be saved, processed, reused, and so on.

We have tried to use a rather narrow definition of email to focus this report on electronic mail, although it will be clear that most email users will also have facilities at hand to browse the World Wide Web, participate in multiuser simulations and games, and so forth. It is not important to draw too fine a distinction between what is email and what is not; the importance of having *some* definition becomes clearer in chapter 3's discussion of access devices and their locations and standards and protocols needed.

Universal Access

The other key concept in this report is "universal access." By this, we simply mean email facilities and services that are

• available at modest individual effort and expense to (almost) everyone in the United States in a form that does not require highly specialized skills or,

• accessible in a manner analogous to the level, cost, and ease of use of telephone service or the U.S. Postal Service.

We do not, therefore, envision that every single person will have access, but that email can achieve the same ubiquity that telephones (including the availability of payphones) and TVs have. Table 11.1 shows the penetration of related technologies into U.S. households, for comparison.

Table 11.1
Availability of Related Technologies in U.S. Households

Technology	Percentage of Households
Television	95
Telephone	93
Video cassette recorder	85
More than one TV	66
Cable TV	64
Pay-per-view service	51
Video game system	40
Video camera	28
Fax	6

Source: Times Mirror (1994).

Note that the above percentages are not distributed uniformly across various sectors of our society. For example, a recent report by Mueller and Schement in 1995 describes telephone access in Camden, New Jersey, by family income, ethnicity, age, and other demographic factors. The report indicates that, overall, only 80.6 percent of households in Camden have telephones; notable disparities include families on food stamps, who lag 20.4 percentage points behind households not on food stamps. For many households, "universal access" means traveling to the nearest working payphone (where receiving incoming messages is sometimes precluded either socially or by the technology). Similarly, universal access to email for many may require using public terminals in shared spaces such as libraries and schools (but where barriers to message reception can readily be eliminated).

Advantages of Universal Email

Email services can be used both for "telephone-type" messages and for other, usually longer, messages or documents that might otherwise be sent using facsimile or hard-copy postal services, both public and private. Compared with the telephone system, one primary advantage of an email service is that it eliminates "telephone tag." It also provides a content record of the interactions that can be retrieved, printed, studied, selectively forwarded, and in general reused. Other advantages are that it permits (but certainly does not require) more deliberative and reflective, but still interactive, conversational dialogs, as well as one-to-many and many-to-many conversations. These features have led to many new social, commercial, and political groupings of people: the "virtual communities" mentioned above, using email as the linkage.[6] It provides a common context among a set of participants.

Compared with postal services, an email service offers much faster mail delivery—usually minutes between any two locations in the United States (although currently, delays up to a day occur with some Internet access providers), compared with one to several days for postal systems. Email systems also afford much more flexibility (both locational and temporal) in that delivery. In the current postal system, a person's mail is delivered to one or two (or at most a few) fixed addresses (e.g., home or office). In most email systems, a person with the proper (portable) terminal equipment can log in to his or her "mailbox" from any location that has electronic access to the system. Today, this means that people can pick up their email from their office, their home, their hotel rooms, another office (perhaps in another city) they are visiting, or any site with a phone jack.[7] In the future, as terminal equipment gets smaller and cellular telephones become more ubiquitous, one will be able to pick up or send email while traveling in a car and flying in an airplane. This results in more geographic independence (where one gets mail) and temporal flexibility (when one gets mail).

These advantages are available in any email system. The additional advantage of a universal email system is that since everyone belongs to the system, a user can send email to anyone, not just a limited group, and receive email from anyone. This makes the special advantages of email available for all of one's correspondence, not just a subset. If the costs of such a service permit attractive pricing, it could take over a significant portion of the business of current postal services[8]—especially when next-generation email systems allow the transmission and viewing of multimedia messages containing high-resolution color pictures, "movie clips" of image sequences, and sound, which could, among other things, support a variety of "electronic commerce."

Disadvantages of Universal Email

The concept of universal email raises serious concerns as well. For example, individual users could get "flooded" with messages, unless some means of "filtering" incoming message traffic is provided. Also, some virtual communities enabled by email could be bad for U.S. society, rather than good; they could conceivably lead to a less-cohesive society, rather than a more-cohesive one.[9] It is also clear that within any email system, some users will be "more equal" than others; they will be able to purchase more powerful equipment, giving them more power over their electronic communication. Some will become more knowledgeable in the features and facilities of the system—permitting them, for example, to assemble tailored mailing lists for broadcast of their messages—allowing them to take advantage of those features for their own personal benefit or gain. Special-interest groups may in particular be motivated to become further empowered by use of these communication tools. Some (but not all) would also consider it a disadvantage that national borders become more transparent to international commerce and influences (Ronfeldt et al., 1993).

Motivations for Universal Email

The apparent advantages of universal email, despite the possible side effects and disadvantages, lead to a number of possible motivations for establishing such a service in the United States, ranging across the spectrum from the utilitarian to the idealistic. At the utilitarian end is efficiency. Electronic mail uses modern information and telecommunications technology to provide a much faster and more efficient means of conveying information from one point to another than current postal systems, which rely on "technologies"—letters written on paper, put in sealed envelopes, and physically transported from sender to receiver—over two millennia old. The increased speed and efficiency of information delivery by email could have many commercial and economic benefits, contributing to increased U.S. economic competitiveness.

At the idealistic end of the spectrum of motivations, the hypothesis is made that electronic mail makes possible much more egalitarian, deliberative, and reflective dialogs among individuals and groups. (See Sproull and Kiesler, 1991, for supporting evidence.) It might therefore lead to new social and political linkages within U.S. society, reduce the feelings of alienation that many individuals in the United States feel, give them a new sense of "community," revitalize the involvement of the common citizen in the political process, etc., and in general strengthen the cohesion of U.S. society.

Different motivations across this spectrum will appeal to different elements of U.S. society. To achieve widespread appeal—and political/economic support—a U.S. universal email service should satisfy a broad spectrum of these motivations, whether the system is "designed" to meet these objectives (e.g., with heavy U.S. government involvement) or evolves through private initiative and entrepreneurship subject to constraints, incentives, or standards that encourage universal access.

Conclusions and Recommendations

This report presents our considerations of the notion of universal access to electronic mail from demographic, technical, economic, social, and international perspectives.

Policy Conclusions and Recommendations

We find that use of electronic mail is valuable for individuals, for communities, for the practice and spread of democracy, and for the general development of a viable national information infrastructure. Consequently, the nation should support universal access to email through appropriate public and private policies.

The goal of achieving universal access has two main subgoals: (1) achieving interconnectivity among separate email systems and (2) widespread accessibility of individuals to some email system.

Universal connectivity among systems appears to be occurring through market forces, although the portability of email addresses and current regulations that distort the prices among potentially competitive communication offerings are likely to remain an issue.

Individuals' accessibility to email is hampered by increasing income, education, and racial gaps in the availability of computers and access to network services. Some policy remedies appear to be required. These include creative ways to make terminals cheaper; to have them recycled; to provide access in libraries, community centers, and other public venues; and to provide email "vouchers" or support other forms of cross subsidies.

The literature reviewed plus information gathered and analyzed in chapters 2 and 5 of this report [*not included here*] make clear the central role of email as the activity that promotes use of electronic networks; the role of these networks as social technologies is salient. Interpersonal communication, bulletin boards, conferences, and chat rooms, of course, also provide information and help individuals find or filter information from other sources.

Much study and discussion, both within our government and elsewhere, focuses on the content, design, and policies related to a "national information infrastructure." If this report demonstrates anything, it is the importance of person-to-person and many-to-many communication within such an infrastructure. Therefore,

It is critical that electronic mail be a basic service in a national information infrastructure.

To the extent that public policy guides the evolution of an NII, it should consider universal access to email as a cornerstone of that policy. Specifically, one-way information-providing technologies—whether broadcasting systems or technologies that provide only search and retrieval—are inadequate. Two-way technologies supporting interactive use and sending or dissemination by all users are key. And everyone should be able to participate:

It is important to reduce the increasing gaps in access to basic electronic information system services, specifically, access to electronic mail services.

Implementation of such policies should begin as soon as possible since it will undoubtedly take as much as a decade before full implementation is accomplished, no matter what strategy is envisioned. We recommend that the gaps that are greatest now and that are still widening be addressed first. Specifically these are deficits in access to computers and electronic networks found in the low-income and low-education segments of the population.

Directory services and addressing mechanisms must be considered core components. Additionally, any obstacles to full connectivity and interoperability must be minimized.

Virtually every study of electronic mail establishes that immediate convenient access is the single most powerful predictor of use. To the extent that national or other policies attempt to redress imbalances caused by the market for electronic access, we conclude that

Policy interventions should give priority to widespread home access.

In addition, and not as a substitute, multiple options for network access located in convenient places (including, for instance, libraries, schools, public buildings, hotel lobbies, business centers, and the like) are important auxiliary access sites. Such common facilities could be considered good locations for help or training centers as well.

Prior studies as well as information presented in chapters 2 and 5 of this report [*not included here*] show little reason to be concerned that citizens will abandon the needs of their local (physical) communities in favor of virtual communities in cyberspace. Rather, communications are typically addressed to a community of concerned individuals, and either for reasons of subject matter or prior acquaintance, these concerns are often (although not necessarily) geographically bounded. Thus, network access can be expected to enhance rather than detract from community involvement.

Provision of community services and activities online should be actively supported.

Local nonprofit providers experience many of the same resource constraints—costs, technical expertise, and so on—that households and individuals face. Engaging people in participatory democracy is not just a matter of giving citizens access but also a matter of enabling the service and information providers. Specific policies might be designed to facilitate and support the development of online civic activities offered by government agencies and nonprofit organizations.

Our study of the technical considerations in providing universal access to email concluded that

There are no fundamental technical barriers to providing universal access to electronic mail services.

We concluded that current and evolving Internet standards for email (SMTP and MIME, in particular), although perhaps not the definitive standards for electronic mail, provide a good basis for further evolution of a universal system. To the extent possible, gateways among dissimilar email systems should be avoided, or be regarded as only temporary measures, because information is lost at least one way, and possibly both ways, in such transactions. Therefore, migration of Internet standards down into organization-level systems appears preferable.

We find that access to, and the location of, physical devices for email use significantly affect universal access. With only about half of U.S. households containing personal computers by the year 2000, a robust set of alternative devices and locations is needed, including keyboard attachments to TV set-top boxes and video game machines, and extended telephones providing email (and likely integrated voice mail) access. Public access is vital, with libraries, post offices, kiosks, and government buildings each playing a role. There might well be a market for "pay" terminals analogous to the ubiquitous pay telephones.

The state of software for "user agents," "knowbots," and similar filtering programs appears capable of handling, sorting, prioritizing, and presenting the large volumes of email that may result from universal access. Similar technologies can give the user sufficient control over content (at least initially using the address or site that is the physical source of the material as an indicator of content; later "filters" may use other cues), so that avoiding objectionable materials should pose no greater problem than it does in other aspects of contemporary life.

We have concluded that email white pages or yellow pages directories will be developed by market forces, and therefore conclude that

There appears to be no need for governmental or regulatory involvement in the development, or centralization, of directories for universal email addresses (both white and yellow pages).

In considering the architecture of a universal email system, we were strongly influenced by the recommendations developed by the CSTB (Computer Science and Telecommunications Board, 1994):

The design of a universal email system should follow "open data network" guidelines, with a small number of transport services and representation standards (e.g., for fax, video, audio, text).

Upon this base, a larger but still quite bounded set of "middleware" services such as file systems, security and privacy services, and name servers may be built. An evolving, growing set of applications can then thrive without requiring redesign of the underlying "bearer" and "transport" portions of the network. This model closely resembles that developed over the last several decades within the Internet development community.

Until more is known about appropriate user-computer interfaces for all segments of our society (see our "Recommendations for Further Research," below), we believe that—to the extent inexpensive computing devices can support it—the "Web browsing" model for user interactions, including access to email services, is an important, highly usable interface model. Within the forseeable future, it is an important means of access to a burgeoning amount of online information and services. Because the cost of computing power continues to drop, we cautiously recommend

The "Web browser" model of user-computer interaction should at least be considered a candidate for the minimum level of user interface for email access as well as other hypertext-style access to information.

This report has considered the need for a simple email address system that gives every U.S. resident a "default" email address by which they can be reached. Such a development would "jump start" a universal access system, because governmental and other organizations could then assume that "everyone" was reachable by this means and design procedures and systems accordingly. The advantages of this approach lead to our recommendation that

A simple email address provision scheme should be developed giving every U.S. resident an email address, perhaps based on a person's physical address or telephone number.

If such a universal addressing scheme were developed, services would then be required, at least in transition, to "migrate" electronic materials received into paper form for persons not capable of, or desiring to, access them electronically. Such services could be provided by third-party entrepreneurs or established agencies and companies such as the U.S. Postal Service or one's local telephone service provider.

The economic analysis presented in chapter 4 suggests that economies of scope and scale on the supply-side, together with the easy substitutability among messaging and communications services on the demand-side, may result in both vertical and horizontal integration—and the formation of strategic alliances—of suppliers in related markets. The growing use of bundled offerings and term and volume discount pricing are consistent with that analysis. The convergence of previously distinct messaging and communications services, and the emergence of a unified communications/messaging environment, raise a number of significant public policy issues. The following are two major areas in which policy may need to be reformed:

1. Uniform regulatory treatment. It is virtually impossible to distinguish among video, voice, and data services in a modern digital environment. An email message may contain audio and video clips, and might substitute for video-on-demand offered by a cable television provider. However, video services can support data communication. Real-time interactive voice conversations can be carried by the Internet using a variety of commercially available software products, and many consumers access the Internet using modems and ordinary telephone lines.

Nevertheless, given their very different histories, voice, data, and video communications services have been treated very differently by regulators. With the convergence of the communications/messaging market, regulatory distinctions are creating artificial distortions in the marketplace and may be creating incentives for customers to use economically inefficient messaging options. The discussion in chapter 4 of this report [*not included here*] of access charges and the "enhanced service provider" exemption is one example of artificial cost differences that arise from regulations designed for one application (standard telephony) that must now compete with other applications. We conclude that

Policies developed separately for telephony, computer communications, broadcasting, and publishing that create artificial distinctions in the emerging information infrastructure should be reviewed, and a consistent framework should be developed that spans all the industries in the unified communications/messaging industry.

Address portability provides an example of the need for a consistent regulatory framework. Portability reduces the switching costs of consumers and increases market competitiveness. It was shown in chapter 4 of this report that with the use of bundling, the portability of telephone numbers could be negated through the use of nonportable email addresses.

Policy makers should develop a comprehensive approach to address, number, and name portability.

Efforts at implementing the above recommendation should be compatible with, and cognizant of, our earlier recommendation that "default" electronic addresses be provided for all U.S. residents. Although there may be some important trade-offs between address portability and simplicity of routing, policy makers should attempt to make this trade-off consistently across all competitors.

2. Open network architectures.   As technologies converge, each business and residence will have the choice of several access technologies and providers who will offer circuit- and packet-based services. In addition, multiple long-distance and international service providers will offer a comparable range of services.

Given the large sunk costs and nominal marginal usage costs of facilities-based providers, competition in raw transport is likely to be unstable. Providers are likely to integrate vertically or form alliances that allow them to differentiate their products. Regulations requiring the nondiscriminatory sale of unbundled transport may not be consistent with emerging vertical relationships and competition.

In the near term, regulation should adopt a light-handed approach that specifies minimum capabilities that can be transferred across networks to allow providers sufficient flexibility to develop enhanced features that differentiate their products. In the longer term, when technologies have more fully converged, subscription to multiple networks by each customer may be inexpensive and widespread, and regulations governing interconnections may not be necessary. Providers may then be free to differentiate their offerings based on market demand.

Our study of the economics of email provision concluded that subsidization for current household access could require approximately $1 billion per year, but we have mentioned (in chapter 4 of this report) interesting commercial experiments providing "free" email to those willing to accept advertising; similarly, "near-free" computers might be provided to those willing to subject themselves to additional advertising (e.g., on a built-in "screensaver" display). So the $1 billion amount may possibly be a mid-level estimate, not a minimum required.

Although email penetration is expanding rapidly, some program of economic assistance to marginal consumers may be necessary to achieve universal levels of services. Obligating service providers to offer subscriptions to large classes of customers at low rates that are financed by contributions from other services is unlikely to succeed in the competitive messaging industry. Instead,

Any email assistance will require public funding from an industrywide tax or from general revenues. Subsidies will need to be narrowly targeted to reach consumers who would not otherwise subscribe.

There are international dimensions to "universal" email within the United States. Policies to influence the development of a national email system should recognize the borderless nature of this technology. Perhaps more than other national systems, an email system will affect and be affected by worldwide standards, policies, and events.

The analysis in chapter 6 of this report [*not included here*] leads to the conclusion that democracy in the nations of the world is positively correlated with interconnectivity. In nations emerging into democracy, or attempting to, connectivity is likely to have a positive influence on democratization. We conclude that

The United States should support increased interconnectivity abroad, since this may aid the spread of democracy.

The results of this study support the conclusion that important results and benefits accrue to those becoming internetted, and that the problem to be addressed is the growing disparity among some society segments in access to that internetting. Universal access to electronic mail within the United States is an important solution strategy; achieving universal access will require dedication, focus, and cooperation by individual citizens, commercial companies, nongovernmental organizations, and government at all levels.

Recommendations for Further Research

Our research has uncovered inadequacies in the statistical data describing the phenomena we studied. We encountered other shortfalls in the existing literature or in current field experiments. We therefore recommend that the following research initiatives be undertaken to permit a better understanding of problems and issues related to universal access to email and related interactive information systems.

· Cost-benefit analysis should be initiated to answer the question: What mass of the U.S. population, if it were network-accessible, is necessary to support electronic delivery of major government services (e.g., filing Medicare claims or income tax forms, delivering at least some of the postal mail, or distributing Social Security benefits or disability benefits) in a cost-effective manner? It is possible that the benefits to many government agencies and other organizations could outweigh costs of subsidization, so that a straightforward business case could be made for universal access.

• A sizable and diverse number of "grass roots" civic networks (i.e., those not designed, like HomeNet, and supported as field research) should be selected and followed from conception through efforts to raise start-up funding, and so on until they have been operating for some years. Getting comparable information across such activities about what works and what does not through early to later stages in the introduction of these networks (including what proportion of them do not make it), plus the kinds of civic, social, and economic roles they play, would vastly enhance what we have been able to learn from cross-sectional studies and site visits at a single point in time.

• CPS data should be collected on a panel basis to monitor access to and uses and effects of computer networks. In particular, the success of policies and markets to close the identified gaps should be tracked and social benefits assessed. This may require revision or extension of CPS questions and administration schedules.

• Most email systems have been designed for use in academic or business settings. Better understanding of the capabilities and limitations of current user-computer interfaces is needed, especially related to electronic-mail handling. Existing interfaces rely on metaphors and analogies common to current users: multilevel "filing cabinets," commands to be issued, "Rolodex"-type address files, and forms to be filled out. How should these interfaces (including perhaps modest extensions of Web point-and-click browsers) evolve so that they can serve the entire range of users, including those in bottom-quartile income and education households? Field experiments concentrating on interface design for these prospective user groups are needed.

Notes

1. A brief history of the ARPAnet and Internet can be found in Lynch and Rose (1993), chapter 1.

2. Documentation on this point may be found, for example, in Sproull and Kiesler (1991).

3. Introductory materials on plans for the NII may be found at ⟨http://nii.nist.gov/⟩.

4. Documentation about the decline in U.S. "social capital" and its effect on the performance of representative government may be found in Putnam (1993) and Putnam (1995). Among the data cited in his 1995 article: U.S. voter turnout has declined by nearly a quarter from the early 1960s to 1990; Americans who report they have "attended a public meeting on town or school affairs in the past year" declined from 22 percent in 1973 to 13 percent in 1993; participation in parent-teacher organizations dropped from more than 12 million in 1964 to approximately 7 million today; since 1970, volunteering is off for Boy Scouts by 26 percent and for the Red Cross by 61 percent.

5. A MUD is variously defined as Multiple User Dimension, Multiple User Dungeon, or Multiple User Dialogue. It is a computer program allowing users to explore and help create an online environment. Each user takes control of a computerized persona/avatar/incarnation/character. The user can walk around, chat with other characters, explore dangerous monster-infested areas, solve puzzles, and even create his or her very own rooms, descriptions, and items. For further information see, for example, ⟨http://www.math.okstate.edu/~jds/mudfaq-p1.html⟩.

6. As one of many examples documenting this, see Klein (1995).

7. Email can also be forwarded automatically to an alternative mailbox (e.g., closer to a vacation spot or sabbatic location).

8. In this regard, it should be noted that the current U.S. Postal Service delivers two things: *information* (e.g., letters) and *bulk material* (e.g., packages). A universal email system should, in principle, be able to take over much of the information delivery functions; it obviously cannot handle the bulk material delivery functions. However, some bulk material consists of catalogs and advertising that may, in fact, increasingly become accessible electronically.

9. Potentially even worse could be hidden virtual communities—online underground communities hiding under encryption or just not advertising themselves.

References

Computer Science and Telecommunications Board (CSTB), National Research Council, *Realizing the Information Future: The Internet and Beyond*. National Academy Press, Washington, D.C., 1994.

Klein, H. K., "Grassroots Democracy and the Internet: The Telecommunications Policy Roundtable—Northeast USA (TPR-NE)," *Internet Society: INE '95 Proceedings*, 1995. Available at http://inet.nttam.com/HMP/PAPER/164/txt/paper.txt.

Lynch, Daniel, and Marshall Rose, *The Internet System Handbook*. Addison-Wesley, Reading, Massachusetts, 1993.

Mueller, Milton, and Jorge Reina Schement, *Universal Service from the Bottom Up: A Profile of Telecommunications Access in Camden, New Jersey*, Rutgers

University Project on Information Policy, Rutgers University School of Communication, 1995. Available at http://www.ba.com/reports/rutgers/ba-title.html.

Putnam, Robert D., *Making Democracy Work: Civic Traditions in Modern Italy.* Princeton University Press, Princeton, N.J., 1993.

Putnam, Robert D., "Bowling Alone: America's Declining Social Capital," *Journal of Democracy*, Vol. 6, No. 1, January 1995.

Ronfeldt, David, Cathryn Thorup, Sergio Aguayo, and Howard Frederick, *Restructuring Civil Society Across North America in the Information Age: New Networks for Immigration Advocacy Organizations*, RAND, DRU-599-FF, 1993.

Sproull, Lee, and Sara Kiesler, *Connections: New Ways of Working in the Networked Organization*. MIT Press, Cambridge, Mass., 1991.

12

Clinton Enlists Help for Plan to Increase Computer Use

Marc Lacey

February 2, 2000

President Clinton sought to build support today for his $2.3 billion initiative to bridge what he calls the digital divide by convening computer executives, including Steve Case of America Online, at an inner-city high school struggling to wire all its computers to the World Wide Web.

Mr. Clinton said the budget proposal he would unveil next week, which requires Congressional approval, will include tax incentives of $2 billion over 10 years as well as expanded grants to encourage the private sector to donate computers, sponsor technology centers in poor neighborhoods, and train those not yet connected to the Web.

Government studies have shown significant differences in Internet access of rich and poor. Households with incomes above $75,000 in urban areas are 20 times more likely to have access to the Web than the poorest households.

Racial disparities also exist, with black and Hispanic families 40 percent as likely as whites to have Internet access.

"It will be tragic if this instrument, that has done more to break down barriers between people than anything in all of human history, built a new wall because not everybody had access to it," Mr. Clinton said.

With the declared goal of making Internet access as common as telephone usage, Mr. Clinton would set aside $150 million to help train new teachers to better use technology.

His budget also calls for the creation of 1,000 community technology centers in low-income neighborhoods, at a cost of $100 million, and the launch of a $50 million pilot project to encourage private industry to provide home computers for the poor.

Another $10 million would go to a special program to help American Indians prepare for careers in information technology.

The centerpiece of the president's digital divide proposal, which he described January 27, 2000 in the State of the Union address as "a national crusade" to create "opportunity for all," would be $2 billion in tax incentives over the next decade to encourage companies to donate computers, sponsor schools, libraries, and community centers, and support technology training for workers.

Under current law, computer makers get a tax deduction for computers they donate to schools. The president's proposal would extend that benefit, which expires this year, until 2004 and broaden it to include donations to libraries and other community sites.

Congressional Republicans have shown support for Mr. Clinton's goal of hooking up more Americans to the Internet. But the specifics of a federal response are still being developed on Capitol Hill.

"I'm a little nervous about having the federal government dictate what gets done in school districts," said Senator Robert F. Bennett, the Utah Republican who heads the Senate High-Tech Task Force.

Mr. Clinton made his budget announcement at Ballou Senior High School in a struggling neighborhood in Washington, D.C. The school, which offers computer courses ranging from basic keyboarding to computer repair, was selected as an example of how schools in poor neighborhoods can keep up in the digital age.

The school's 140 computer terminals are now partially linked to the Internet. But several private companies and labor unions are working with officials there to begin technical training programs, upgrade the computer skills of teachers and wire the rest of the campus.

IV

Reality Check: Tracking a Moving Target in High-Tech Time

There is increasing evidence that the digital divide is largely disappearing under the relentless forces of decreasing costs for equipment and access, the greater value of email, and the wealth of shopping, entertainment, and information on the Web. Adam Clayton Powell III believes the persistence of a belief in such a gap is as much old news as the Dow breaking 1,000 (it was past 10,000 at this writing). "Misled by stereotypes, misinformed about survey techniques, and misdirected by interest groups," Powell lays much of the blame on the media. As with most innovations, there may have been such a gap in 1996 or 1997—as the Internet caught popular attention and was quickly used by early adopters. But the trends rapidly reversed, though the use of old data and unsophisticated analysis of the data did not catch up to reality.

The analysts who are cited in this section do not all agree on the interpretation of the data. But they all come to the same general conclusion: gaps are shrinking and the have-nots are not necessarily the groups we have been lead to believe they are.

In contrast to the NTIA and Vanderbilt studies, which highlight race and ethnicity as the focus of gaps, these more recent and sophisticated analyses (Stanford, Cheskin Research, and Forrester Research) find other variables most telling. The study by Nie and Erbring characterizes education and age as the critical factors determining Internet access and use. Cheskin discovered that computer availability in Hispanic households increased 50% faster in 1998 and 1999 than in the general population. The Harvard Kennedy School/NPR/Kaiser Foundation survey found that the most recent computer owners were more likely to come from groups who have historically been less likely to be computer owners.

The Forrester survey is the most comprehensive, being a representative sample of more than 80,000 U.S. households. It found that, contrary to some perceptions, Hispanic Americans (often lumped into "minorities" in other surveys) are more likely than Caucasians to be online, as are Asian American households. However, its large sample size allowed it to use statistical methods to determine that income was the best predictor for a household to be online, though age, education, and technology optimism played measurable roles. Though African American households lagged behind—based on income disparities, not ethnic causes—figure 14.1 lends support to the closing of any gap, as the rate of growth of online penetration was the highest for this group.

Taken together, these studies confirm that there are gaps, much as could be found in automobile ownership, newspaper subscriptions, or life insurance protection. But they confirm what Powell promotes: that the divide is not consistent across stereotypical groups and, most of all, it is rapidly narrowing even before the applications of major national initiatives.

The issue of gaps in the classroom has been a constant theme of the have/have-not issue since the dawn of the personal PC (see, for example, chapter 12). Over the 20-year history of PCs in the schools, lower-income districts have lagged behind wealthier school districts—as they have in textbooks, athletic equipment, or student/faculty ratios. Still, it's a receding problem. In 1982 a survey mentioned in chapter 4 found that two-thirds of the wealthiest school districts had at least one microcomputer, compared to two-fifths of the poorest schools. In the 1998–1999 school year, the article reprinted in chapter 15 reported that 90% of American schools had Internet access (and presumably therefore computers). More astounding was the slimness of the difference between the wealthiest and poorest communications: 94% of the former and 84% of the latter were online. A gap to be sure, but a small and surmountable one. And the reason, once again, has more to do with economics than with politics, a point made in the op-ed article from *The Wall Street Journal* that is included as chapter 16.

Charitable efforts, as reported in "This Internet Start-Up Looks to Conquer an Online Divide" (chapter 17), are individually too small to have much of an overall impact. The article does suggest that such efforts may be motivated by a perception of a chronic problem. But even here there is reinforcement of how the landscape is changing so rapidly that such charitable efforts may be unnecessary (we never had foundations giving away television sets in poor communities). Or better yet, the changing landscape makes their job easier and their funding go further. The Computers for Youth program it reports on provided free PCs to needy families along with three months of free Internet access. Thereafter recipients had to pay the designated ISP a monthly fee, though at an unspecified reduced fee. However, by the time the program was running, free Internet service providers had emerged, while others were offering deals such as six months free with a one-year contract. (That would average to $10.98 per month over the year.)

13

Data from Three Empirical Studies, 2000

Numerous studies addressing the Internet and/or information technology have been undertaken for a variety of needs. In many cases, only a small portion of each study is directly relevant to questions of the digital divide. Following are useful and relevant data, using a variety of methods, gleaned from a range of broader findings.

Internet and Society: A Preliminary Report

Norman H. Nie and Lutz Erbring

[Editor's note: *This study is based on data on a panel of households recruited as a random telephone sample of the U.S. population. In order to use the Internet for the purpose of efficient multi-channel data collection, each household in the sample—with or without prior Internet connection—was equipped with a WebTV® set-top box, with free Internet access and email accounts. The data for the study were collected in December 1999, from a national random sample of 4,113 individuals in 2,689 panel households. The margin of sampling error is about ±1.5% for results from the complete survey, and about ±2.5% for the subset of Internet users.*]

Myth and Reality of the "Digital Divide"

• *There are some demographic differences in Internet access.* (See figure 13.1.) Twenty-one percent of differences in Internet access can be explained by demographic factors. By far *the most important factors facilitating or inhibiting Internet access are education and age,* and not income—nor race/ethnicity or gender, each of which account for less

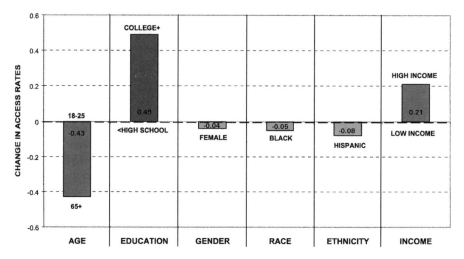

Figure 13.1
Differences in rates of Internet access: Effects of age, education, gender, race/ethnicity, and Income.

than 5 percent change in rates of access and are statistically insignificant. By contrast, a college education boosts rates of Internet access by well over 40 percentage points compared to the least educated group, while people over 65 show a more than 40-percentage-point drop in their rates of Internet access compared to those under 25. Age really reflects generational differences, and thus shows what to expect in the future.

• *There are few demographic differences in Internet use.* (See figures 13.2, 13.3.) Only 6 percent of differences in Internet use can be explained by demographic factors: Thus, *once people are connected to the Net they hardly differ in how much they use it and what they use it for*—except for a drop-off after age 65, and a faint hint of a gender gap. Demographic differences in Internet use involve at most an hour and a half a week, mainly reflecting people's time budgets and work status; and they involve hardly more than half an additional Internet activity, in the latter case reflecting levels of education. Instead—and above all—Internet use increases dramatically, both in terms of amount of time and in terms of range of activities, the longer people have been connected to the Internet, and this fact will make for steady growth in the future.

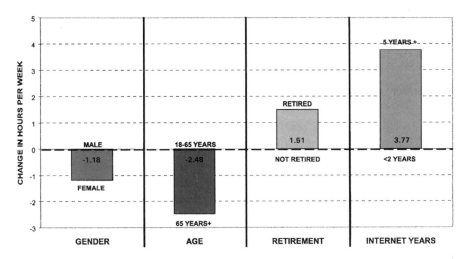

Figure 13.2
Differences in hours of Internet use: Effects of gender, age, retirement, Internet years.

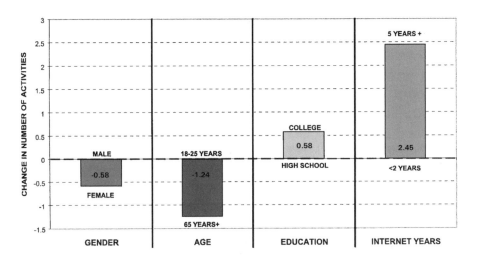

Figure 13.3
Differences in range of Internet activities: Effects of gender, age, education, Internet years.

The Digital World of Hispanics in the United States

Cheskin Research

Introduction

It is no secret that the U.S. Hispanic market has become fertile ground for companies who want to expand their market share or increase revenues. And, with the emergence of the Internet as a vehicle for the new economy, Hispanic consumers represent an untapped market in this new digitally connected world. While today's interest in the Hispanic market is not unexpected, the lack of past interest on the part of technology-producing companies is. Software and hardware manufacturers have paid little attention to this potentially lucrative segment. The result is a disparity in household computer ownership and access to the Internet between general and Hispanic markets. This disparity has translated into what has come to be known as the digital divide.

Research suggests there is a strong opportunity for companies to take the lead in narrowing the digital divide between the haves and have-nots. Why? Because consumption of technology is driven by information, and the Hispanic consumer has been routinely bypassed by traditional marketers.

[Editor's note: *Data are from a telephone survey of 2,017 Hispanic households that was conducted between February 1 and February 18, 2000. A nationally representative Hispanic surname sample was used. To be eligible to participate in the study, respondents needed to self-identify as having origins in a Spanish-speaking country and be 18 years of age or older.*]

Highlights

1 The Digital Divide Is Narrowing

Traditionally it had been believed that the Hispanic market was not worth investing in because it did not hold the promise of a strong economic future. However, technology adoption among Hispanic households is growing faster than previously believed [figure 13.4]. Currently 42% of U.S. Hispanic households have a computer. Using this data along with other documented statistics, we see that in the past

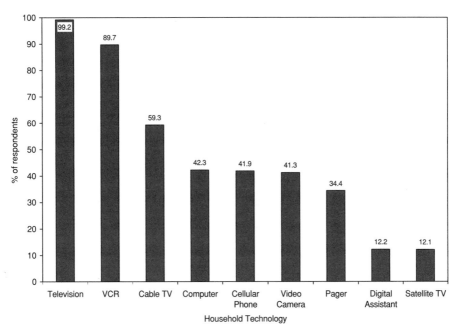

Figure 13.4
Technology penetration—households.
Note: Percentage base; all respondents = 2,017.

2 years, household computer penetration has increased approximately 43% in the general U.S. population and about 68% among U.S. Hispanics.

2   The Gap Is Due to Lack of Information, Not Just Economics

While the perception of high cost is still a strong barrier to computer ownership, lack of information and understanding of technology and its value are impediments that seem to actually be driving this [figure 13.5]. The same holds true for Internet usage where a key reason for not being online are the perceptions that it is not needed or enough is not known about it. Technology companies have not traditionally targeted this market so many of these consumers have not yet become aware of the convenience and utility of computers. Computer manufacturers who provide easy Internet access along with relevant benefit awareness may be able to significantly extend the reach of their brand.

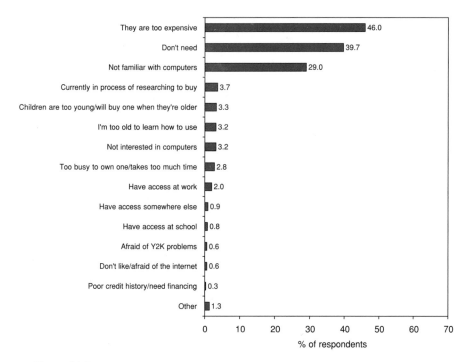

Figure 13.5
Reasons for not having a computer in the household—households.
Note: Percentage base; Households with no computer = 1,164.

Survey of Americans on Technology

National Public Radio, Kaiser Family Foundation, and Kennedy School of Government

[Editor's note: *This data is from a telephone survey conducted between November 15 and December 19, 1999, with a nationally representative sample. It is based on interviews with 1,506 adults, 18 years or older, including an oversample of African Americans.*]

4. When it comes to computers, would you say you are keeping up or being left behind?

	Keeping up	Being left behind	Don't know
Total	49	49	2
Adults under age 60	56	43	1

5. *(Asked of respondents who are being left behind)* Why do you think you have been falling behind?

	You don't have enough time	You don't have enough knowledge	It's too expensive	You're not that interested	Don't know
Total	22	23	18	36	2
Adults under age 60	27	22	20	30	1

20. *(Asked of respondents who do not have a computer at home to use)* What is the main reason you don't have a computer at home? Is it because:

	Total (%)	Adults under age 60 (%)
You don't know enough about computers to choose which one to buy	8	10
Computers are too expensive	33	44
You don't have time to learn how to use one	7	6
You don't need one	47	37
Don't know	5	4

21. *(Asked of respondents who do not have a computer at home or work to use)* Do you think it is a problem for you not having a computer?

21A. Is it a very serious, somewhat serious, or not very serious problem?

21/21A *Summary*

	Very serious problem	Somewhat serious problem	Not very serious problem	Not a problem	Don't know
Total	2	10	11	77	0
Adults under age 60	2	12	10	76	0

21. *(Asked of respondents who have a computer at home to use)* Do you have access to the Internet or email on your computer at home?

	Yes	No	Don't know
Total	79	21	0
Adults under age 60	77	22	0

Computer Use Summary

	Total (%)	Adults under age 60 (%)
Use either at home or work	70	81
Use at home	60	69
Have Internet/email	47	53
Don't have Internet/email	13	16
Use at work	44	53
Have Internet/email	29	34
Don't have Internet/email	15	19
Use only at home	26	27
Use only at work	10	12
Use at neither	30	19

[Analysis of study's authors:]

These Gaps May Be Narrowing   Nearly half (48%) of Americans under age 60 who make less than $30,000 now have a computer at home, and 31% have access to the Internet at home. Moreover, the most recent computer owners are more likely to come from the groups who have historically been less likely to be computer owners. Recent computer owners under age 60 (those who purchased their first computer within the past two years) are more likely than longer-term owners to be low-income (30% versus 14%) and to have a high-school education or less (59% versus 33%).

Racial Differences   While there has been much talk about the digital divide by race, we find that gaps between Blacks and Whites under age 60 are more pronounced in the home than at work. We also find they are more pronounced at lower-income levels than at higher-income levels. There is a gap of 11 percentage points between Blacks and Whites using computers at work (46% vs. 57%); but there is a larger, 22 point gap between Blacks and Whites who have a computer at home (51% vs. 73%). Similarly, a gap of 8 points exists between Blacks and Whites using the Internet at work (21% vs. 29%) compared with a larger 19 point gap in access to the Internet or email at home (38% vs. 57%). Although there is a 17 percentage-point gap in home-computer ownership between low-income Blacks and low-income Whites, the differences virtually disappear at upper-income levels.

Have-Nots under Age 60 Generally Share Positive Views about Technology with the Haves   The majority of people without computers under age 60, like people with computers, tend to say that computers (76%, 89%) and the Internet (56%, 76%) are making life better for Americans. Most have-nots and haves say that computers will widen the income/opportunity gap (42% and 47%) or make no difference (43% and 38%), though a few say that computers will narrow the gap (13% and 13%). Further more, the have-nots (85%) and haves (87%) say they are not concerned they might lose their jobs because of advances in technology. While have-nots (74%) are more likely to say they are being left behind by technology than haves (35%), only around one quarter of have-nots feel left out because they do not use a computer at work or at home (25%) or feel that not having a computer is a problem for them (24%). The main reason that have-nots under age 60 give for not having a computer is that they are too expensive (44%).

14

The Truth about the Digital Divide

Ekaterina O. Walsh with Michael E. Gazala and Christine Ham

Income Divides Consumers into Digital Haves and Have-Nots

The "digital divide"—the gap between the Internet haves and have-nots—is grabbing headlines, with much of the coverage suggesting that members of ethnic minorities lag behind online. Forrester's research confirms that a digital divide exists, but not all minorities show up on the wrong side of it. Our January 2000 representative mail survey of more than 80,000 U.S. households reveals that:

• *Asian and Hispanic Americans lead in online access.* Internet penetration among Asian American households already matches that of mass consumer technologies like cable TV, while Hispanic American households are 9% more likely than Caucasian ones to be online. Despite being the fastest-growing online group last year, African American households still lag behind all other groups in Internet adoption (see figure 14.1, part 1).

• *At-home Internet access grows for all ethnic groups.* In 1999, connectivity to the Net from home increased by at least 11% percent for all ethnic groups. Again, Asian and Hispanic American households lead (see figure 14.1, part 2.) Because African Americans are least likely to own a PC, they are also least likely to connect from home (see figure 14.1, part 3). Focusing solely on PC owners, we find no differences in quality of access: Across the board, about 60% purchased their computers in 1998 or 1999, virtually all home PCs feature modems, and most users dial in at 56 Kbps.

• *Income drives Internet access ...* Although a combination of factors determines consumer likelihood to be online, income is the strongest predictor—across ethnic groups, online penetration rises as income rises. Other drivers of Internet use include age, education, and technology

US online penetration by ethnic background

		Percent online in January 2000	Percent online in January 1999	1999 growth rate
Caucasian-American	(C. Am.)	43%	34%	27%
African-American	(Af. Am.)	33%	23%	44%
Hispanic-American	(H. Am.)	47%	36%	33%
Asian-American	(As. Am.)	69%	64%	8%
All households		43%	35%	23%

Ethnic groups are ordered by number of US households (most to least)

1-2   **Locations where households connect to the Internet**

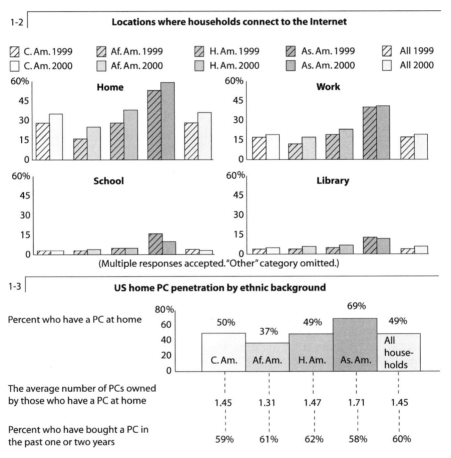

C. Am. 1999   Af. Am. 1999   H. Am. 1999   As. Am. 1999   All 1999
C. Am. 2000   Af. Am. 2000   H. Am. 2000   As. Am. 2000   All 2000

Home   Work   School   Library

(Multiple responses accepted. "Other" category omitted.)

1-3   **US home PC penetration by ethnic background**

Percent who have a PC at home

	C. Am.	Af. Am.	H. Am.	As. Am.	All households
	50%	37%	49%	69%	49%
The average number of PCs owned by those who have a PC at home	1.45	1.31	1.47	1.71	1.45
Percent who have bought a PC in the past one or two years	59%	61%	62%	58%	60%

Source: Forrester Research, Inc.

Figure 14.1
Internet and PC penetration among ethnic groups.
Source: Forrester Research, Inc.

optimism (see figure 14.2). Ethnic background alone does not explain the existence of a digital divide: Once statistical analyses take into account the impact of income, age, education, and technology optimism, ethnic background does *not* materially influence online adoption (see the March 3, 1999 Forrester Brief, "The Digital Melting Pot").

• *... therefore, African Americans' online usage lags behind.* More than one in four African American households lives on less than $15,000 per year, compared with only 7% of Asian, 14% of Hispanic, and 17% of Caucasian American households that do so. As long as income remains a critical driver of online adoption and household incomes differ markedly across ethnic groups, the United States will be stuck with a digital divide.

The Digital Divide Closes Online

Once online, the digital divide virtually disappears. Regardless of ethnicity, consumers use the Internet for the same reasons and to do the same things (see figure 14.3, part 1).

• *Communicate.* A shared motivation—cheap and quick communication —compels almost all consumers to go online. Sending email is the most popular online activity for all consumers, and more than two-thirds of respondents in each ethnic group say that it prompted them to get wired. Furthermore, ethnic background appears to have little impact on the uptake of newer online communication technologies like chat and instant messaging.

• *Access information.* Online consumers of all ethnic groups mine the Internet for information on everything from the weather to nutrition guides. Only minor differences exist in the *types* of information that interest various ethnic groups: African Americans, for example, are more likely to seek health and job information, while more Asian Americans use search engines and browse newspapers and magazines.

• *Have fun.* The quest for entertainment consistently influences how consumers of all ethnic backgrounds use the Internet. Again, only minor differences exist in the types of entertainment they seek—African Americans are more likely to play games online and Asian Americans are more likely to download music.

• *Shop.* At first glance, the data shows deeper eCommerce penetration among Asian Americans—they are 30% more likely than any other ethnic group to buy online. But examination of specific online purchases by ethnic group reveals that all consumers progress almost in lock step

Factors influencing Internet adoption

	C. Am.	Af. Am.	H. Am.	As. Am.
Median annual household income	$40,000	$31,000	$40,000	$65,000
Median age	47	44	40	36
College educated*	29%	24%	26%	60%
Technology optimists	51%	61%	58%	76%

*The college-educated category includes those who have
either a college, graduate, or professional degree

Income is the main driver of Internet adoption

	C. Am.	Af. Am.	H. Am.	As. Am.
Less than $15,000	11%	7%	13%	35%
$15,000 to $24,999	25%	19%	35%	56%
$25,000 to $34,999	37%	36%	40%	71%
$35,000 to $49,999	48%	44%	50%	75%
$50,000 to $69,999	59%	51%	62%	74%
$70,000 to $99,999	64%	55%	68%	69%
$100,000 or more	68%	65%	72%	79%

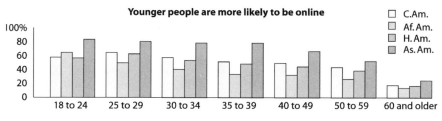

Younger people are more likely to be online

☐ C.Am. ☐ Af.Am. ◩ H.Am. ▨ As.Am.

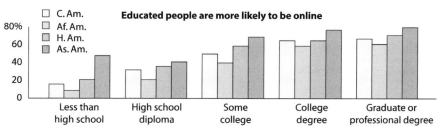

Educated people are more likely to be online

☐ C.Am. ☐ Af.Am. ◩ H.Am. ▨ As.Am.

Technology optimists are more likely to be online

	C. Am.	Af. Am.	H. Am.	As. Am.
Percent of technology optimists online	58%	39%	57%	75%
Percent of technology pessimists online	28%	22%	33%	51%

Source: Forrester Research, Inc.

Figure 14.2
Ethnic background does not materially influence Internet adoption.
Source: Forrester Research, Inc.

Across ethnic groups, consumers use the Net for the same reasons

	C. Am.	Af. Am.	H. Am.	As. Am.
Communication				
Send email	92%	86%	89%	92%
Use instant messenging	21%	19%	23%	21%
Participate in chats	16%	17%	21%	22%
Seek access to information				
Use search engines	73%	63%	71%	77%
Seek medical or health information	32%	40%	36%	30%
Read daily newspapers and magazines	27%	36%	32%	43%
Seek job information	21%	38%	30%	30%
Entertainment				
Play games	25%	33%	26%	18%
Visit sports sites	20%	21%	20%	22%
Download music	12%	17%	16%	20%

Note: Percentages are based on number of online households.

All consumers buy convenience goods the most

	C. Am.	Af. Am.	H. Am.	As. Am.
Of online households				
Research purchases online	44%	40%	43%	57%
Purchase online	51%	40%	49%	61%
Of online purchasing households				
Amount spent online in the last three months of 1999	$254	$225	$254	$331
Convenience items				
Books	61%	60%	56%	65%
Music	48%	57%	52%	54%
Videogames	41%	38%	41%	42%
Clothing	38%	40%	33%	36%
Videos	31%	37%	36%	39%
Software	47%	48%	47%	48%
Flowers	22%	25%	26%	29%
Jewelry	10%	12%	11%	12%
Researched items				
Airline tickets	40%	43%	43%	60%
Hotel reservations	29%	31%	31%	42%
Computer hardware	29%	25%	29%	42%
Consumer electronics	18%	17%	19%	35%
Furniture	3%	6%	4%	4%
Replenishment items				
Health and beauty aids	20%	23%	24%	26%
Food and beverages	14%	16%	16%	17%

(Multiple responses accepted. Some categories omitted.)

Source: Forrester Research, Inc.

Figure 14.3
Ethnic groups' online activites are all the same.
Source: Forrester Research, Inc.

through a retail adoption cycle—buying convenience items the most, researched products second, and replenishment goods the least (see figure 14.3, part 2).

How to Reach Ethnic Groups Online

Our findings about various ethnic groups' online use have two implications for companies targeting ethnic groups on the Internet:

1. *Ethnic flavor alone does not lure visitors.*   The immaterial impact of ethnic background on online behaviors highlights the need for sites to offer more than a generic ethnic label to attract visitors. Online users are not only Asian, African, Hispanic, Polish, or Irish Americans—each of them also has specific individual interests, ranging from arts and gardening to hunting and fishing, that are stronger drivers of surfing behavior.

2. *Ethnic sites should specialize.*   The era of the broad-based portal is coming to an end—Forrester expects that only three will remain by 2004 (see the December 1999 Forrester Report, "The Parting Of The Portal Seas"). Niche sites hold the best chance of survival, and this trend applies to ethnic sites, too. With their clear differentiation, batanga.com—which specializes in alternative Hispanic music for 16- to 28-year-olds— and minorityinterest.com—promising to connect minority users with minority-owned businesses—have an edge amid the clamor of broad-based ethnic portals.

15

Internet Access Spreads to More Classrooms, Survey Finds

Pamela Mendels

December 1, 1999

Anyone seeking a gauge of how fast computer technology is spreading through the American public school system need only look at a recent report published by a major education market-research company.

Some highlights of the report:

• In the 1998–1999 school year, there was an average of one computer for every six students in schools. Five years earlier, the figure was one for every 11 students.

• Today, 90 percent of American schools report having Internet access. Three years ago, when researchers first began asking schools about access, the figure was 32 percent.

• About 71 percent of schools have Internet access in at least one classroom, indicating that access is spreading beyond school libraries and computer labs. More than half of schools have a home page on the World Wide Web. Almost half—49 percent—are opting for high-speed Internet access through T1 lines, a jump from 35 percent in 1998. And 54 percent of schools report that a majority of their teachers are now using the Internet in instruction.

The report, "Technology in Education 1999," is an annual look at computers in the schools by Market Data Retrieval, a unit of Dun & Bradstreet Corp. that specializes in the education market. It is based on a survey answered by officials at almost half of the 86,700 public schools in the United States during the 1998–1999 school year.

Kathleen Brantley, who oversaw the report as director of product development for the company, said the big trend that emerged from the 148 pages of statistics and graphs is the growing presence of the Internet in schools. "The explosion of the Internet continues," she said. "We also see that the Internet is migrating out of the library and computer labs and into the classroom."

But the numbers also indicate that the country has yet to reach a goal set by the United States Department of Education: that there be one modern computer for every five students in public schools. The survey found a ratio of one for every 10 students.

The Internet invasion is not coming without a big price tag. The report estimates that schools spent about $5.53 billion on technology in the last school year, or about $119 per student. As a result, Brantley said, the taxpayers footing the bill increasingly want to know whether the investment is paying off. "The real question is how much and how effectively are the machines being used," she said.

In addition, Brantley said, the numbers show a continuing "disturbing" pattern that many have come to call the digital divide. Schools with high poverty rates and a high percentage of minority students are less likely to have up-to-date technology than others. For example, 94 percent of schools in the wealthiest communities have Internet access, while 84 percent of the schools in the poorest areas do.

For B. Keith Fulton, director of technology programs and policy at the National Urban League in New York, these numbers mean that the public school system is falling down on the job when it comes to assisting those with the greatest need to familiarize themselves with computers. Poor and minority children often do not have a computer to tinker with at home, so it is especially important that technology be available to them at their schools, he said.

"Citizens should be able to expect a decent public education," Fulton said. "To the extent that schools are not providing students with meaningful connectivity, they are failing their mandate to provide a good public education."

Fulton also said he believes more attention needs to be paid to how the Internet is being employed in the classroom. "Access is part of the picture," he said, "but access doesn't mean use, and use doesn't always mean meaningful use."

It is a point echoed by William L. Rukeyser, coordinator of Learning in the Real World, a group based in Woodland, Calif., that advocates more skepticism about the benefits of technology in the classroom. He said the survey findings point to an urgent need for policy makers to turn their attention to basic pedagogy: where the Internet improves education and where it does not. Calculating the number of computers in schools, he said, is not the same as measuring the amount of learning taking place at keyboards.

"We may find our dollars are better spent making sure there are a relatively small number of very up-to-date pieces of equipment focused on those areas where it has proved its effectiveness," Rukeyser said.

In addition, he said, educators should be asking some tough questions about educational content, like whether dazzling graphics on CD-ROMs and Web sites are a hindrance, rather than an aid, to education. "Is there a chance kids will concentrate on the sizzle and not pay attention to the steak?"

16

Cheap Computers Bridge Digital Divide

John Simons

In his State of the Union address [January 2000], President Clinton plans to ask Congress for as much as $50 million to provide computers and Internet access to poor households. Earlier this month Bill Bradley bemoaned the comparatively low rates of Internet access among such groups; Al Gore frequently boasts that the administration has a $2.25 billion program to link schools and libraries to the Internet. "It's the new new thing in politics," says Timothy Adams, a Washington-based consultant who is studying the digital divide for the George W. Bush presidential campaign. "Every politician wants to be tech-savvy yet also grounded in representative politics. It's the perfect compassionate message."

But is the digital divide really a problem that requires a government solution? At first glance, the numbers suggest so. Households with incomes of $75,000 and higher are at least 20 times as likely to have access to the Internet than those at lower income levels and nine times as likely to own a computer. Even at the highest income levels, Blacks are slightly less likely than Whites to own a computer or have Internet access at home. And while Blacks make up 10% of the nation's work force, they hold only 5% of information technology jobs. Hispanics comprise 9% of the overall work force, and occupy just 4% of IT jobs.

But if the digital divide is defined solely as a question of who does and does not have the ability to surf the Web, then it's hardly an intractable crisis. The average price of a fully loaded desktop computer has fallen 44%, to $844, in the past three years, according to market-research firm PC Data Inc. That's still a big investment for a lower-income family, but most analysts foresee those price tags dropping even further.

PC ownership has reached a near-saturation point among middle- and upper-income families. If computer makers wish to maintain the extraordinary revenue growth they've seen over the last half-decade, they will soon be forced to seek out new first-time buyers. Some PC companies no doubt will push hard to find willing buyers among the 13.5 million U.S. households with annual incomes less than $25,000, 90% of which do not own a computer. "It's a viable market, and the demand is there," says Eric Schmitt of Forrester Research.

For those who can't afford a new computer, there will always be a brisk market for secondhand PCs. In addition, smaller, less expensive hand-held devices will offer alternatives to computers at even lower prices. Internet access rates are likely to fall too. In fact, in the never-ending fight for "eyeballs" online, companies such as AltaVista, Excite At Home and Yahoo! have recently announced plans to offer free Internet service.

Predictably, some of these trends have already begun to close the divide. This year, Forrester Research expects African American households to outpace all other demographic groups in the rate at which they will make their initial forays online. Even the scarcity of minorities in information industries is a problem the market will likely mitigate. The Information Technology Association of America (ITAA) estimates that some 400,000 jobs in the sector are vacant because companies can't find skilled workers. Each year, as a result of severe worker shortages, software and hardware manufacturers expend precious political capital lobbying Congress to raise the annual cap on workers they can hire from overseas. And every year, after much debate, Congress raises the yearly limit.

But Silicon Valley realizes it needs to develop more homegrown talent. ITAA will unveil a new "digital opportunity" initiative under which its member companies will offer internships to talented minority students.

Some companies have already created their own programs. Cisco Systems Inc. started its Cisco Networking Academy two years ago. It donates equipment to high schools and community centers in empowerment zones. Students learn how to build, design, and maintain networks. Last year, the company spent $20 million on the academies, which now exist in some 2,500 locations; this year they've budgeted $30 million. A graduate of Cisco's two-year program can enter the job market with a starting salary between $30,000 and $60,000 per year. Hewlett-Packard, 3Com, Intel, Lucent Technologies, and Microsoft run similar programs.

Government can play a small but useful role. As part of the 1996 Telecommunications Act, telecom companies pledged to deploy new services—such as high-speed Internet access and digital cable—to rural areas and inner cities. The Federal Communications Commission should keep a watchful eye on megafirms like America Online–Time Warner to make sure they live up to this commitment. Policy makers should also consider offering tax incentives to companies that provide technical school-to-work training. For the poorest of the poor, government might consider subsidizing public street-corner Internet kiosks, as it did with public telephones decades ago. But we don't need massive new government programs to bridge the ever-dwindling digital divide.

17

This Internet Start-Up Looks to Conquer an Online Divide

Timothy Hanrahan

Elisabeth Stock is one of the few Internet entrepreneurs not trying to strike it rich.

You couldn't tell from the array of blue-chip partners Ms. Stock has lined up in the past year, which includes Microsoft Corp., Citigroup Inc., and iVillage.com Inc. Ms. Stock has a dot-com pedigree in the form of an engineering degree from Massachusetts Institute of Technology and has earned her stripes by setting up a complex supply system to refurbish and reprogram Pentium-class personal computers. She's taking aim at a vast market—Black and Hispanic families—and has earned raves from her backers.

"Elisabeth had done a business plan you could've started a billion-dollar company with," says Chip Raymond, president of Citigroup Foundation.

So why isn't an initial public offering in the future for Ms. Stock? Because while dot-coms have made multimillionaires out of untold 25-year-olds, dot-orgs don't go public.

Given her resume, the 31-year-old Ms. Stock could probably command a boatload of venture-capital dollars and the attention of legions of marketers. But that isn't her goal—instead, as the executive director of the not-for-profit group Computers for Youth (CFY) ⟨http://www.cfy.org⟩, she's trying to bring affordable Internet access to the homes of minority children who otherwise wouldn't have it, and back it up with relevant Web content and full-bore technical support.

"People think the digital divide is about access or technology, but it's about a lot more," she says. "There's all these other pieces—tech support, content and training."

Complicated Puzzle

Putting those pieces together isn't easy.

A warm Saturday morning in December finds Ms. Stock in the South Bronx, leading a small army of volunteers who have been enlisted to distribute PCs at KIPP Academy. Twenty kids, all with at least one parent or older sibling in tow, have come into school to take in a three-hour training session—and take home a personal computer. Many will have Internet access by sundown.

KIPP is made up entirely of Black and Hispanic students, 95% of whom get free or subsidized lunches, a key statistic in measuring relative economic need. KIPP also happens to be one of the most demanding public middle schools in the borough, while being relatively small. Those are two of the reasons its students were the first to receive computers from CFY.

By the end of the 1999–2000 school year, all 220 students at the school and 30 teachers will receive computers. But first come the training sessions—five weekend sessions from CFY have been held since late October.

This particular Saturday, Computers for Youth volunteers hand out user names and passwords to the students and set up 20 PCs—one per family—in two brightly painted classrooms across the hall from each other. Two volunteer trainers use overhead projections on chalkboards to walk students and their parents through Windows 98 menus and arcane Word functions. Nearby, other volunteers are helping debug problems that students from the previous training session haven't been able to solve. One student forgot his email password and has popped by the school to get it; in just a week, he had more than 100 messages in his in-box.

Bridging the Divide

As volunteers swirl around classroom desks helping kids keep up with the instructors' sessions, Ms. Stock looks in control.

"You look so calm," says Morra Aarons, a public-relations manager for iVillage.

"I just look calm," Ms. Stock responds. After all, it's only the third training session she's done.

These training sessions are just the beginning. A crucial piece of bringing Internet access to the children is distributing used PCs to families, to be sure. But that's just the start: In Ms. Stock's view, such efforts to bridge the "digital divide" in the United States will fail if the children don't find online content tailored for them or are frustrated because they can't get the technical support they need.

The digital divide is the name given to the gap in Internet usage between rich and poor and between Black and White. The Commerce Department's findings last July that Internet use was higher among wealthier families came as no surprise. What did grab headlines, however, was that regardless of household income, Blacks and Hispanics use the Internet less than Whites and Asians do.

If this remains true, the fear is that many families could be left out of the high-tech explosion that has changed the face of not only American business but also American culture. The Internet boom has created vast wealth for entrepreneurs bright enough or lucky enough to get in on the ground floor of successful start-ups, but it's also changing the lives of people in countless ways big and small. It's meant filing taxes electronically, sending email or chat messages to distant friends and family members, or shopping for a better job or that Ricky Martin compact disk without leaving the home.

Going Online

These are the kind of things inner-city families have been missing—and that Ms. Stock hopes her program will give them. Audrey Greenidge, an eighth grader at KIPP who received her computer through Computers for Youth in late November, already sees a change in the way she does her homework.

"It helps to get a computer at home—you're able to get more done," she says. "At school, the computers were mostly used by other people."

Now that kids have computers at home, teachers are assigning homework that requires students to go on the Web—take a recent assignment to write a report on diamonds, quartz, and coal. Teachers are also asking that homework be typed, not handwritten—and instead of note-books, kids are starting to bring in computer diskettes.

Before getting the computer, Audrey "used to come home and go back out to the library," says Gail Greenidge, adding that now her daughter "can do her research here." Neither mother nor daughter has made an online purchase yet, but Ms. Greenidge says she's done some "browsing and window shopping."

Ms. Greenidge has two worries about Internet access: potentially inap-propriate conversations in chat rooms (she's told her daughter to stay within her age group when chatting online) and the fact that the Internet ties up the family's phone line. Like she does with television-watching, Ms. Greenidge is considering putting a limit on how much time her daughter can spend online.

"It's not a problem yet, but I can foresee a problem—so I have to set a schedule," she says.

Computers for Youth's focus on the home is relatively unique. While President Clinton has pledged to bring Internet access to all Americans, his vision is of providing that access in schools and community centers. Ms. Stock, however, believes that providing PCs for family households goes most directly to the disparity in Internet access. "We figure if the problem is in the home, let's solve the problem in the home," she says.

Ms. Stock got the idea for her program during a stint as a White House fellow in the office of the Vice President, during which she devel-oped a program, known as Computers for Learning, that allowed federal agencies to donate computers directly to schools.

At the time, though, she recalls thinking: "Hey, this is a good idea, but wouldn't it be better if we got computers from businesses, whose com-puters are newer—and put computers in the home."

Finding Resources

In December 1998, she met with Dan Dolgin, who had recently founded Computers for Youth, thinking he'd be a competitor. Instead, he offered her the top job with the group, which she accepted in February 1999. Mr. Dolgin, a corporate lawyer and investor, remains chairman.

After that came the tough business of raising funds, building partner-ships, and tracking down companies that were willing to donate PCs, software, and services. Within a year, she had persuaded Microsoft to donate about $150,000 worth of software, New York City Internet provider Panix to offer low-cost Internet access, and iVillage to publish content on its site customized for Computers for Youth ⟨http://www. ivillage.com/click/features/projectconnect⟩. Funding came from the likes of Home Box Office, Citigroup, and the U.S. Department of Education.

Other partners include help-desk firm C3i, which will train high-school students to man help desks for Computers for Youth users with the help of software donated by International Business Machines Corp.'s Lotus Development unit; umbrella volunteer group New York Cares; and Solid Oak Software, which donated Cybersitter filtering software. A crucial piece of the puzzle was provided by the New York City Board of Education, which is allowing Computers for Youth to use warehouse space in Long Island City to store donated machines before they're distributed to students.

Mr. Raymond, who heads Citigroup's philanthropic arm, says giving $15,000 to Computers for Youth wasn't a tough call once he met Ms. Stock: "A person who's this enthusiastic, with her background, who's willing to start a not-for-profit when you could go off and make a lot of money? I'm very impressed."

Colleen Farell, Microsoft's community and media-relations manager for New York, cites "the thoroughness of the program ... the whole infrastructure" that Ms. Stock had developed.

Ms. Stock's current challenge is to finish distributing the 250 computers at KIPP—she is about halfway done—and figure out which school should be next. She selected KIPP in part because of its strong academics and its dedicated students. Now, she wants to choose the next school, and ramp up the pace of PC rollouts.

"Once this thing purrs, we can expand it" quickly, she says. She is aiming to distribute another 500 computers by the end of the school year: about 200 to homes and 300 for use within schools as part of various projects.

Ms. Stock also faces the quickly changing economics of the Internet. Currently, Computers for Youth pays for families' first three months of Net access; after that, families must pay Panix, ⟨http://www.panix. com⟩, a reduced monthly rate. Ms. Stock considered using a provider of free Internet access, but decided that free services were too new and unproven, and their banner ads too intrusive. Moreover, she says, Panix has a "track record of excellent service."

Computers for Youth will continue seeking ways to cut costs, Ms. Stock says, but adds that if the tumbling prices of new PCs fall far enough, refurbishing donated PCs may not make sense anymore. But no matter: If PCs get really cheap, she says, Computers for Youth will devote more of its efforts to training, content, and support.

"The question [people ask] is 'How do we use this?'" she says. "That's why we feel that the training is so important. If you've never sent and received an email, you don't know what the hype is all about."

V

What's It All Mean?

This final section tries to pull some of the material together. It is likely that one person's gap is another person's crevice.

Jorge Schement, co-author of the study in chapter 5 and a long-time chronicler of the social and cultural side of universal service issues, provides useful insight into gaps in chapter 18. Gaps that have involved information goods (televisions, radios) have quickly disappeared. They require a one-shot investment. Information services (telephone, cable) have lingered. Services require ongoing payments. His conclusion is that Internet access is a service issue. Therefore policy should concern itself with its diffusion (presumably rather than with providing the devices themselves). However, Schement also recognized that the diffusion of telephone and cable service has defied decades of policy-tinkering to eliminate all gaps, which may raise a red flag on how to approach Internet access policy. Moreover, just as broadcast television proliferated because the service was "free" to the consumer, the likely spread of free or advertising or other privately subsidized Internet access should quickly move the Internet into the information goods category.

Adam Clayton Powell III is far more direct than Schement. Yes, there may have been a gap for a short while in the first few years following the popularization of the Internet. But any gap is closing, if not gone. The continued insistence that there is a digital divide, says Powell, is the result of stereotypes and misleading survey data, well-meaning but misguided interest groups, and a mass media machine that keeps the perception alive. He argues that federal initiatives aimed at eliminating a nonexistent divide are misdirected.

As the editor of this volume, I get the last word, in print at least. Picking up where Powell leaves off, I add further indicators that any gap is rapidly closing well before the impact of federal dollars have had a chance to filter into the system. Furthermore, if we were serious about gaps among groups, we would look at other areas where the disparities in costs are far greater than the relatively few dollars involved in Internet access and computer ownership. My policy recommendation: declare the war against the digital divide won and move on to issues with higher stakes.

18

Of Gaps by Which Democracy We Measure

Jorge Reina Schement

There was a time when gaps in the social fabric ripped the picture of America as the land of opportunity. Franklin D. Roosevelt addressed the reality of that image at his second inaugural: he looked out beyond his audience and declared, "I see one-third of a nation ill-housed, ill-clad, ill-nourished."[1] In so doing, he tapped into one of the most enduring apprehensions within American culture. Americans, then, found Roosevelt's gaps terrifying. Today, we find a second group of gaps discomforting.

That gaps fix our attention shouldn't surprise us. After all, we have built our edifice of democracy on the promise of freedom and justice for all, and over the centuries we have come to emphasize the *all*. Unlike the Europeans left behind, who accepted a social order where some were meant to rule and others to be ruled, we agreed to no such determination. And we still don't.

Entering the Information Age, we carry our convictions with us. No matter the new era, we firmly believe that access to communications technologies is the primary policy tool for enabling *all* citizens to participate in those economic, political, and social activities fundamental to a democratic society that is also a good society. We see an accessible National Information Infrastructure (NII) as the essential ingredient for overcoming social fragmentation and, consequently, for enabling participation. In this world, communication creates society, and, in essence, the NII creates the weave that holds us together. So, when we observe or imagine that some are falling behind, we pause as the promise of democracy falters—thus our anxiety over gaps, especially information gaps.

A decade of research has documented the existence and persistence of a number of gaps in access, of which the following have received some attention (with the groups identified as lagging in parentheses):

• Telephone access (minorities; women with children; Native Americans; renters; the unemployed; some states like New Mexico, Texas, West Virginia);
• Internet access (African Americans; Native Americans; rural households outside of towns; women in certain income groups; the elderly);
• Households with PCs (minorities, especially African Americans and Native Americans; households below median income; women in certain income groups; the unemployed; high-school graduates); and
• Households with cable (women in certain income groups; renters; Whites).

At first glance, there appears to be a bewilderment of groups lagging behind the majority when it comes to access. Yet, many researchers and policy makers see these "gaps" more simply; most of the groups affected can be classified into a familiar category—women and minorities—while the cause appears quite simply to be income. So, where's the crisis? We have subsidy policies in place to assist poor households when applying for telephone service, which has been deemed essential. As for the others, we have no consensus on the necessity of cable, PCs, nor Internet access. What gaps exist must be there because of disparities in income, something no democracy protects one against.

This picture, simple, familiar, and comfortable, is also wrong. To be sure, income affects access—the more you have of one, the more you have of the other. However, other factors influence access in ways that perplex researchers and complicate the picture. For example, minority households below median income lag behind majority households in telephone penetration, even when they have the same income. Whereas minorities lag behind Whites in PC ownership, Hispanics appear to exhibit the highest rate of increase in buying PCs. And, while Whites list both children and jobs as motivators for purchasing PCs, Blacks (a group at zero population growth) prioritize children, while Hispanics (the group with the most children) prioritize jobs. When it comes to premier cable subscriptions, Blacks lead all other groups—as they do in the purchase of advanced telephone services. Elderly households are more likely to subscribe to a telephone than are young households with children, even in the same income bracket. Upper-middle-class Black households lag behind upper-middle-class White households when it comes to Internet access, and, for the moment, women lag behind men—but that gap appears to be narrowing. In other words, income alone explains not one of these gaps. Other factors contribute, sometimes in degrees that challenge our intuition.

Even so, do all of these gaps demand our attention? The question has merit; after all, in a world of limited resources, sound policy requires careful application. Moreover, in such a world, one may reasonably ask whether the gap is persistent or transitory. In theory, gaps that persist cause more damage to the promise of democracy than those likely to close after a reasonably short time. As a result, we acknowledge the potential magnitude of gaps at the same time that their symptoms confuse us.

Under these circumstances, an analysis of historical gaps can be instructive. In the first place, all new technologies diffuse unevenly; some individuals will adopt them early on, while others will lag after the majority. That said, information and communication technologies display some contrasting patterns of diffusion. Consider radio, television, and VCRs versus telephone, electricity, and cable.

In 1925, less than 10% of all households owned radios. By 1930, ownership stood at 46%. Ten years later, as the Depression lingered, Americans still managed to increase ownership of radios to 82% of all households. They bought radios at an astonishing rate, so that by 1950 radio had achieved saturation. In that year, less than one household in ten owned a television. However, fifteen years later, less than one household in ten remained without. Television's complete adoption took less time than radio. Videocassette recorders (VCRs), though available in the 1970s, occupied less than 2% of households in 1980. By 1990, nearly 70% of households owned VCRs, and, at the end of the decade, penetration stood at 90%.

In each of these examples, any gaps that might have existed closed rapidly. In fact, the one medium for which we have data, television, shows that, by 1956, 90% of households in the top income quartile had already adopted TV, whereas only 55% of households in the bottom income quartile had done so. Yet ten years later, no gap existed. In other words, it seems reasonable to infer that the early diffusion of radio, TV, and VCRs produced gaps; however, the alacrity with which Americans bought up those devices erased each gap in a short period of time.

Three information technologies present an unmistakable contrast. From 1878, with the establishment of the first practical exchange, 80 years passed before 3 out of 4 households boasted a telephone. And, though the adoption of radio sets proved immune to the Depression, telephone penetration dipped in correlation with personal expenditures. Telephones did not reach a flattening of the adoption curve until 1970 with 93%, and lodged itself there in the thirty years since. Growth in the provision of electricity to households begins at a modest 8% in 1907. It progresses steadily, peaking at 68% in 1929, dips slightly through the Depression years, and finally picks up again in 1937. From there, electrification grows steadily until it reaches 99% of households in 1956. Cable service first appears at the end of World War II in Pennsylvania. For the first three decades it experiences little growth, reaching 10% penetration in 1973. From that point on, however, households begin to switch over so that its penetration now reaches approximately two-thirds of households. Here also we have reliable data on gaps for only one medium, the telephone. Since the late 1970s, numerous gaps in telephone service have been documented involving the poor, women heads of households, African Americans, Latinos, and residents of inner cities.

What ties all these gaps together is their persistence. In each case, they have resisted a string of policy remedies. Nor do they simply reflect differences in income; they persist even when examined within the same income group, e.g., African Americans vs. Whites in households earning less than $20,000.

What should we make of gaps that pass and gaps that persist? Clearly, gaps that resist closure pose the greater threat to participation. What we know is this: Information *goods*, like radios and TVs, diffuse very rapidly; whatever gaps might have been created close quickly. Information *services*, especially those that require deployment of infrastructure, diffuse much more slowly. Sixty years to saturation for electrification; 55 years and counting for cable; 100 years for the telephone. The reason is not hard to discern. Goods require a one-time purchase for which the household can save, whereas information services require a decision to pay every month. That explains why the purchases of radios skyrocketed during the Depression, while the telephone and electrification faltered. The requirement of a deployed infrastructure added further constraints.

That said, we should keep in mind that gaps are a natural feature of the diffusion of any technology; however, their temporality varies widely. Thus, to insure access, we must pick and choose carefully those gaps that deserve our attention.

So, what about gaps in access to the Internet? That Internet service provision requires periodic payments and the deployment of infrastructure places it closer to the telephone than to TV. Any downturn in the economy will cause some households to drop the service. Moreover, poorer households will experience an inability to maintain the service, just as they do today with telephone and cable. Therefore, given the importance of the Internet to the promise of participation, policy makers should concern themselves with the diffusion of Internet service and seek policies to support its widespread availability.

By identifying information access gaps as a stumbling block to the advance of an Information Age commonwealth, we bring to the fore one of the essential elements in the invigoration of American democracy for the 21st century. By engaging access as a public discourse, we live democracy as the founders intended—lively, dynamic, and enlightening. In the Information Age, we must recognize those gaps that threaten access, understand them, and decide through public discourse how best to fill them in. As we breathe life into the Republic, we will demand access so that all citizens may participate in the economic, political, and social life of a democratic society that is also a good society.

Note

1. This sweeping vista is often attributed to Roosevelt's first inaugural, when he addressed a people frightened by events out of their control. In fact, the line comes from his second inauguration in 1937, at a time when the Great Depression was inching toward recovery. Roosevelt wanted to keep Americans focused on the work still to be done. As a stand-alone sentence, it captures his penchant for balanced prose and visual phrases. By the way, 1937 represents the first time a president was sworn in on January 20.

19

Falling for the Gap: Whatever Happened to the Digital Divide?

Adam Clayton Powell III

The New York Jets have just won the Super Bowl. It must be true: There's a story on the front page of the *New York Times,* and there are color pictures in *Sports Illustrated.* And indeed it is true. Or, rather, it was true, a few decades ago. Only a truly inexperienced sports writer would suggest that the New York Jets are the current champions of the NFL.

Did you hear that the Dow Jones industrial average has topped 1,000? That, too, is old news, as even the most junior financial writer must know. How about this one: There is a broad and widening gap on the Internet between White and minority Americans. This familiar claim, often asserted as a fact by policy makers and digerati alike, is also based on old information. Reinforced by White House press releases and presidential candidates' speeches, the idea is so ubiquitous that even the usually well-informed have come to believe that White Americans are online and minorities are not.

Not so. It may have been true in 1996 or 1997, when the Internet was only a few years old as a popular medium and personal computers cost thousands of dollars. But today, with dirt-cheap Internet access and computers approaching the costs of television sets, assertions of a "digital divide" or "racial ravine" are as correct as identifying Joe Namath as football's current MVP or pinning last week's Dow at 1,000.

Misled by stereotypes, misinformed about survey techniques, and misdirected by interest groups, the media have treated the digital divide as a crisis requiring government intervention. As a result, billions of dollars might be spent to address needs that no longer exist.

To understand how this happened, start with stereotypes. East Coast journalists typically equate "minority" with "African American," portraying the country as divided between Black and White. This view omits the fastest growing minority group, Hispanic Americans, who in just a few years will be the largest minority group in the country.

Confusing "minority" with "African American" also leads journalists and analysts to forget that it is not among Whites but among Asian Americans that Internet and computer use are approaching levels of penetration comparable to those of the telephone, television, and indoor plumbing. So even using the old survey data, it was always inaccurate to claim that minority Americans were not online in large numbers.

But the issue of dated information is crucial, especially because a year or two in "Internet time" is the equivalent of a decade for older media. The findings of the most frequently cited "digital divide" study, released last summer by the U.S. Department of Commerce, were presented and widely reported as new information. The study was actually an analysis of surveys in 1998 and earlier. When it was released, more-current information was already available from market research firms, but only a handful of news organizations reported the newer data.

The Commerce Department study made page one headlines with its conclusion that the United States faced a "racial ravine" dividing online White Americans from information-poor minorities. "For many groups, the digital divide has widened as the information 'haves' outpace the 'have nots' in gaining access to electronic resources," it said. "Between 1997 and 1998, the divide between those at the highest and lowest education levels increased 25 percent, and the divide between those at the highest and lowest income levels grew 29 percent."

That sounds impressive, but if you look more closely you may spot a crucial methodological flaw. Among reporters for the major daily newspapers, only John Schwartz of the *Washington Post* noted the problem. "Last year's study did not collect information about out-of-home access," wrote Schwartz. "It is not possible, therefore, to say whether the digital divide is growing based on access from all places." In other words, the Commerce Department's claim of a "widened" gap was not supported by the data it cited, because the surveys asked different questions from year to year.

"We never stated that we have any information about widening with regard to anywhere access," says Larry Irving, who directed the government study before he resigned as assistant secretary of commerce. "But certainly we can prove the in-home access gap is widening."

Yet according to every survey taken in the last few years, Americans get their online access at work and at school in far larger numbers than at home. According to "The Internet News Audience Goes Ordinary," a 1999 report from the Pew Research Center for the People and the Press, 62 percent of employed Americans go online through their jobs, and 75 percent of students go online from their schools. The Commerce Department study reported only on use of personally owned computers, thus excluding the millions of users (including this writer) who are online every day but do not own a computer. This is like assuming you don't need a driver's license unless you buy a car.

Regardless of whether the questions in the federal survey were correctly phrased, they were asked in 1998. Surveys conducted this year have found not only that minorities are not falling behind but that they are catching up.

"If you missed Christmas [1998], you missed a big surge," says Ekaterina Walsh, author of "The Digital Melting Pot," a report based on 1999 data collected by Forrester Research of Cambridge, Massachusetts. "Quite a lot of people got cheap PCs. We were surprised ourselves, because we were projecting lower numbers for online penetration and commerce [than the study found]. Even a month made a big difference." Walsh adds that the federal report may undercount or ignore WebTV®, which in 1998 was one of the lowest-priced devices enabling consumers to go online.

"I think we did miss a certain amount of information with regard to lower-priced PCs since December," concedes Irving, the former Commerce Department official. But he stands firm on the question of whether the department's study was misleading because it tracked only computer use at home. "No one has been tracking out-of-home access, as far as we know," he says.

Larry Irving, meet Bob Mancuso. Mancuso, marketing manager for Nielsen Media Research in New York, says his firm produces a regular report on out-of-home Internet access and use. Forrester Research also provides tracking data on out-of-home use.

The *Orlando Sentinel* was one of the few newspapers that noted the problem with focusing exclusively on Internet use at home. The *Sentinel* also reported inconsistencies among the 1994, 1997, and 1998 federal surveys, noting that the earlier surveys did not even ask specifically about computer ownership; they asked whether respondents owned a modem. *Sentinel* reporter Maria Padilla also quoted comments from Walsh and other researchers challenging the government's conclusions. "Race has nothing to do with whether you adopt technology or not," Walsh told Padilla.

Donna Hoffman, an associate professor of management at Vanderbilt University who studies Internet access and popularized the term digital divide, says racial differences do indeed disappear when you measure access and use, rather than modem or computer ownership. "We do not find gaps in usage, given access," Hoffman says. But she defends the federal study because, however shaky its conclusions, it could have an impact on the policy debate, encouraging government spending on computers for poor people (a policy that Irving also favors). "Getting PCs into the homes of all Americans is critical," she argues.

Hoffman concedes that the research by Nielsen and Forrester, using 1999 data, was more current than her studies and the federal government's, which were based on data from 1998 or earlier. But she says older data are still useful. "We track events over time the better to understand the evolution in access and usage," she says. "We have learned an enormous amount about technology usage by carefully studying these events over time. The fact is that the data show a digital divide for those time points. The data also allow us to understand the likely impact of policy initiatives."

There is no shortage of those initiatives. Within hours of the federal report's release, President Clinton, Vice President Gore, the National Association for the Advancement of Colored People, and the National Urban League all announced programs to buy computers for minority Americans. But the recent data from Forrester and Nielsen suggest that such programs may be misdirected. According to Forrester, Hispanic Americans were slightly ahead of White Americans in computer use earlier this year, and African Americans were closing the Black-White gap at a rate that could lead to parity within the next 12 months. In terms of Internet use, the truly disadvantaged may well be Native Americans, who were not covered by the federal report. Data from the Black College Communication Association and other sources also indicate disparities between educational institutions, including lower Internet access at predominantly minority colleges and universities. This, too, was lost in the focus on home computer ownership.

"Questions of colored folk and cyberspace are often plagued by over-statements of the bad news, understatements of the good news, and misplaced concern about the importance of computers," says Omar Wasow, an MSNBC commentator and founder of BlackPlanet.com and other black-oriented Web sites. "For example, a few years ago people were concerned that women were dramatically underrepresented on the Internet. Yet because women were signing up at America Online and other access providers at an incredible clip, in a few short years women have practically achieved parity in their online access ... The critical statistic is not what are the current rates of usage but rather [what are] the current rates of adoption."

Wasow cites the history of another electronic medium. "We forget that once upon a time televisions were a rare and expensive device that only a few households were lucky enough to possess, and now every home has nearly a TV per person," he says. "Over time, most advanced technologies that are available only to an elite few become widely dispersed among the broader population."

In other words, there is no debate about the television-rich vs. the television-poor in America. Every American who wants one has a television set. And now that some personal computers cost less than TVs and Internet access is cheaper than cable (or even free), the data do indeed show that every American who wants one is getting a PC.

But the media echo chamber has drowned out updated information with old studies and stereotypes. Even informed technology observers have mistaken last summer's federal report for current information. In the cover story for the August issue of *Yahoo Internet Life* magazine, Farai Chideya of ABC News wrote that "the average Web user is different from the average American: more likely to be white or Asian ... and less likely to be Latino, black or a blue collar worker." Her source? That Commerce Department report, based on interviews in 1998.

"Although middle-class blacks and other minorities are getting online in substantial numbers, there remains an enormous disparity between whites' computer use and blacks'," wrote the usually perceptive Internet observer Jon Katz in a late-summer [1999] column on the Freedom

Forum Web site.[1] His source? The new edition of the widely respected book *Technology and the Future*, edited by Albert Teich, the director of science and policy programs at the American Association for the Advancement of Science. And what was the book's source? The Commerce Department study. So Mayor Giuliani, where's the ticker-tape parade for Joe Namath?

Note

1. ⟨http://www.freedomforum.org⟩

20

Declare the War Won

Benjamin M. Compaine

Technologies in general and information technologies in particular are being developed and implemented at historically unprecedented levels. For those who are motivated to learn about the impact of information technology quickly discover the mantra: smaller, faster, cheaper, better. That is, anything touched by silicon—the raw material of computer chips—has been impacted by Moore's Law since the development of the microprocessor.

What much of the research lacks in the attempted documentation of a digital divide is recognition of the forces and trends shaping the information landscape, particularly the economics of the Internet and computers. This concluding chapter addresses this particular gap.

The Economics of Online Access: In Brief

The economics of online access involve the consumer's capital cost—equipment and its upkeep—and the operating costs—subscription and connection fees. Sociocultural factors address the McLuhanesque nature of screens versus paper, keyboards or dictation versus pens and pencils. The two have some relationship: if wireless connections and paper-like reading devices are economical (we know they are technologically feasible), then some of the sociocultural nuances could be diminished.

The following pages focusing on the economics of being online suggest where the technology could go next. For some discussion of the social and cultural nature of being online, see Compaine's "The New Literacy" as well as the work of Sherry Turkle, among others.[1]

Consumer Costs

There is a cost to consumers even when the content is "free." Users must pay, in some form, for any information they access via the media. There is no free lunch. For broadcast television and radio, the direct cost is periodic investment in television and radio receivers, antenna, and occasional repairs.[2] Readers, listeners, and viewers must subscribe to newspapers and magazines, purchase books and records, subscribe to cable, or rent videos or a pay-per-view showing. Table 20.1 identifies examples of the monthly costs of some of these media. Consumer spending on media was estimated to be an average of more $49 per month per person in 1999, not including online access.[3]

The monthly total is realistic as an average, given that a much higher figure is readily reached by many households: figure $31 for a cable subscription, $15 for the newspaper, $10 for a few magazines for different family members, $25 for a few paperback books for parents and kids (more if a best-seller hardcover is included), $30 for a family night at the movies (popcorn not included), $15 for five or six video rentals for the month plus perhaps a few CDs.

In addition, households need one or more television sets and radios; the average household had 2.4 television sets and 5.6 radios in 1996.[4] More than 84% of households had videocassette players, four times the penetration of 10 years earlier.[5] Indeed, consumers increased the proportion of their personal consumption expenditures on media from 2.5% in 1980 to 2.9% in 1996.[6]

Just as consumers had to buy radios, phonographs, televisions, and VCRs to make use of previous waves of new media technologies, to make use of online media they must have access to other devices. Initially these were personal computers but were supplemented by less expensive options such as dedicated TV set-top boxes. One brand was WebTV®, a Microsoft subsidiary that used the TV set as the display.[7] Another was Netpliance's I-Opener, which sold a dedicated Web browsing and email device for $299.[8] From home, consumers must have telecommunications access to the Internet, via a telephone line, cable wire, or wireless. Does cost create a barrier?

The simple answer is, of course. Any cost is a barrier. The real question is: Is it a fatal or unfair barrier given the standard of living (refer-

Table 20.1
Monthly and Capital Cost of Traditional Media, 1999–2000

Medium	Monthly Cost	Capital Cost
Daily newspaper subscription		$0.00
Atlanta Journal & Constitution	$17	
Pottstown (PA) Mercury	14	
The Wall Street Journal	15	
USA Today	10	
Cable Television, standard tier	$31 (1998 national ave.)	$250 (per 27″ TV set)
Home Box Office	9.95	
Pay per view movie	3.95	
Pay per view special event	19.95 and up	
Direct Broadcast Satellite	$29.99 (2000 DirecTV Total Choice)	$0–$99 for dish and one receiver $250 (per 27″ TV set)
Books		$0.00
Bag of Bones, Stephen King	$28 list, $19.60 discount	
Technologies of Freedom, Pool	16.50 (paper)	
Silver Palate Cookbook	$25 list, $17.47 discount	
U.S. Statistical Abstract	$50 (paper)	
Babe—The Gallant Pig	$5 list, $4 discount	
Magazine subscription		$0.00
PC Magazine	$2.90 (2 issues)	
Fortune	5.00 (2 issues)	
The Atlantic Monthly	1.25 (1 issue)	
Time	4.30 (4.3 issues)	
Consumer Reports	2.00 (1 issue)	
Ave. total per consumer spending on all media	$49.43	

Sources: Newspapers—From each newspaper's Web site, February 10, 1999, Cable—Seth Schiesel, "FCC Notes Lack of Cable TV Competition," *The New York Times Interactive*, January 14, 1998. Magazines—from Web sites, Feb 11, 1999. Books—from Amazon.Com, February 10, 1999. DBS—from DirecTV price list at Web site, May 3, 2000 and *Parade* magazine ad for Dish Network, May 7, 2000; Hardware cost—from Best Buy advertisement, May 7, 2000. Total per consumer: see endnote 3.

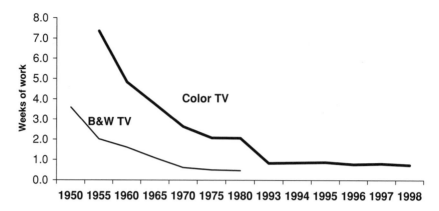

Figure 20.1
Cost of television sets, selected years, 1950–1998.
Sources: Television set prices, 1950–1976: Christopher Sterling and Timothy Haight, *The Mass Media: Aspen Institute Guide to Communications Industry Trends*, New York: Praeger Publishers, 1978, pp 360–362. 1979–83: *U.S. Statistical Abstract*, 1985, p. 777, from *Merchandising, 62nd Annual Statistical and Marketing Report*. 1993–1996: U.S. Bureau of the Census, Current Industrial Reports, Manufacturing Profiles, annual. Wages: U.S. Bureau of Labor Statistics, *Employment and Earnings*.

ring here to the United States, but applicable to societies of similar wealth)? How does access to the Internet compare to the cost and value of other media? Figure 20.1 looks at the costs of television sets from 1950 to 1998. The measurement is in number of weeks of work at the average weekly pay for private-sector wage earners. In essence it shows that the first television sets were expensive: equal to 3.6 weeks of earnings. By the late 1990s, the cost had declined to under four days of work. Meanwhile the quality improved as well. From nine-inch black and white screens with high-maintenance tubes to 27-inch solid-state color and remote control, the cost by any measure fell continuously and substantially throughout the decades.

The cost of the hardware associated with online information has followed even a steeper declining curve. Table 20.2 shows examples of the costs associated with access to the Internet in 1999. Based on historical trends, the capital cost of hardware is likely to decrease in both current and real dollar terms, the cost of access fees is likely to decline, and the cost of information is likely to stay constant or decrease as the audience online expands.

Table 20.2
Capital and Operational Costs for Consumer Internet Access, 1999

Access device	Street cost
Personal computer*	$848
Dedicated Web device**	$299
Internet Service Providers	**Monthly cost**
American Online	$21.95 unlimited use
	19.95 with annual contract
	4.95 for 3 hours + 2.50/hour
juno.com	$0, basic service
	8.95, premium service
AT&T Broadband—cable	29.95 unlimited for cable subscribers
	39.95 for non-cable subscribers
Telocity 640kps DSL	$49.95, free modem
Telephone charges	Varies depending on service level and location. None if using flat rate (non-measured) service to local POP. May be one to two cents per minute for measured service or more for more distant POP.
Internet-accessed Content Providers	**Monthly cost**
The Atlanta Journal-Constitution online	$0.00
The Mercury (Pottstown, PA)	0.00
The Wall Street Journal Interactive	5.00
USA Today online	0.00
ZDNet (includes *PC Magazine* & others)	0.00
U.S. Statistical Abstract	0.00
Consumers Report	2.00
Time, Fortune, Newsweek	0.00

Notes: *HP Brio 200, 64 mb w/ CD-ROM, 56K modem, 15″ monitor. PC Connection catalog, v. 221, April 2000.
**i-opener with keyboard and display, www.netpliance.com, September 14, 2000.
Monthly charges: from company Web sites, May 4, 2000

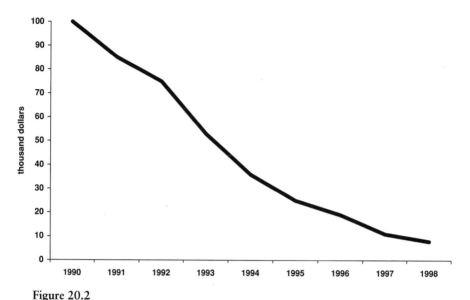

Figure 20.2
Cost of MIPS, 1990–1998.
Sources: Eva Freeman, "No More Gold-Plated MIPS: Mainframes and Distributed Systems Converge," *Datamation,* March 1998. Data from Hitachi Data Systems.

Figure 20.2 charts one of the measures of computer costs over the decade of the 1990s, the decline in computer processing costs. It is consistent with Moore's Law. As the story goes, in 1965 Gordon Moore, a founder of Intel, which has developed most of the central processing units (CPUs) used in personal computers, was preparing a speech. When he started to graph data about the growth in chip performance, he realized there was a striking trend: Each new chip contained roughly twice as much capacity as its predecessor, and each chip was released within 18 to 24 months of the previous chip. If this trend continued, he reasoned, computing power would rise exponentially over relatively brief periods of time.

Moore's observation described a trend that has been maintained for at least 35 years. It is the basis for many planners' performance forecasts. In 26 years the number of transistors on a chip had increased more than 3,200 times, from 2,300 on the Intel 4004 in 1971 to 7.5 million on the Intel Pentium II processor that was the standard in 1999.[9] Meanwhile, other components also decreased in cost while increasing in capacity:

mass storage, modems, CD-ROM drives, even monitors. Between 1996 and 1998 alone the retail cost of personal computers fell nearly 23% annually.[10]

This brought the retail price of Web-ready full-featured (for that date) personal computers to about $600 or about 1.4 weeks of average weekly earnings. This was a level not reached for color television sets until the mid-1980s. By 1999 multiple vendors offered Web-enabled PCs for free. They might be provided in return for recipients providing personal demographic information or willingness to be exposed to added advertising as they use the Web.[11] Or they were provided to consumers willing to sign a long term contract with an Internet Service Provider.[12]

Adoption of Technologies

Compared to other popular technology-created goods and services, the rate of adoption for PCs and the Internet is historically unprecedented. And given the ultimate overwhelmingly high penetration rates of the other technologies, as seen in Figure 20.3, it would seem reasonable to expect that both computers and similar intelligent devices, along with Internet access, will reach similar penetration much faster. Of the 11 products in Figure 20.3, only two (electrification and telephone) relied on direct government programs to targeted populations to help with those on the margin.

Computer and Internet Adoption Rate

The rate of adoption of personal computers and the Internet had been stimulated by at least five trends: rapidly declining costs and increasing power of the hardware; improving ease of use; increasing availability of points of presence (POPs) for local Internet Service Provider (ISP) access; decreasing cost of Internet access; and network externalities associated with email and chat.

Rapidly Declining Costs and Increasing Power of the Hardware

Figure 20.2 best measures this phenomenon based on the cost of computer capabilities. The difficulty in directly graphing the decline in computer cost alone is that capabilities and features have been increasing

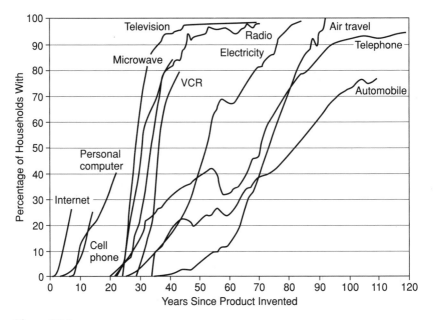

Figure 20.3
Rate of household adoption of selected products.
Source: W. Michael Cox and Richard Alm, *Myths of Rich & Poor* (New York: Basic Books, 1999), p. 162.

while absolute prices went down. For example, this author bought his first personal computer in 1981 for about $3000 (with a loan from his employer). It was an Apple II+, with an 8-bit central processing unit (CPU), probably running at 1 mHz, 64 kilobit of memory, two floppy drives that each stored about 160,000 bits and a crude monochrome monitor. A 300 baud modem added later cost $300. Word processing and the VisiCalc spreadsheet were the two useful applications.

My latest PC, purchased in September 1998, was $2400, running a 32-bit Pentium II CPU at 400 mHz, with 128 mb (that's 2000 times more memory), 13.6 gb of hard disk storage, a 17-inch high-resolution color monitor, a 56 kps modem and a host of other features not even dreamed of in 1981: sound and speakers, 100 mb removable mass storage, CD drive, and so on. By early 2000 a similarly configured PC, but with a CPU 100% faster, was available from the same vendor for $1700.[13]

This is the high end and far more than most households need. Dell, for example, offered a quite capable PC system for $779 that included a year of Internet access as well as Microsoft word processing and spreadsheet software. As has been noted previously, various specialized devices for Web only or dedicated email use became available for as low as $99. There is every reason to expect the declining cost curve to continue in hardware. By 2000 the hardware had become so low-cost that numerous vendors were providing free or subsidized computer systems in conjunction with signing up for service contracts of Internet access at market rates.

Improved Ease of Use, via Apple Macintosh and Microsoft Windows "Point-and-Click" Operating Systems

Before the graphical interface (GUI in tech jargon), operating a PC took a certain determination and level of learning that most casual users found on the losing end of the cost-benefit equation. The breakthrough of point-and-click, first developed by Xerox then implemented in the Apple Macintosh and later Microsoft Windows, greatly lowered the technical barriers to entry. Similarly, the original Internet and first iteration of the World Wide Web were character based, meaning they required lots of typing of commands to make things happen. It was not until the Mosaic browser was popularized by Netscape in 1994 that the Web and with it the Internet became transparent enough to interest a mass, nontechnical audience.

The next breakthrough in ease of use, just starting to fulfill a long-held promise, is reliable voice recognition. In 1999 several programs became available for under $100. Combined with ever more capable computers, voice recognition will further lower the skill level required to access information, create documents, and otherwise perform functions that have heretofore required some modicum of skill in operating a keyboard and mouse.

Increasing Availability of Points of Presence (POPs) for Local Internet Service Provider Access

At the end of 1999 there were 5,078 Internet Service Providers in the United States, up 233 from a year earlier. These were the "on-ramps" to the Internet. Among these 184 were considered "national" ISPs by virtue having a presence in more than 25 area codes.[14] By the spring of 1998— barely four years after Netscape introduced the Web to the mass audience, 92% of the U.S. population had access by a local phone call to seven or more ISPs. Fewer than 5% had no access by other than a toll call.[15] As might be expected, the few areas that are underserved tended to be lower in population—primarily rural counties.

Decreasing Cost of Internet Access

Only 2.55% of the population lived in counties with three or fewer ISPs, while more than 85% of the population lived in counties with 21 or more competitors.[16] Greater competition is generally associated with lower prices and higher quality of services. Meanwhile, several services have developed advertiser-supported models that offer no charge to consumers. In 2000 these include Juno.com, NetZero.com, and Bluelight.com. The latter claims that it offers local access to 96% of the United States. In 1996 AT&T Worldnet introduced the first flat-rate unlimited-use consumer ISP service for $19.95 per month. Previously most services, such as America Online, charged about $9.95 for only five hours of use, then a per-hour rate, typically $2.50. After Worldnet, most services followed suit at similar prices. Popular services charged $20–22 per month in 2000, with some as low as $8.95, as well as the advertiser-supported free services. Discounts of 10% or more were often available for yearly contracts.

Network Externalities Associated with Email Utility

Network externalities refers to the increase in value to all users of a network as more users join the network. When only a few businesses and households had telephones, they were of limited value. The postal network, on the other hand, was of great value because anyone could reach anyone else. In the early days of email, systems were proprietary. That is, large companies had their own internal email not connected to the outside world. Online services, such as CompuServe and America Online, had email systems that only allowed exchange with other members of that service. If I subscribed to Prodigy and a friend subscribed to AOL, we couldn't exchange email. Thus, email was not an application that drove many people online.

But as the Internet juggernaut accelerated, consumer demand and commercial practicality quickly forced—or encouraged—the various networks to open their systems to sending and receiving email over the Internet, using standard protocols. Thus, in the early 1990s there were roughly 15 million email accounts worldwide. By the end of 1999, there were 569 million.[17] In the United States there were about 333 email boxes. Accounting for multiple accounts and home/office overlap, an estimated 110 million American were using email, or 52% of Americans more than 14 years old. This compared to about 7% six or seven years earlier.

Internet Relay Chat (IRC) has undergone similar growth. IRC is the basis of chat rooms, which allow users to engage in real time text (and increasingly voice) conversation. Like email the early chat rooms were service-specific, but chat is now available across the Internet, using software that is available for free.

Trends vs. the Digital Divide

The overwhelming weight of the data, from the NTIA surveys to the Forrester Research study, all point in a direction that is historically consistent and socially positive. New and expensive technologies have to start somewhere and almost invariably that means with two groups: those who find it undeniably useful—often commercial entities—and those who can simply afford it. Similarly, where infrastructure must be built, the provider will start their buildouts aimed at audiences who are most likely to understand the value and be amenable to their service. Again, that typically means a focus on commercial ventures and wealthier residential areas.

The attraction of this market-driven self-interest is that it creates an invisible cross subsidy for those who follow. The early adopters pay higher per-unit costs that reflect lower production volumes of manufactured products—such as PCs—or start-up costs of services, such as Internet access via the cable system. But as production builds, unit costs decline, product costs decline, and manufacturers are able to lower prices. In the case of personal computer devices, that process is compounded by advances in component technologies, such as hard disk drives, as "box" manufacturers increase their own output.

The builders of networks—traditional and new, telephone, wireless, cable, and even electric distribution firms—similarly know that the marginal cost of adding users to a network is low and thus highly profitable. Once the fixed cost of the network has been covered, additional users not only cost them little to add, but network externalities actually make their service of greater value to current and new customers. Thus they have an incentive to lower price and increase utilization.

To summarize the trends:

• The United States has seen an unprecedented rapid adoption of the Internet and email between 1994 and 2000 among all strata of the population.
• Many other similar technology-inspired products achieved near-universal adoption without massive government or even private programs: radio, television sets, and VCRs among them.
• Prices for computers and similar devices have been falling constantly and substantially, to levels equal to a decent color television set.
• Though services such as telephony and cable have tended to lag behind in adoption rates due to ongoing fees, free Internet access is available using a broadcast TV and radio model in territories that include most of the population.
• Current rates of adoption for those groups variously included on the unwired side of the early divide are greater than for the population as a whole.
• As a result, some gaps have already disappeared. For example, from 1994 to 1998 there was high visibility of the gender gap: Initially more than two-thirds of Internet users were male. By 1999 that was history. It simply reflected that early users came from computer science and engineering disciplines that were more heavily male.
• Among those who do have access to computers and the Internet, patterns of use are similar across income, gender, and ethnic lines.

From a policy perspective, there are other reasons the digital divide is less a crisis than a temporary and normal process.

Concerns for Rural Users

Surveys such as those from NTIA and Vanderbilt inexplicably link "poor" and "rural" together. For decades telephone service prices were

Table 20.3
Auto Insurance in Three Communities, 2000

City/Town and ZIP	Lowest Rate*	Low to High Gap
Philadelphia, PA 19122	$3940	+$3323
Carlisle, PA 17013	1070	+ 2253
Atchison, KS 66002	617	—

Note: *For identical coverage on 1996 Ford Taurus GL, married male driver, age 50. Used lowest quote if more than one.
Source: ⟨http://www.insuremarket.com⟩, May 4, 2000.

adjusted so that rural dwellers paid roughly the same for service as urban dwellers, despite higher cost in servicing the former.

There is an assumption that rural dwellers need help with telecommunications networks because they live in low-density territories that are more expensive to wire. There are, to be sure, poor rural families. But the subsidies in the past also went to middle-class farmers and wealthy ranchers who, when unable to get cable, thought nothing of installing $10,000 satellite dishes. Meanwhile single working mothers in the cities and mom-and-pop store owners paid telephone rates that helped subsidize the rural subscribers.

There is also scant attention paid to the economic benefits of living in rural areas that may more than compensate for having to pay rates closer to full cost for telecommunications. Assuming that there is general agreement that access to an automobile is as important as access to a computer and the Internet for one's livelihood, there are huge real gaps in costs for auto insurance. Table 20.3 shows that a resident of a low-income neighborhood in Philadelphia might pay more than six times as much for auto insurance than a resident in rural Atchison, Kansas, and nearly four times that of a resident of the suburban town of Carlisle, Pennsylvania, about 120 miles west of Philadelphia. It could be argued that the rural residents of Atchison could readily absorb a doubling or tripling of their $25 monthly phone bill and still come out way ahead over their Philadelphia counterpart when looked at in the context of cost of living in rural areas. Similar gaps exist in other large-ticket items, such as the cost of urban housing compared to rural areas. As a percentage of total household budgets, telecommunications, including cable or DBS fees, would under any scenario be substantially less than items such as housing and auto insurance. Similar reasoning would apply to schools in rural versus urban communities.

Voluntary Non-users

In the statistics showing nonsubscribers to telephone or cable service, PC ownership or Internet connectivity, there has been scant attention paid to voluntary non-users. There is both anecdotal evidence and increasing statistical verification that large numbers of individuals are voluntary non-participants, for which no manner of programs of financing will change until they see the personal value. In chapter 13, the Cheskin Research study of Hispanic households found that the second most voiced reason for not owning a computer, nearly 40%, was "don't need." Another six percent had similar reasons—"too old" or "not interested." This is generally consistent with the NPR/Kaiser Foundation/ Kennedy School survey in the same chapter. Of those characterizing themselves as being "left behind" in computers, barely 20% blamed cost. A third were just not interested. In the interviews reported from Camden, NJ, in chapter 5, the authors found households that were willing to pay $20 or more per month for cable but not $10 for a dial tone.

Among the fourth of households that did not subscribe to cable or DBS in 2000, it is reasonable that many, if not most, passed on the opportunity by choice. At the extreme, in cities like Cambridge, Mass. and Berkeley, Calif. there are sizable pockets of households that take satisfaction in not having a TV at all, or at best an old black and white TV with a rabbit-ear antenna to bring out of the closet for special news events. Many elderly are quite happy watching the existing over-the-air stations and see no need for 85 channels of cable options. I'm personally surprised at the number of people I know who see no need for an ATM card—it's their preference to go to the bank once a week to get some cash.

Thus some portion of various gaps will always be with us. The number of those who *want* PCs and Internet access but who don't have it because of cost is somewhat smaller than the absolute non-user number.

Schools, Libraries, and the Rush to Wire

The policy of helping schools and libraries with their education and information missions in light of changing technologies is on more solid historical and policy footing than policies directed at individuals and households. Still, there remain caveats that seem to have been given little attention in the digital divide debate.

Foremost among them is the type of aid that should be given schools and the conditions, if any, that should be attached. Currently, the Universal Service Fund levy—a tax by another name—on telephone bills is providing billons of dollars earmarked for wiring institutions to the Internet and providing related equipment. With the money available, schools are spending sums for construction and hard wiring far in excess of what it might take to install an improving breed of wireless technologies.

Perhaps even more questionable, as seen in chapter 10, is that schools are scrambling for the funds sometimes without having a clear sense of what they will do with their wired buildings. And where there is the semblance of a plan, it is often in the absence of a sound pedagogical footing: teachers who range from being downright opposed to change to lacking an integrated strategy for use with the curricula. Rare is the development of new curricula that truly takes advantage of the information and communication capabilities of networked PCs.

Having computers available in the schools is an unassailable necessity, just as is having a school library. That there are differences between the libraries in wealthier school districts and poorer ones has long been a reality as well. However, as seen in table 20.4, by 1999 those differences were small and continuing to narrow further, at least along minority and income lines. Schools with high minority enrollments (50% or greater) had one computer per 6.5 students. This compared to one computer per 5.0 students in schools with under 5% minority enrollment. Results were even slightly better when comparing poor students with wealthier ones. In schools where over 50% of students qualified for the federal free lunch program there was one computer per 6.2 students compared to one per 4.9 students in schools with no such students. Thus, a wealthy school

Table 20.4

Computers and Internet Access in Minority and Poorer School Districts

Measurement criteria	% students in school				
	None	Under 5%*		Over 50%	
		1998	1999	1998	1999
Minority enrollment		5.3	5.0	7.1	6.5
Free lunch program	4.9			N.A.	6.2
		% Schools with Internet Access			
		1997	1999	1997	1999
Poverty-level students		78	94%	59	84

Note: * 0–10% for Internet access

Source: Technology in Education: A Comprehensive Report on the State of Technology in the K–12 Market, Market Data Retrieval, 1999. Figures 16, 17, table 33.

with 1,000 students might have 204 PCs, while the poorest schools of similar size had 161 PCs. That would translate to a potential of about six hours of computer time per student per week available in the wealthiest schools to almost five hours per student in the very poorest.

Finally, poorer schools were a minimal 10% lower in Internet access in 1999, with 84% of the schools with the poorest students having access compared to 94% of the wealthiest. As significant, the poorer schools were closing the gap rapidly. Between 1997 and 1999 the poorer schools had a 42% improvement in access, compared to half that rate for the wealthiest schools. Moreover, most if not all these improvements came prior to significant expenditures from the E-rate programs of the Universal Service Fund, indicating they are the result of local budget commitments.

There is also reason to believe that the poorer schools, having been later to the game, are benefiting from lower costs for equipment and the improved performance of PCs compared to those that would have been purchased by the "cutting-edge" schools at higher prices a few years earlier.

As a policy matter there are or can be mechanisms in place to manage whatever discrepancies remain, primarily at the state level but in federal programs as well. Decisions of how much to spend on hardware, software, and training are not new to budgeters. With the declining cost of hardware, increasingly it will be teacher training—and teacher enthusiasm—that can and should be the focus of the educational policy process as it applies to new learning and teaching approaches.

Public libraries have long been the preferred societal mechanism for leveling the information access field. As with the schools, district-to-district discrepancies in resources is not a new issue. Acquiring Internet browsing devices, printers, Internet access and subscriptions, online archives, and databases are part of the budgeting process. At some point—if not yet—all libraries will have to realize that online access reduces the need for periodical subscriptions and many reference works that accounted for portions of their budgets. The digital library will have to take away allocations that heretofore went to the analog library.

Furthermore, libraries may take advantage of the virtual world by reducing the need for bricks and mortar. Although it may be awhile before digitized fiction and biographies become more practical than a printed book, the increased availability of reference material online should reduce the need for library expansions. Moreover, once digital, it makes no sense to require patrons to come to the library to use a terminal if the same data can be accessed from home connections. The library card of the future may be in the form of a password that gives holders access to the "subscriptions" the library has. The savings in real estate could thus become available for services for those users who do not have home access. Making these sorts of changes in priorities is not easy after centuries of buildings and books.

In many communities the cost of high-speed access will be covered by cable systems that have been obligated to provide access to libraries, schools, and other municipal facilities under the terms of their franchise agreements with their municipalities.

Democracy Versus Entertainment

Jorge Schement, in chapter 18, sees this digital divide debate about the existence of and responses needed, if any, as a "lively, dynamic and enlightening" process that is one of the joys of democracy. And so it is.

However, it is more tenuous to equate access to the Internet or to cable as one on which the republic depends. Politicians in particular are prone to wrap their rhetoric on the digital divide in terms of furthering democracy. And in many respects this is a political issue as much as a social one. Typical is the FCC's William Kennard in chapter 8: "Our society is not represented by a chat among a homogeneous few, but rather a democratic chorus of many different voices and divergent views."

Similarly, in their introduction to chapter 9, Cooper and Kimmelman write that a widely held goal of the Telecommunications Act of 1996 was "the opportunity to harness enormous technological advancements for the social and economic benefit of all citizens."

And yet ... Television had raised the expectations of many social theorists for education and the political process. The Kennedy-Nixon presidential debates of 1960 seemed to lend some hope for these expectations. But despite television's important roles in forming public opinion during the Vietnam War and creating shared experiences during events such as the O.J. Simpson trial in 1996, for the most part it is a source of simple entertainment. Ratings for national network news shows, never high, have been moving steadily down. The all-news cable networks get a viewership rating of 0.5% while special-interest networks such as C-SPAN, all public service all the time, have even lower viewership. Home shopping shows do better. The old commercial networks, though way down from their pre-cable peaks, still get 15% or so of households each during prime time. Is it a national policy priority to keep cable rates low to provide Americans with "Buffy the Vampire Slayer" (a popular teen-oriented show in 2000)?

The Internet is similarly a mixed bag. Undoubtedly being connected has its value. But surveys have found that services such as chat rooms (sex is popular), sports, and game playing top the list of activities. It is wonderful having access to news and finance and diverse opinions from providers who would never have a worldwide audience pre-Internet. But as the research presented in this volume and elsewhere repeatedly confirms, once digitally enabled, all groups—by income, ethnicity, gender, and education—fall into almost identical patterns of usage. Connecting those not yet connected will likely result in a continuation of this pattern.

One Person's Take on the Digital Divide

In the early 1980s, under a program of the U.S. Information Agency, I was sent on an educational and cultural mission to several countries to talk to various government officials, educators, and academics about information policy issues. One of my stops was Israel. Here I found myself lecturing about the convergence of computers and communications, about the impending competition to newspapers by online information, and about the reasons for increasing competition in telecommunications to people who carried automatic rifles to accompany third-graders on a class trip. I felt somewhat embarrassed trying to speak of these issues as those requiring national policy debates—as they were in the U.S. Congress and among many stakeholders at the time—when my audience faced daily concerns about their existence.

It is, perhaps, a huge testimony to the overall prosperity and well-being of American society at this point in history that an issue such as the digital divide can marshal the attention and commitments it has. A society that has more important issues, such as feeding and housing its people, providing for safety and security, and creating general well-being would place access to entertainment and information well down on the list of priorities. It is a positive sign that we can even turn our attention to information access issues.

Let there be no misunderstanding of this conclusion. There are those households and institutions that are disadvantaged, in information access as in other arenas. It is endemic to the democratic capitalist system and to any other system that has been tried. By the same token, American society has tried various policies to take the hardest edge off those gaps. But where goods or services are truly important to people history demonstrates that here has been great success in minimizing differences among groups (radio, television, and cable come most immediately to mind in this context).

Information access is important. But where does it sit among the schedule of other phenomena for which there has been little or no concern about gaps and advocates who demand government programs to remove them. Having access to an automobile and to have a license to operate one was certainly as critical to one's livelihood in the second half of the 20th century as having access to email may be today. Certainly there have been gaps between those who could afford an automobile and its ongoing operating expenses and those who could not. Were there studies of income and ethnicity and gender to document the auto have and have-not gap? The real question is not whether some group of citizens has more of something than another. It is abundantly obvious that that is true and will continue to be true.

The forces and trends summarized in this chapter suggest (to me anyway) that there is little short-term damage to be had by allowing the self-evident forces of declining cost, natural acculturation, and growing availability to take their course. At some point before the end of this decade—likely sooner rather than later—the adoption curve will flatten. At that point it will be time to take stock of whether a true divide exists, who is on each side, and then debate what policies can best address the resolution.

Perhaps it is fair to propose that the digital divide is disappearing on its own. Public policy in a few years can then turn its attention to the much smaller skirmishes that may be needed to help out with the digital crevice left at the fringes.

Notes

1. Benjamin M. Compaine, "The New Literacy: or How I Stopped Worrying and Learned to Love Pac-Man," in Benjamin M. Compaine, ed., *Understanding New Media* (Cambridge, Mass: Ballinger Publishing Co., 1984); Benjamin M. Compaine, "Information Technology and Cultural Change," in Benjamin M. Compaine, ed., *Issues in New Information Technology* (Norwood, NJ: Ablex Publishing Corporation, 1988). Sherry Turkle, *Life on the Screen: Identity in the Age of the Internet* (New York, Touchstone Books, 1997).

2. Even the programming that is apparently "free" has some cost in the form of marketing costs that are part of the prices we pay for goods and services that advertise. How much that cost really is and how much different prices would be if there were no advertising (and hence less competition and thus hypothetically perhaps *higher* prices for many goods and services) is left to another venue.

3. *Statistical Abstract of the United States, 1999*, p. 580, table 920. Source of the table is *The Veronis, Suhler & Associates Communications Industry Report*, annual.

4. Ibid., p. 581, table 921.

5. Ibid.

6. Calculated by adding books, newspapers and magazines, video, audio and computer products, radio and TV repair, and motion picture theater admission by personal consumption expenditures. From U.S. Bureau of Economic Analysis data in *The U.S. Statistical Abstract*, 1985 and 1998.

7. John Markoff, "Microsoft Deal to Aid Blending of PCs and TVs," *The New York Times Interactive*, April 7, 1997, at ⟨http://www.nytimes.com/library/cyber/week/040797webtv.html⟩.

8. At ⟨http://www.netpliance.com⟩, September 14, 2000.

9. "What is Moore's Law?" Intel Corporation, ⟨http://www.intel.com/intel/museum/25anniv/hof/moore.htm⟩. Accessed February 12, 1999.

10. James Padinha, "Taking PC Prices Out of the Equation," TheStreet.Com, February 3, 1999, at ⟨http://www.thestreet.com/comment/economics/713190.html⟩.

11. Don Clark, "Free_PC to Offer Free Computers in Exchange for Exposure to Ads," *The Wall Street Journal Interactive*, February 8, 1999 at ⟨http://interactive.wsj.com/articles/SB918431496866451000.htm⟩.

12. Margaret Kane, "ISP Offers Free PCs to Subscribers," *ZDNet*, February 17, 1999, ⟨http://www.zdnet.com/zdnn/stories/news/0,4586,2210090,00.html⟩.

13. Dell Web site, ⟨http://www.dell.com⟩, May 5, 2000.

14. *Directory of Internet Service Providers*, 11th ed., Boardwatch, 1999.

15. Thomas A. Downes and Shane M. Greenstein, "Do Commercial ISPs Provide Universal Access?" in Sharon Eisner Gillett and Ingo Vogelsang, eds., *Competition, Regulation and Convergence: Current Trends in Telecommunications Policy Research* (Mahwah, NJ: Lawrence Erlbaum Associates, Publishers, 1999), p. 195.

16. Ibid., p. 204, table 12.1.

17. "Year End 1999 Mailbox Report," Messaging Online, ⟨http://www.messagingonline.com⟩ accessed May 5, 2000.

Epilogue

Benjamin M. Compaine

"Falling through the Net: Toward Digital Inclusion": This is the title of the 2000 update to the "Falling through the Net" series from the National Telecommunications and Information Administration.[1] It was made available in October 2000 and was based on data primarily current to August 2000, twenty months after the data cutoff for the previous report issued in 1999 (chapter 2). Its principal findings confirm the narrowing of the previously reported gaps:

The Data Show that the Overall Level of U.S. Digital Inclusion is Rapidly Increasing:

• The share of households with Internet access soared by 58%, rising from 26.2% in December 1998 to 41.5% in August 2000.
• More than half of all households (51.0%) have computers, up from 42.1% in December 1998.
• There were 116.5 million Americans online at some location in August 2000, 31.9 million more than there were only twenty months earlier.
• The share of individuals using the Internet rose by 35.8%, from 32.7% in December 1998 to 44.4% in August 2000. If growth continues at that rate, more than half of all Americans will be using the Internet by the middle of 2001.

The rapid uptake of new technologies is occurring among most groups of Americans, regardless of income, education, race or ethnicity, location, age, or gender, suggesting that digital inclusion is a realizable goal.

Groups That Have Traditionally Been Digital "Have-Nots" Are Now Making Dramatic Gains:

• The gap between households in rural areas and households nationwide that access the Internet has narrowed from 4.0 percentage points in 1998 to 2.6 percentage points in 2000. Rural households are much closer to the nationwide Internet penetration rate of 41.5%. In rural areas this year, 38.9% of the households had Internet access, a 75% increase from 22.2% in December 1998.

• Americans at every income level are connecting at far higher rates from their homes, particularly at the middle-income levels. Internet access among households earning $35,000 to $49,000 rose from 29.0% in December 1998 to 46.1% in August 2000. Today, more than two-thirds of all households earning more than $50,000 have Internet connections (60.9% for households earning $50,000 to $74,999 and 77.7% for households earning above $75,000).

• Access to the Internet is also expanding across every education level, particularly for those with some high school or college education. Households headed by someone with "some college experience" showed the greatest expansion in Internet penetration of all education levels, rising from 30.2% in December 1998 to 49.0% in August 2000.

• Blacks and Hispanics, while they still lag behind other groups, have shown impressive gains in Internet access. Black households are now more than twice as likely to have home access than they were twenty months ago, rising from 11.2% to 23.5%. Hispanic households have also experienced a tremendous growth rate during this period, rising from 12.6% to 23.6%.

• The disparity in Internet usage between men and women has largely disappeared. In December 1998, 34.2% of men and 31.4% of women were using the Internet. By August 2000, 44.6% of men and a nearly indistinguishable 44.2% of women were Internet users.

• Individuals 50 years of age and older—although still less likely than younger Americans to use the Internet—experienced the highest rates of growth in Internet usage of all age groups: 53% from December 1998 to August 2000, compared to a 35% growth rate for individual Internet usage nationwide.[2]

To be sure, the study found that disparities remained: those with disabilities, such as impaired vision, were less likely to have Internet access than the general population. Blacks and Hispanics had not caught up to the national average, even accounting for income disparities, although the rate of increase was much higher than the overall average. The newest hurdle, broadband access, as might be expected initially, has greater penetration in high population density than in lower density areas.

Still, "Toward Digital Inclusion" could have been the title of this book, and it sums up what has been the trend since the inception of the digital age. It was rather predictable from the history of other important information technologies: that we would naturally start off with disparities among groups, but they would narrow. Those familiar with Moore's Law and network effects (see chapter 20) could have easily predicted that costs and accessibility would bring both the appliances and the services down to costs affordable by the overwhelming majority of residences and businesses that choose to avail themselves of the services.

As a side note, Adam Clayton Powell's suggestions in chapter 19 that the mass media have done a poor job at reporting on digital divide phenomena is bolstered by the lack of coverage of NTIA's study. A search of the online archives of *The New York Times* and *The Wall Street Journal* found no mention of the digital inclusion report, as opposed to extensive and prominent reporting of the earlier "digital divide" reports.[3] *The Washington Post*'s single article's headline focused on the fact that more than half the households now had computers. *The San Francisco Chronicle* still headlined that the digital divide was growing, while *The Chicago Tribune's* lead focused on the subsidiary finding that people with disabilities lagged behind.

Thus, the myth is likely to persist despite the facts.

Notes

1. "Falling through the Net: Toward Digital Inclusion," National Telecommunications and Information Agency, U.S. Department of Commerce, October 2000. Accessed at ⟨http://www.ntia.doc.gov/ntiahome/fttn00/contents00.html⟩.

2. Ibid, Executive Summary.

3. Searches for "digital divide" and "digital inclusion" at ⟨http://www.nyt.com⟩ and ⟨http://interactive.wsj.com⟩, January 17, 2001.

Source Notes

Chapter 1, "Falling through the Net: National Telecommunications and Information Administration," public domain. From an NTIA report posted online at ⟨http://www.ntia.doc.gov/ntiahome/fallingthru.html⟩, 1995.

Chapter 2, "Falling through the Net: Defining the Digital Divide," public domain. From an NTIA report posted online at ⟨http://www.ntia.doc.gov/ntiahome/fttn99⟩, 1999.

Chapter 3, "The Evolution of the Digital Divide," reprinted with the permission of Donna Hoffman, Vanderbilt University, 2000.

Chapter 4, "Information Gaps: Myth or Reality," originally appeared in *Telecommunications Policy* (March, 1986).

Chapter 5, "Universal Service from the Bottom Up," reprinted with the permission of the authors, 1996.

Chapter 6, "Universal Access to Online Services," from *Telecommunications Policy* 21:1, © 1997 by Elsevier. Reprinted by permission from Elsevier Science.

Chapter 7, "Universal Service Policies as Wealth Redistribution," reprinted from *Government Information Quarterly* 16 (1999), by permission from Elsevier Science.

Chapter 8, "Equality in the Information Age," originally published in *51 Federal Communications Law Journal 553* (1999). Reprinted by permission of the journal and author.

Chapter 9, "The Digital Divide Confronts the Telecommunications Act of 1996," © Consumers Union of U.S., Inc., Yonkers, NY 10703-1057, a nonprofit organization. Reprinted by permission for educational purposes only. No commercial use or photocopying permitted. Visit ⟨www.ConsumersUnion.org⟩ and ⟨www.ConsumerReports.org⟩, 1999.

Chapter 10, "The E-rate in America: A Tale of Four Cities," available at ⟨http://www.benton.org/e-rate/e-rate.4cities.pdf⟩. © 2000 by Benton Foundation.

Chapter 11, "Universal Access to E-mail: Feasibility and Societal Implications," chapters 1 and 7. © 1995 by RAND. Reprinted by permission.

Chapter 12, "Clinton Enlists Help for Plan to Increase Computer Use," © 2000 by The New York Times Co. Reprinted by permission.

Chapter 13a, "Internet and Society," reprinted by permission of Norman H. Nie and the Stanford Institute for the Quantitative Study of Society, 2000.

Chapter 13b, "The Digital World of the U.S. Hispanic," © 2000 by Cheskin Research.

Chapter 13c, "Survey of Americans on Technology," was reprinted by permission of the Henry J. Kaiser Family Foundation of Menlo Park, California. The Kaiser Family Foundation is an independent health care philanthropy and is not associated with Kaiser Permanente or Kaiser Industries, 2000.

Chapter 14, "The Truth about the Digital Divide," reprinted by permission of the author and Forrester Research. © by 2000 Forrester Research, Inc.

Chapter 15, "Internet Access Spreads to More Classrooms, Survey Finds," © 1999 by The New York Times Co. Reprinted by permission. Accessed via The New York Times on the Web, December 1, 1999.

Chapter 16, "Cheap Computers Bridge Digital Divide," © 2000 by The Wall Street Journal. Reprinted by permission of The Wall Street Journal via Copyright Clearance Center. Accessed January 27, 2000.

Chapter 17, "This Internet Start-Up Looks to Conquer an Online Divide," © 2000 by The Wall Street Journal, January 20, 2000. Reprinted by permission of The Wall Street Journal via Copyright Clearance Center.

Chapter 18, "Of Gaps by Which Democracy We Measure," from *Information Impacts* magazine, accessed December 19, 1999 at ⟨http://www.cisp.org/imp/december_99/12_99schement.htm⟩. Reprinted by permission of the author.

Chapter 19, "Falling for the Gap," from *Reason* (November 1999). © 2000 by the Reason Foundation, 3415 S. Sepulveda Blvd., Suite 400, Los Angeles, California, 90034, ⟨www.reason.com⟩. Reprinted by permission.

Chapter 20, "Declare the War Won" was prepared for this volume.

Contributors

Benjamin M. Compaine is Senior Research Affiliate at the Internet & Telecoms Convergence Consortium at the Massachusetts Institute of Technology. His Web site is at ⟨www.compaine.com⟩.

Robert H. Anderson, Head, Information Sciences Group at the RAND Corporation.

Tora K. Bikson, Senior Social Scientist at the RAND Corporation.

Andy Carvin, Senior Associate, Communications Policy at the Benton Foundation.

Cheskin Research is a strategic market research and consulting firm specializing in multicultural markets.

Mark Cooper, Research Director, Consumer Federation of America.

Lutz Erbring, Professor of Mass Communication Studies at the Free University of Berlin.

Timothy Hanrahan, reporter for *The Wall Street Journal.*

Donna L. Hoffman, Professor of Management at the Owen Graduate School of Management, Vanderbilt University, and Co-Director of the Electronic Commerce Research Laboratory.

The Kaiser Family Foundation is a nonprofit, independent national health care philanthropy and is not associated with Kaiser Permanente or Kaiser Industries.

William E. Kennard, Chairman of the Federal Communications Commission.

Gene Kimmelman, Co-Director of the Washington office of Consumers Union.

Marc Lacy, writer for *The New York Times*.

Sally Ann Law, behavioral scientist.

Pamela Mendels, writer for *The New York Times*.

Bridger M. Mitchell, vice president of Charles River Associates.

Lloyd Morrisett, retired President of the John and Mary Markle Foundation and one of the principal creators of the Children's Television Workshop.

Milton Mueller, Associate Professor and Director, Telecommunications and Network Management Program at School of Information Studies at Syracuse University.

The National Telecommunications and Information Administration is the arm of the U.S. Department of Commerce charged with advising the Executive Branch on domestic and international telecommunications and information technology issues.

Norman H. Nie, Research Professor of Political Science at Stanford University and Director of the Stanford Institute for the Quantitative Study of Society.

Thomas P. Novak, Professor of Marketing and Electronic Commerce at the Owen Graduate School of Management, Vanderbilt University.

Adam Clayton Powell III, Vice President, Technology and Programs, at The Freedom Forum in Arlington, Virginia.

Jorge Reina Schement, Professor of Telecommunications and Co-Director of the Institute for Information Policy, School of Communications, Pennsylvania State University.

Ann Schlosser, Assistant Professor of Marketing at Vanderbilt University.

John Simons, former technology policy reporter with *The Wall Street Journal* and a Markle fellow at the New America Foundation.

Ekaterina O. Walsh, technographics analyst at Forrester Research in Cambridge, Massachusetts.

Mitchell Weinraub, Senior Director of Operations and Engineering at AT&T's Digital Media Center.

Index